CW01091428

THE
WINGED BULL

BY

Dion Fortune℠

S.I.L (Trading) Ltd
38 Steeles Road
London, NW3 4RG

First Published in by 1935 The Inner Light Publishing Co
This edition published 1998 by SIL Trading Ltd.

ISBN 1 899585 45 1

© Society of the Inner Light 1998

All rights reserved. No reproduction, copy or transmission of
this publication may be made without written permission.
No paragraph of this publication may be reproduced, copied or
transmitted save with written permission or in accordance with
the provision of the Copyright Act 1956 (as amended).
Any person who does any unauthorised act in relation to this
publication may be liable to criminal prosecution and civil
claims for damages.

Dion Fortune © is a registered trademark.

A CIP catalogue record for this book is available from the
British Library.

Design & Typesetting by Clinton Smith
Design Consultants, London.

Printed and bound in Great Britain.

The Society of the Inner Light has no branches nor authorised
representatives and expresses no opinion on other groups.

SIL Trading Ltd is the commercial extension of The Society of the Inner Light - Registered Charity No; 207213

Its aims and objectives include the propagation of theology and metaphysical religion.

THE WINGED BULL

Novels by Dion Fortune

The Sea Priestess
The Demon Lover
The Goat-foot God
The Secrets of Dr Taverner
Moon Magic

Works on Magic and the Esoteric;

Applied Magic and Aspects of Occultism
Esoteric Orders and their Work and the Training and Work of an Initiate
The Cosmic Doctrine
Machinery of the Mind
The Mystical Qabalah
Psychic Self-defence
Through the Gates of Death
Glastonbury: Avalon of the Heart
The Esoteric Philosophy of Love and Marriage

Hitherto unpublished material with commentary by Gareth Knight;

An Introduction to Ritual Magic. (Thoth Books, Leicester)

Forthcoming titles from Thoth Books, Leicester, including hitherto unpublished material by Dion Fortune with a commentary by Gareth Knight.

The Circuit of Force
Principles of Hermetic Philosophy

Reprinting by Thoth Books with a commentary by Gareth Knight;

Spiritualism in the Light of Occult Science
Mystical Meditations on the Collects
Practical Occultism in Daily Life
Sane Occultism

Forthcoming titles from Windrush Press, Moreton on the Marsh. Leicester, including never before published original material and commentary by Gareth Knight.

Principles of Esoteric Healing *by Dion Fortune*
The Pythoness (Margaret Lumley Brown), *one of Dion Fortune's closest collaborators.*

'For of old the Sun, our sire,
Came wooing the mother of men,
Earth, that was virginal then,
Vestal fire to his fire.
Silent her bosom and coy,
But the strong god sued and pressed;
And born of their starry nuptial joy
Are all that drink of her breast.'

WILLIAM WATSON

CHAPTER 1

There was a sky-fog in Central London that made the heavens look like dirty metal and caused the street lamps to be lit at three o'clock in the afternoon. The British Museum, seen across its hazy forecourt, looked like the entrance to Hell. Ted Murchison had no wish to return to his brother's house at Acton before the hour of the evening meal. He disliked his sister-in-law, and the house was full of kids that needed a spanking and didn't get it. He turned in at a gateway in railings that dripped soot and fog-dew, and set out across the wide expanse of gravel in the gathering gloom.

It suddenly struck him as he mounted the steps of the portico that if the fog grew worse he would have the devil's own job recrossing that wide expanse without any landmarks. But he didn't care. He wasn't going back to Acton to kick his heels till supper-time. The Museum would be warm and lighted, and would give him something to think about and distract his mind from the memory of the interview which had just ended. He had gone up for that interview on a personal introduction from his brother, and had failed to get the job. Now he had to go back to Acton and tell his brother that he had failed to get it, and hear his comments on the failure. And his sister-in-law's comments, too. She was a strong believer in kicking a man when he is down as the best way of helping him to rise.

A rush of hot air smote him in the face as he entered the building. It was warm, as he had expected, and he was glad of the warmth, for there was no overcoat under the old trench-coat that he wore. A relic of the War, it had been good in its day, and had outworn a succession of cheap overcoats. Coats like that did not come his way nowadays. His father had been a colonel in the Old Contemptibles, and one of the first to fall. He himself had joined up straight from school. When he came out of the army there was no money to give him a start in life, and no one to care whether he had a start in life or not. So he took the first job that offered, and when that proved to be a blind alley, took the next one; and as that was a shady employment agency, he came perilously near gaol before he tumbled to what was afoot.

So the years had gone by. Clerking without shorthand. Salesmanship on commission. Anything and everything that would enable him to hand over thirty shillings a week to his sister-in-law at Acton. In normal times he was the type that goes out to the Dominions, but the Dominions were not taking men without capital during the post-war depression. His brother never proposed advancing him the capital. Thirty shillings a week is not to be despised in the home of a clergyman whose principles oblige him to bring into the world an annual baby, whether he has anywhere to put it or not.

With demobilization Ted Murchison's halcyon days were over. He had been an officer and a gentleman, even if a very young one. Digging out the old trench-coat to wear in this drizzling fog had turned his mind back to those days. He had been lucky in his colonel, and his year in the army had done something for him that churches and universities between them had failed to do. As he handed over his hat and coat to the attendant in the muggy warmth of the Museum, he speculated upon what had become of the rest of the members of his mess. Had any of them missed the boat as he had, or were they all getting on in the world and raising families to fight in the next war? Marriage had been out of the question for him, and life had not been any easier in consequence. He was thirty-three now, and was beginning to steady down. There were times when he thought he had quite steadied down. There were other times when he doubted it. The handling his colonel had given him had stood him in good stead during those difficult years and steered him past much miscellaneous trouble.

Brangwyn had been the chap's name. He wondered what had become of him. No one knew whence he came when he joined up, and no one knew whither he went when he had been demobbed. He was of the soldiering type, but was not a professional soldier. He had been a most marvellous handler of men, both in billets and in action. There was less crime and fewer casualties in his command than in any other down the line. As a lad in his teens, Ted Murchison had adored him. As an older man, with wider experience, he realised more and more clearly that his old chief was a man of no ordinary calibre.

The Museum, though warm, was not brightly lit, for the fog hung in wreaths down the long galleries and haloed the lights with a golden haze. It was not the best of conditions under which to see the exhibits, and Murchison was sauntering idly down the central aisle, lost in thought, paying no attention to his surroundings, when suddenly he was startled out of his oblivion by the sight of a face staring at him through the gloom with a curious, questioning expression, as if its owner were about to speak to him. It was a good-humoured face, though slightly cynical, and its eyes seemed to probe his very soul. They looked at each other, he and the owner of the face, without speaking. There did not seem to be any need of speech between them, for thought flowed from one to the other unchecked. He knew that the owner of the face thought he was a damned fool, but liked him. The impulse was on him to speak to this stranger, but an intuition told him that the stranger was a foreigner and would not understand the spoken word. Then he suddenly realized that the face was larger than human, and it was high above his head; he saw the shadow of a vast wing stretching away into the gloom; a vast hoof upon a plinth was planted beside his knee. It was one of the winged, human-headed bulls that guarded the temples of Nineveh that he had been communing with!

Realization gave him something of a shock. He had been so sure the beast was alive, and it had seemed to have something very important to communicate to him; something that would have altered his whole life if he could have learnt it. He gazed up into the quizzical, cynical face that gazed back so steadily, and it seemed to him as if it had a life of its own, a very definite life, despite his disillusionment as to its nature. He had a curious sensation that he had made a friend. That winged bull would know him again, in the same way that some of the beasts at the Zoo get to know visitors who have a flair for animals. He knew that by day the great bull stares out into space over the heads of the sightseers, and that it was only an optical illusion caused by the shadows which made it appear to be looking at him; nevertheless, he believed that even if he returned in broad daylight he would catch its eye, and that there would be recognition in it. He made up his mind that he would return, and return again and again to visit his new-found friend; he had a dashed sight more in common with it, graven image though it was, than with most of the humans he had known during his thwarted life. He believed the bull knew it, too; it knew he would return, it knew they had a lot in common.

Reluctantly he turned away and moved off down the gallery; an attendant was eyeing him in much the same way that the bull had eyed him, though with considerably less goodwill. He passed slowly on down the Egyptian Gallery, and the shadowy gods on their pedestals sat quietly watching him. They, too, were alive with a strange life of their own in the uncertain light of the mist-filled gallery; but they had not the energy of his Babylonian friend, nor did he get en rapport with them in the same way, though he felt their life, till he came to an enormous arm in rose-red granite outstretched with clenched hand upon its pedestal; an arm so vast that it was inconceivable what manner of statue it had come from, ending in a Hand of Power, if ever there was one.

Murchison remembered the Ingoldsby Legend of the Hand of Glory that could open locked doors; but this rose-red granite arm was utterly different in the feeling it gave him from that sinister relic. It was its benignity that impressed him; the benignity that controlled the awful power it possessed. It was an utterly different kind of god to the crucified God in the Christian churches; but it was a good god nevertheless; and it was very much of a god; let the orthodox say what they would.

Reluctantly he moved on again. Another attendant was eyeing him. It did not do to admire the exhibits overmuch or one was suspected of wanting to steal them; though how anyone could make off with that mighty, 20 foot arm was beyond imagination.

He drifted on at random up the broad, shallow stairs, and presently found himself in the Mummy Room and stood gazing thoughtfully at the desecrated dead. A scanty handful of fog-bound sightseers were gathered around the official lecturer, and Murchison joined them. The lecturer exasperated him by patronizing both the dead and the living. Were not the ancients men like unto us? he asked himself. Why should one credit them with the mentality of imbeciles? They had known enough to build the pyramids.

The party was gathered around the leathery individual lying curled up in his imitation tomb. The lecturer was explaining that the ancientest ancients buried their dead like that because that was the attitude in which they slept, and the less ancient ancients buried their dead out flat, because that was the attitude in which they slept. Murchison wondered whether they ever turned over in bed at night, same as other folk - put the question, and got snubbed.

He quitted the party, and drifted off towards the gallery where aboriginal godlets vie with each other in ugliness. But on the threshold he halted. This was altogether too much of a good thing. These, too, had come alive under the influence of fog and dusk, and he backed away, startled. The place smelt of blood.

Murchison turned and went striding away down the long galleries in search of the exit. He had had enough of these presences, and he wanted to smoke. Their effect was altogether too queer. Something in him that the dragging years had numbed into a merciful insensibility woke up and began to ache again. He thought of fighting men on the march, and longed for open spaces and high winds. He was a man, and he wanted a man's job, not this wretched quill-driving for a pittance in the dingy offices of shady concerns. Murchison struggled against a rising tide of anger with life; but it does not do to be angry with life unless one has private means, lest one's last state be even worse than one's first.

Murchison took his hat and coat and went towards the exit. As he approached the glass doors he saw that it was now quite dark outside, but it was not until he passed through them that he realized that a black wall of fog, opaque as a curtain, pressed against his face. He hesitated for a moment. Then suddenly stepped forward into the clinging, smothering darkness, which closed behind him as water closes over a swimmer.

There was no sound whatsoever in that impenetrable blackness; for not only does fog blanket sound, but all traffic was at a standstill. Murchison wondered whether the end of the world had arrived at last, after so many abortive prophecies; or whether, under the influence of his new friend, the man-bull, he had slid back to the dawn of creation, and this was the formless void before the spirit of God moved upon the face of the waters. He stood motionless, staring with unseeing eyes into the slowly swirling invisibility. Any moment he might see the spirit of God come through and the darkness part, and vast forms of great winged bulls formulate out of the formless mist.

Then a sudden horror smote him at the thought that it might be hideous godlets, creatures of the slime, that would formulate first. But he rejected the thought. Those things in the Aboriginal Gallery had belonged to the decadence of a race, not its prime. No, the things he would see formulate out of the mist were noble, and beautiful, and very strong.

He remembered Hans Anderson's story of the toys that came alive at night and held their revels in the moonlit nursery. The gods on their pedestals had been alive right enough, even before he had left the building. As soon as the last of the readers in the great library had been given his hat and pushed out, would they get off their pedestals and begin their revels? His friend, the door-keeper of the gods, relieved from duty, might come out and join him for a chat and a smoke in the courtyard. He wished he would. He liked him a darned sight better than any human he had ever met before, with one exception, his boyhood's idol, the colonel of the regiment in which he had held his brief commission.

Someone passed him in the smother, and, desiring to be alone with the gods, he advanced a few paces diagonally across the broad portico, felt the edge of the steps under his feet, and passed down them, setting off at random across the wide stretch of invisible gravel. A queer feeling came to him that in so doing he had committed himself beyond all possibility of return. He had left the flagged path that would have guided his feet to the gate, despite the murk, and was astray in black vacancy. He had left the lighted and landmarked ways of men and was adrift in primeval darkness. And who, in that darkness, would come to meet him? The hideous godlets? The spirit of the Ancient of Days, with a long white beard and a golden crown? Or a mighty rose-red Arm that parted the clouds and gave light? His choice fell upon the Arm. He was sick to death of his brother's God, 'A grasping de'il, the image of himsel', Got out of books by meenisters, clean daft on Heaven and Hell.'

His brother had asked him once whether he thought God would ever forgive him for his attitude towards Him; and he had asked his brother whether he thought he would ever forgive God for His attitude towards him? Anyway, He was a spiteful brute, if all that was said of him were true; and a poor judge of human nature, for He regarded some pretty awful specimens with favour, if their statements were to be believed. Ted Murchison had had enough of Him, and He could go to His own Hell and stop there, for all he cared. He stood alone in the breathless smother and called mentally to his new friend, the winged bull of Babylon.

'I am upon your side!' he cried aloud in his imagination. 'Come to me, O winged one. Door-keeper of the gods! Open to me the doors!'

His chant ceased abruptly. By what name should he call upon his new friend? For names were needful in order that the gods might be invoked. Man-headed, eagle-winged, bull-footed, how should he name him? 'Rushing with thy bull-foot, come!' The words of the old school crib came back to him. 'Evoe, Iacchus! Io Pan!'

Murchison stood alone in the fog-bound darkness of the forecourt of the British Museum and cried aloud, 'Evoe, Iacchus! Io Pan, Pan! Io Pan!'

And echo answered 'Io Pan!'

But a voice that was not an echo also answered, 'Who is this that invokes the Great God Pan?'

CHAPTER 2

Murchison was so startled by the immediate response to his invocation that he involuntarily exclaimed, 'Good Lord!' which was the invocation of his brother's 'graspin' de'il,' and had nothing whatever to do with the deity he had been invoking with such fervour a moment ago. He heard a footstep on the gravel beside him, and held his breath. A hand touched his arm.

'You seem to have lost your way pretty thoroughly,' said a voice, and Murchison came back to earth with a bump.

'Unless you are going to call on the Keeper of the King's Books, you are decidedly wide of the mark,' continued the voice. 'Would you like me to put you on the track of the gate? I have a pretty good sense of direction. I think you will find me a reliable guide.'

The voice was that of an educated man, and it had the indefinable something that is only to be found in the voice of one who habitually associates with educated men. It was also a strangely resonant voice. He had only heard one other voice as resonant as that. Curious how his mind kept on going back to his brief soldiering that afternoon. He was so astray among his thoughts that he neglected to answer his interlocutor, and the invisible voice went on again.

'I think you had better come along with me, whether you want to or not. No, I am not a policeman, but you don't appear to me to be in any state to take care of yourself at the moment, and Christian charity compels me to lend you a hand as far as the gate. Or, since you were calling upon the Great God Pan, you may prefer to call it pagan charity. But in any case you had better come with me lest you get yourself locked in and have to spend the night in these insalubrious precincts.'

Murchison, feeling very foolish, allowed himself to be led by the arm through the darkness, made a desperate snatch at his scattered wits, and managed to say:

'I'm frightfully sorry. I am afraid you must think me an awful fool. I'm not drunk, really. I - I was just thinking of something else, and got lost in the fog.'

'Hullo? I have heard that voice before somewhere. I never forget a voice. Now, who is it?' exclaimed his invisible companion.

Murchison stiffened. He wondered what sort of confidence trick was about to be played upon him, and did not answer.

'Quite right,' continued the voice, 'never tell a stranger your name in the dark. But I'll tell you my name, however, for I am pretty certain I know you. My name is Brangwyn. Now can you place me?'

If the Great God Pan had appeared in person the effect upon Murchison could not have been more overwhelming. It took him so long to collect his wits and answer that his companion began to think that he had been mistaken in identifying him; but at last he managed to say:

'Good Lord, sir, is it you?'

'Yes, it's me all right, and from your mode of address I think you must have been one of my cubs. Now which is it? Roberts? Atkinson? Murchison? Yes, I believe you are Murchison. Am I right?'

'Yes,' said Murchison, and that was all he could find to say. When one has offered one's soul to the devil, according to all the traditions of one's upbringing, and the god of one's youth suddenly accosts one out of the darkness, the association of ideas is irresistible. Murchison had been deeply stirred by the uprushing rebellion at his thwarted life; his wits were astray in the fourth dimension and could not readily be recalled, and the sudden voice in the darkness that answered his invocation had seemed to turn all his imaginations into reality, and the old gods had verily come again for him. They were all about him, pressing in upon him; for his mind had turned bottom-side up with the shock and reaction that had caught him off his guard, and for the moment subconsciousness had superseded reason and taken charge of his affairs.

Brangwyn could not see his companion's face in the murk, but he listened attentively to the timbre of his voice, for his quick ear told him that something was very much amiss with this man, and that he was under high emotional tension. He remembered well the alert, eager youngster of the last years of the War, and wondered what the years of peace had made of him.

'How has life used you since last we met?' he asked.

'I'm still alive,' said Murchison, with a curt laugh.

A dull orange glow loomed up through the haze ahead of them.

'I expect those are the lamps by the gates. At least, I hope they are,' said Brangwyn. 'Now, if I can continue to pilot you successfully, I will steer you into a certain teashop of my acquaintance in Southampton Row and ask you to join me at a cup of tea.'

14

Murchison accepted with more than the eagerness that is normally due to the offer of a cup of tea, and Brangwyn wondered if he were down and out and starving. Queer things happened during the peace to fellows who had been temporary gentlemen during the War. But he was wrong. It was not food for which Murchison was starving, but something quite different.

Now that there were the street lamps and the kerb to guide them, it was easier going. Bloomsbury is a land of right angles, and it was only a matter of knowing how many streets to cross until the right turning was reached in order to find Southampton Row. Once there, the lit-up shops gave them all the guidance they needed, and in a few moments they turned into a big café whose brightness almost blinded them after the gloom in which they had been groping for so long.

Brangwyn led the way to a corner table, and for the first time was able to see the face of his companion as they sat down opposite each other.

So this is what the alleged peace had made of that fine youngster? If he had seen him in the street he would not have known him. There was a family likeness to what he had been, but no more.

He studied him closely. He was looking rather dazed and self-conscious, Brangwyn thought, and wondered what had been at the bottom of that extraordinary outcry of 'Io Pan' in the foggy forecourt of the British Museum. It was exceedingly curious that the fellow should have turned up when he did, for he had just been thinking that the type of man he was looking for was the Murchison type. Big-boned, upstanding, Nordic. The Viking breed, in fact; and Murchison, if he remembered aright, was a Yorkshireman, and therefore probably of Viking stock. He studied him closely, after handing him the menu to distract his attention from the inspection. It would not do to be sentimental because the fellow was down on his luck. Nor must he jump to the conclusion that, because the youngster had been the right sort, the man was all that could be desired. Strange things can happen to men in the vital 10 years between 20 and 30, especially in times of stress. He must be cautious, and not let impulse, masquerading as intuition, lead him astray. A mistake would have very far-reaching repercussions.

Murchison looked up from the menu, having made his choice, and for the first time met the eyes of the elder man that had been fixed on him so steadily. He, too, had been making use of the menu for other purposes than those it was intended for, and under cover of its perusal had contrived to pull himself together. Crumpets were agreed upon, and the waitress departed, leaving them alone together. They had the place to themselves, all other wayfarers having been driven home by the fog.

Brangwyn had no mind to come straight to the point. He wanted to walk round his companion sniffing before he committed himself. It would not be fair to rouse the fellow's hopes and then dash them. So he turned the talk on to old comrades and wartime experiences, and Murchison followed him thankfully, for he had no mind to be asked about himself, since he had nothing good to tell, and had no love for pitching a hard-luck story.

So they chatted contentedly over their tea and cigarettes, and Brangwyn watched the likeness to the lad he had known come back into the face of the man opposite him.

'Have you far to go tonight, before you get home?' he asked at length, when empty plates gave them no further excuse to defy a hovering waitress who obviously wanted to get rid of them and go home herself.

'Acton,' said Murchison curtly, brought down to earth abruptly by the word.

'Good Lord, you'll never get there,' said Brangwyn, secretly delighted, and grabbing his opportunity. 'Let me put you up for the night at my place. I've got bachelor quarters just round the corner. We'll brew rum punch over the fire and make a night of it.'

Murchison agreed eagerly. This was a treat beyond all expectation. Brangwyn had all his old fascination for him. He could imagine nothing more delightful than to sit up half the night yarning with him; and, above all, to meet him on an equality; for there is a great gulf fixed between 20 and 40, but the gap between 33 and 53 is by no means unbridgeable. The younger man was now mature, and the elder still in his prime.

They left the shop together, and found that the fog had lifted considerably, which was fortunate, for Brangwyn's abode was by no means easy to find, even by daylight, and he had been wondering whether he had promised more than he could fulfil in inviting his companion to go home with him.

They left Southampton Row, and went down an alley, crossed a square, and went down another alley. It was a cross-country journey, and the district was distinctly insalubrious; Brangwyn was not sorry to have a companion when he saw the lounging groups in alley entrances, for this was a night on which an assault could be committed with impunity.

Despite the slum to which it had been reduced, the district had a

16

charm of its own, and even the extremes of grime and dilapidation of the houses could not destroy the grace of the Georgian architecture, though what the drains must be like it was better not to inquire.

They turned south, into a street of mean shops, and Brangwyn inserted a key in a narrow door beside an Italian restaurant on the corner, and entered. Sufficient light from the street lamp shone through the fanlight to reveal the worn oilcloth of the entry, and a long flight of dingy stairs leading upwards into darkness and flanked on either side by a wall bereft of handrail. It was an unprepossessing abode, and Murchison concluded that Brangwyn must also have come down in the world since the War, for he had been reputed to have money.

At the top of the stairs there was another door, and this also Brangwyn unlocked with a latch-key, though why both doors should require keys was difficult to understand, for no other entrance opened into the slot-like passage and stairs. Brangwyn switched on the light and held the door open for his companion to enter, and Murchison found himself in another world.

The entire upper part of the corner house and its two neighbours had been reconstructed, leaving the facade intact, so that there was nothing outside to hint at what was within. To all appearances the three houses were as dingy as the rest of the street, for such painting as had been done to their woodwork had been carefully matched with the surrounding grime, and dingy Nottingham lace curtains were stretched against the glass of the windows, hidden from the eyes of the occupants of the house by inner curtains of thin golden silk.

A whole floor had been pulled clean out of the corner house, making the lounge hall into which they entered spacious and lofty. A great chimney of mellowed brick, salved from the discarded party wall, occupied the rear angle of the fan-shaped apartment; on its wide, flat hearth a pile of wood and peat awaited lighting, though the place was warm almost to stuffiness with central heating. Thick soft rugs lay about on the dark polished parquetry of the floor, and a divan and two vast armchairs flanked the hearth. Books lined the walls from the floor to the gallery, supported on massive posts of old timber that had once been floor-joists, and on to the gallery opened doors that were presumably bedrooms and what house agents call the usual offices.

Brangwyn bent down and put a match to the pile on the hearth.

'I believe in plenty of fire-lighters,' he said, as the flames roared up the chimney. 'Those are the sort of little things that make all the difference to life, and you never can get women to understand them.'

'Take this chair,' he continued, 'and mind how you sit down; it is on wheels instead of casters.'

Despite the warning, Murchison felt the chair go from under him, and sat down sooner than he meant to.

Brangwyn stretched out a hand to a cocktail cabinet and drew it towards him, for it also was on wheels. Murchison noted that all the heavy furniture was mounted on small, rubber-tyred wheels, and marvelled that no one had ever before thought of such a simple device for increasing comfort and minimizing labour. He drew his great chair up to the now blazing fire with a single easy kick of his heel, and stretched out in luxurious comfort, giving himself up to his brief hour of enjoyment. This was the way a man ought to live. Solid comfort, but no show or fuss; and, above all, no servants to make themselves a nuisance and pinch the drinks. He remembered that even in the front line Brangwyn had always believed in being comfortable, and managed to be so, too, within 24 hours of the biggest push. Moreover, he believed in everyone he was responsible for being comfortable also, as being the best way to get the best work out of them.

Brangwyn was a tall, slight, dark-skinned man; and his black hair, brushed straight back from his forehead, was greying over the ears and receding over the temples. That was the only difference the years had made to him, thought Murchison, as he watched him picking and choosing among a formidable array of bottles. Murchison had never seen him in mufti before, and thought it became him better than uniform; for that ascetic looking scholar's head had always seemed rather incongruous sticking out of a tunic, though his bearing was soldierly enough.

The cocktail Brangwyn finally evolved, after much thought and care and accuracy, was amber-coloured and aromatic, not quite like anything Murchison had ever met before; but it had an authentic kick in it, as was evidenced by the sudden glow of his chilled skin and the livening up of his dazed brain. It amused him to observe that Brangwyn, who looked so ascetic, could be so fastidious in every detail of his way of living. Everything about him seemed to have had the most careful thought lavished on it, though nothing in itself was of any great intrinsic value. Even the compactness of the cocktail cabinet had been forced to find room for three sets of glasses, amber, green and rose, to set off the complexions of the various kinds of drinks, and in its recesses he caught a glimpse of a pile of small black bowls, with silver bases, and wondered what manner of tipple was imbibed out of these.

'Getting a trifle warm, don't you think?' said Brangwyn.

18

Murchison had thought for some time past it was getting decidedly warm, what with the cocktails, fire and central heating. Brangwyn rose and opened a cupboard in the wall, inset among the books, and revealed an array of what looked like voluminous silk dressing-gowns ranged on hangers; he selected a dark crimson one, and then paused and eyed Murchison and selected another of peacock blue shading off to emerald.

'Like this?' he questioned. Murchison did not quite know what was expected of him, and returned a polite non-committal affirmative.

'Then shed your coat and collar and get into it,' said Bran 'The slippers are in the pocket.'

Murchison did as he was bid, shedding coat, waistcoat and collar after the example of his host, and girding himself about with the flowing silk, amazed to find the extraordinary change that came over his mood as the folds fell about him. In this garb he could have invoked the Great God Pan without any embarrassment.

'I always change my kit when I come indoors,' said Brangwyn. 'I find it helps me to think.'

'It's dashed nice stuff,' said Murchison. 'What does it smell of? It's got the same flavour as the cocktails.'

'Sandalwood,' said Brangwyn.

'But you don't put sandalwood in the cocktails?'

'No, essential oil of santal.'

'How do you get it to mix?'

'Smear it round the glass, and the spirit picks up the aromatic essence.'

They sank into a companionable silence after another round of cocktails, watching the fire change and glow and fall apart in caves of flame. The peat and the pinewood of which it was made smelling sweet and aromatic, blending harmoniously with the sandal-flavoured cocktail. Murchison had never realized before the way in which odour and flavour reinforce each other.

He found Brangwyn an extraordinarily interesting study, apart from the liking and respect he had always had for him. He had evidently brought the art of living up to the level of an applied science. Murchison approved with a sigh of envy. That, beyond all question, was the right way to live; but it needed cash, and plenty of it, for the development of its fine flower, and he, for his part, had had to bring the art of doing without to the level of a science.

'You like my little place?' Brangwyn broke the silence conversationally.

'I like it immensely,' said Murchison. 'But don't you find it rather noisy, what with kids playing in the street, and barrel-organs, and chuckings-out from the local pub? Especially in summer when the windows are open.'

'We never hear them,' said Brangwyn. 'I put sheets of good thick plate-glass inside the windows, and the ventilation comes down the old chimneys with the aid of electric fans.

'I suppose you wonder why I elect to live in a slum?' he continued. 'I am like Oscar Wilde; I can manage without necessities so long as I can have luxuries. I dropped a good deal of money through the War; rents are high in decent parts, so I picked up this bit of slum property cheap because it was too far gone to be worth reconditioning. I didn't attempt to recondition it. I gutted it. I left the front alone because if I had put in decent windows I should have only have had 'em broken twice a week and been assaulted every time I opened the front door. It isn't tactful to make yourself out to be better than your neighbours in this part of the world. They think I am going out disguised for a crime when they see me in my best togs, and entirely approve. If anyone comes around inquiring if I live here, the entire street swears I am non-existent without waiting to be asked. It suits me excellently.

'The chaps in the shops underneath are my tenants; in fact the lad in the bookshop is a manager, not a tenant, because book-collecting is one of my hobbies. The fellow in the Italian restaurant has to look after me as part of his rent. It works admirably. You should see him supervising the charwomen. I will give him a ring when we want supper, and he will come up the back stairs and produce it out of his hat.'

CHAPTER 3

Whether it was the drinks, or the smell of the sandalwood, or all this warmth and light after his drab existence, Murchison could not have said, but he felt his whole personality changing and unfolding and flowering as he lay back in the big chair sharing the tranquil silence. The warmth of the fire was lulling him to sleep, and as he drowsed with half-shut eyes it seemed to him as if the face of the bull of Babylon was superimposed upon that of his host, so that the two had become one; and the arm that lay along the padded arm of the big chair, its loose, crimson sleeve catching the fire-light, was the rose-red granite Arm of Power. Whether his dream would have led on to the coming of the Great God Pan himself, was mercifully concealed, for his host arose and phoned for a meal, and they adjourned to a small but beautifully equipped little dining-room, where a dark, lively Italian, the owner of the restaurant, served them with admirable food, openly adoring Brangwyn, and apparently quite accustomed to waiting on birds of paradise. Murchison had felt somewhat embarrassed at appearing before Brangwyn's domestic staff in his flowing robes, but Italians take that sort of thing in their stride.

The proprietor-waiter informed Brangwyn of the ingredients of every course; Murchison would have found this exasperating were it not for the light it threw upon his host as an epicure. Brangwyn evidently sensed his irritation, for he murmured in a low voice when the little man was momentarily absent from the room. 'One tips an hireling, but one appreciates an artist,' and Murchison got a yet further insight into his host's nature. The excitable little man, in his second-hand dress-suit, proprietor of a cheap eating-house in a slum, was to be treated as an artist because in his queer way he was an artist.

As Murchison had expected, the talk swung round to his own affairs when they returned to the lounge after dinner. He felt grateful to Brangwyn for his leisurely, Oriental style of diplomacy. It is so much easier to face a thing when one comes to it gradually. But, even so, he was almost rudely secretive in response to the leads his host gave him,

21

because his need was so great, and he was so desperately anxious not to appear to cadge. Brangwyn could learn nothing of his affairs save that he made his home with his brother, had not got any special line of work, and was disengaged at the moment; he guessed the rest, and thought well of his one-time subaltern for leaving him to guess it.

But even the reticence of self-respect can be carried too far, and there were things Brangwyn greatly wished to know about his guest, though he was careful to hide his interest. The fellow might be suitable; and, again, he might not, and he did not wish to commit himself beyond the point where he could readily back out if the latter proved to be the case. But there are more ways of killing a cat than choking it with butter, and he thought that Murchison had had enough butter, and that it was time to cut the cackle and come to the 'osses. He shot a sudden, authoritative question at him:

'What were you up to when I met you, calling upon Pan in front of the British Museum?'

Murchison jumped as if he had been stung, and his fair skin blushed painfully.

'Raising the devil, I suppose,' he muttered resentfully, greatly disliking his host's reference to the matter.

'Why did you wish to raise the devil?'

'Living with my brother, who's a clergyman, and his wife, who's a clergyman's wife, is apt to make you want to raise the devil if you can't raise the wind.'

Brangwyn saw that nothing was to be obtained by the direct method, so tried the indirect one, watching for reactions.

'It appeared to me, from what I know of the matter, and I have studied it a good deal, that you were well on the way to obtaining the presence of Pan when I interrupted you.'

Murchison did not answer, but Brangwyn fancied he pricked up his ears.

'Have you ever seen the invocation performed effectually?' he continued.

'No,' said Murchison uneasily.

'I have, and the results are very striking.'

'Does Pan appear in person?'

'How would you define Pan?'

'Ah, you have me there. I haven't any idea on the subject, save that he gave his name to panic.'

'Panic is what he produces in the unprepared, but in those who are

22

prepared for his coming he produces a divine inebriation.'

'Oh, does he?' said Murchison sulkily, 'I prefer beer myself.'

Brangwyn saw that it was inadvisable to pursue the matter further, as the subject seemed a sore one. But as it was sore, he concluded that it was also vital, and ticked off the chief point in favour of the candidature of the unsuspecting Murchison for the matter he had in view. Murchison was reaching out well beyond the veil, whether he knew it or not, and whether he could be got to admit it or not, and as Brangwyn's interests lay exclusively beyond the veil, this was as it should be in a prospective employee.

He came to the point abruptly, 'Murchison, would you care to consider the offer of a post as secretary-chauffeur with myself. Live in and five pounds a week? It's only temporary, I am afraid, because I am liable to be called abroad at any time, and then the arrangement would have to come to an end, but I would help you to get fixed up with something else after you had finished with me.' That gave him a bolt-hole if Murchison did not come up to expectations.

Murchison's first reaction was a horrible suspicion that he was being offered charity, and the suspicion made him ungracious.

'What would the duties be?' he asked unemotionally, though his heart was fuming over inside him at this extraordinary piece of luck that had come his way after the long years in the wilderness.

'The duties,' said Brangwyn, a little puzzled by his manner, 'would be a certain amount of chauffeuring, as my eyes are not equal to long runs, but mainly odd jobs. Cope with correspondence; tackle tradesmen; keep an eye on Luigi and the chars, and stand between me and the world generally. I am engaged in some rather special work, and there are times when I can't be interrupted; and I want someone with the sense to handle things for me on his own initiative at those times.'

'My usual salary is three pounds a week and keep myself,' said Murchison sullenly. 'Why are you offering me a salary like that? It isn't my market price.'

'Because it is a position of trust and requires initiative,' said Brangwyn tactfully, 'and because the hours are irregular. I believe in paying enough to make the job worth while, and then I secure satisfactory service. Moreover, you will have to dress decently and generally keep up appearances, so it isn't all net profit.'

Murchison was mollified. He looked up with a sudden quick smile that completely changed his face. 'I'd like the job first-rate,' he said. 'I'll do my best for you, you know that.'

'Splendid!' said Brangwyn. 'You can fetch your belongings tomorrow. Meanwhile, I suggest we think about turning in. I hope you won't mind if I put you in my sister's room until I can get one fixed up for you.'

'Your sister's room?' demanded Murchison in sudden horror, all his dreams of a delightful bachelor menage falling about his ears.

'Yes, my sister keeps a couple of rooms as a *pied à terre,* but she doesn't use them much. I can fix you up quite comfortably upstairs. There's a whole lot of space I have never made any use of in this place.'

Brangwyn rose and led the way up a corkscrew wooden stair in the corner on to the gallery that ran round the room at half its height. He opened a door and entered a small room furnished as a sitting-room, passed through it into a bathroom, and then on into a bedroom, Murchison following him.

'A complete flat, you see,' he said, with a wave of his hand. 'all ready for occupation. We always keep the bed made in case she appears unexpectedly.'

'Is she likely to appear unexpectedly at the present moment,' asked Murchison anxiously.

'I trust not,' said his host negligently.

'What time is breakfast?' Murchison thought that he would not be sorry when the night was safely over.

'Tennish,' said Brangwyn, 'I am a night-worker, I am afraid. But if you ring through on the house-phone in the sitting room, Luigi will bring you rolls and coffee or tea and toast, any time you fancy. Then we have a decent breakfast between 10 and 1. Tea about three, and supper latish, when I've finished work. I find that a better way of breaking up the day than the usual arrangements, which spoils your morning sleep, sends you to bed when you are just beginning to wake up, and lays you dead in the afternoon.'

Murchison acquiesced readily enough. He would have acquiesced if his new employer had suggested cannibalism.

Good-nights having been said, Murchison strewed his clothes all over the room in the manner his sister-in-law had never been able to break him of, and then gathered them up hastily in case the redoubtable Miss Brangwyn returned unexpectedly. He wondered what sort of an old dame she would prove to be. Was she lean and cantankerous, or placid and whale-like? Would she keep an eye on his doings and report to her brother, or want to use him as a lounge lizard? She was the one fly in the ointment of what promised to be a perfect existence, and he found it hard to take her philosophically. Then he remembered his employer's words to the effect that the post was only temporary, and a sudden pang shot through him; he must be careful not to strike his roots too deeply lest the wrench of pulling them up should be too great.

He got into the heavy silk pyjamas that had been lent him, comparing them with the flannelette ones that were waiting in vain for him at Acton. He considered the bed, with its great square frilled pillow and deep rose-coloured eiderdown, but did not feel like sleep. It was by no means late, and he suspected that he had been pushed politely out of the way while his employer got on with whatever it was that occupied him o' nights. He wandered into the sitting-room to see if he could find a book. There were plenty of books here, just as there were downstairs. Miss Brangwyn was evidently a lady with catholic tastes in the literal, but by no means the theological, sense. Modern science and ancient philosophy jostled each other on her shelves, together with many modern novels and a very representative selection of the poets. *Embarras de richesse* here, thought Murchison, moving from shelf to shelf round the little room. He picked out a book at last. Jung on the Psychology of the Unconscious. What a book for an elderly female who ought to be knitting socks while she read missionary reports! He opened it and glanced at the fly-leaf, saw there a book-plate, looked more closely, and lo, his friend the Babylonian bull stared him in the face, wings neatly folded over his back, great bull-foot advanced, and on his plinth the name Ursula Brangwyn.

Murchison nearly dropped the book in his astonishment, not to say horror. He thrust it hastily back into its place on the shelf, got into bed, turned out the light, and put his head under the bedclothes.

It may have been this last act, or it may have been Brangwyn's cocktails that made him dream. For dream he did, and dreams of a quality he had never had before. He was a vivid dreamer, as are many men whose lives are shut in and inhibited; but his dreams were not particularly vivid that night. They reminded him of the times when he slept through his brother's services and the dronings mingled with his dreams. He thought he heard an organ being played in the distance, and the chanting of a mighty choir drawing near and dying away and drawing near again. He dreamt of the War, and searchlights playing up and down the sky, only they were coloured searchlights, of the colours of the robes he and Brangwyn had worn at dinner. All these things he seemed to be seeing and hearing between sleeping and waking, and they were vague and a long way off.

Then suddenly his dreams came to a focus and became crystal-clear and vividly bright, and he dreamt that at the foot of his bed a woman's head, bodiless, hung in mid-air, no larger than an orange, but vividly living, gazing at him intently. He sat up in bed in his dream and stared back at it open-mouthed, unable even to think. There was a curious likeness to Brangwyn about it. It might have been Brangwyn's daughter, if he had ever had a daughter. It neither spoke nor stirred, but it was alive, for the eyelids blinked from time to time. Then it slowly faded, and he woke up to find that he actually was sitting up in bed, but gazing into the blank emptiness of midnight.

He switched on the bedside stand-lamp and looked round the room. The door was shut and locked as he had left it; but even if it had not been, the vision could not possibly have been of a living woman because of the smallness of the head. He switched off the light and dropped back on to Miss Brangwyn's frilled pillow in disgust. He had dreamt of beautiful females before; they were no particular novelty, and he had read enough of popular psychology, which interested him, to know that night was compensating him for the denials of the day. He dropped off to sleep again, and slept dreamlessly till morning.

CHAPTER 4

Murchison awoke at his usual hour of seven o'clock, tubbed, dressed, and, as breakfast was a long way off, phoned for tea and toast. Luigi appeared in person, in a clean white jacket, and beamingly did the honours, evidently feeling that the responsibilities of hospitality rested upon his shoulders in the absence of his master. Murchison thought that the man who could win the adoration of a box of tricks like Luigi must be a good man to serve. Luigi had evidently been informed of his status in the house, and made a formal speech of welcome with many polite bows. Mistaire Brangwyn was a gentleman it was an honour and a pleasure to sairve. Mistaire - (a strange sound followed here, resembling the uncorking of ginger-beer) was fortunate, most honoured, most blessed, in being admitted to his service.

Murchison replied that he only hoped he would be able to achieve in his department the same lofty standard that Luigi had achieved in his.

Luigi bubbled with delight at this appreciation, and assured Mistaire - (more ginger-beer was uncorked) that he himself was also fortunate, honoured and blessed in having such a collaborator, and that his cooperation was always at his disposal.

Murchison replied that he thought that if they pulled together they ought to be able to make a good job of it. Luigi bowed himself out beaming, and Murchison saw how right Brangwyn had been when he said the tips would not buy the loyalty of a man like Luigi.

Murchison got rather bored hanging about waiting for the 10 o'clock breakfast. He did not like to wander about the house uninvited, nor to go out to get a paper, for he did not know how he would get in again in the absence of a latch-key. He felt that it would be more tactful to stop where he was till sent for, lest he drop unsuspected bricks, for he did not know the ways of the household, and had a suspicion that they were odd.

The air, though fresh, was over-warm for his taste, and he went over to where a diffused amber light came through some draperies and thrust them aside, concluding that here was the window, only to be checked by a sheet of plate-glass behind which was a filthy piece of Nottingham lace curtain and an even filthier sash-window. Peering through a rent in the Isabella coloured net, he saw the dreary facade across the way, and in a bow-window a foreign-looking female hunting small game in her infant daughter's hair. He looked down into the street, and saw a coster slowly shoving his barrow and apparently bawling, but no sound reached him through the thick plate-glass. Murchison dropped the amber silk curtain back into place again. It was certainly a mercy to have all the sights and sounds, and in summer presumably the smells, of that insalubrious neighbourhood shut out, but he wondered how he was going to like spending his days shut away from sunlight and fresh air in that somewhat high temperature, which he guessed to be in the neighbourhood of seventy.

He could not complain of stuffiness, however, and, looking up at the ceiling, he saw an ornamental metal grid, and judged from the slow movement of a curtain in its neighbourhood that air was being pumped into the room thereby, and presumably drawn out through another orifice which he could not identify. It was, he knew, the way most big buildings were ventilated, but, all the same, he found it hard to reconcile himself to it, and to convince himself he was not being stewed and stifled.

He shed his coat and prowled about in his shirt-sleeves, and felt better. The temperature would be all right if you had nothing much on, but in a thick suit and winter underwear it was decidedly oppressive. Then he shed a bit more, and yet more, until finally, hearing a step on the stair, he hastily seized the silken peacock robe that lay over a chair and flung it about him as a dressing-gown in case the visitor should be Miss Brangwyn.

But it was Brangwyn himself, in a robe of amber silk, and he smiled when he saw Murchison's peacock plumage.

'Ah,' he said, 'I see you have realized the value of the robes. All the same, that is not the right shade for the first thing in the morning. One is of the earth, earthy, at that time of day. And brogues, my dear fellow, do not go well with it. Let me beg of you to wear the appropriate slippers. So much more pleasant for both the feet and the carpets.'

Murchison, blushing and feeling a fool, did as he was bid, kicking off his thick, clumping brogues and pulling on the soft, heelless, glove-like kid slippers that matched the robe. Silently as two cats in a jungle they made their way down the corkscrew stairs to the dining-room and took their places at a table laid and decorated with every imaginable shade of amber, yellow and orange, gay as a sunrise.

Luigi did not appear, to Murchison's relief, who found that a little of the temperamental Italian went a long way, with his perpetual chatter of recipes. He himself was accustomed to shovel down whatever was set before him without paying any particular attention to it, which was just as well in his sister-in-law's menage, and spared him a good deal.

Everything was to hand, and they waited on themselves. The porridge, in a fireproof casserole, was ready made, but the bacon was artistically laid out in a shallow copper pan, waiting for the current to be switched on in the electric grill, and they ate their porridge to the accompaniment of its frisky spittings as it cooked, and the silver tinklings of the coffee as it trickled through the percolator.

'That porridge,' said Brangwyn, 'is ground between stones instead of steel rollers, and it comes fresh every week. Incidentally, I may mention, it takes all night to cook it. It is my belief that one should take thought in these small matters. Most people don't. They only take thought in big ones, and then it is usually too late. How much simpler to pay attention to your porridge instead of having your appendix out. Yet most people prefer the latter. I make a fine art of the simplest processes of living, thereby inducing a high degree of efficiency, and I hope to have your cooperation in the matter, Murchison, for I regard it as important.'

Murchison thought that the five pounds a week was going to be earned all right with all this finickiness, but acquiesced politely.

Brangwyn, who was watching him closely, continued, 'You know, my dear fellow, if you were designing a car you would study every detail of every part, right down to the air vacuum in its wake. How much more should one study the details of the machinery of living that make for smooth running and economy of power?'

'I had always thought you were a kind of monk,' said Murchison. 'I had expected to see you eating one of those nut rissoles that set solid inside you, instead of doing yourself jolly well, as you seem to.'

'Yes,' said Brangwyn thoughtfully, 'I always do myself as well as I can, except when I'm fasting. Why not? It has always appeared to me that only fools and slovens do otherwise. Yet what's this breakfast? Porridge, bacon, coffee, toast and butter, honey. But everything is the best of its kind, and I scoured the country till I found where the best was to be had. Most of it comes by post direct from the folk who produce it. It costs very little more than the worst of its kind. I don't suppose there is a shilling's difference between the actual cost of what is on this table and the cost of what you would get in a cheap boarding-house. The only difference is that everything has been thought out. Someone once asked

Opie what it was he mixed his colours with to get such brilliant effects, and he said he mixed 'em with his brains. Luigi and I mix our recipes with our brains, and that makes all the difference. Now tell me, don't you feel, sitting there in your flowing robe, beside my yellow breakfast table, as if you were much more alive than you felt when you ate your breakfast yesterday?'

'My God, yes!' said Murchison, thinking of the leathery kidneys and tea that could have tanned them which he had partaken of twenty-four hours ago amid sounds of contention and smells of back-fired gas. There was a curious feeling of satisfaction to be derived from the simple perfection of this breakfast. The wheels of life moved smoothly and easily; his self-esteem seemed established on a firm basis. More things were soothed than the stomach by this minor artistry.

They were tranquilly digesting their breakfast with the aid of cigarettes which, in accordance with Brangwyn's theory that sophisticated smokes should be kept for later in the day, were homely papers, when host once again shot a sudden, revealing question at guest:

'What did you dream of last night?'

Murchison sat up as if a pin had been stuck into him. He hated these sudden questions that could not be parried because they could not be foreseen, and that laid bare the secret recesses of his soul; that forced him to speak of the things that should never be spoken of and exposed his secret self to ridicule. His first impulse was to deny that he had dreamed, or to make up an imaginary dream for his employer's delectation; but he knew that if his employer were a Freud fan, an imaginary dream would be just as revealing as the genuine article. He therefore determined to offer nothing but the truth, even if not the whole truth.

'I dreamt of a church service. Scraps, you know, nothing definite. Music, mainly. And of the searchlights we had during the War, only coloured, like our robes. Then I woke up for a bit, and then went to sleep again and didn't dream any more till I woke up for good at seven.'

Exceedingly innocuous, thought Murchison. Even the fiercest libido-hound will find it hard to make anything of that.

'Anything else?' came the inexorable question. Murchison writhed and felt like rebellion, but five pounds a week is five pounds a week, and he answered sullenly;

'Oh, just the usual lovely houri.'

'Could you describe her?'

'Yes,' said Murchison furiously, looking ready for murder. 'She was damn like you. And now I suppose you'll say I've got a schoolgirl crush on you?'

'Not at all,' said Brangwyn placidly, quite unperturbed by the other's simmering resentment. 'There are a lot more things in the subconscious than are dreamed of by our mutual friend, Dr Freud. Forgive my eccentricities, but I am interested in some of the remoter branches of psychology, and one can learn a great deal about a person from their dreams, as you appear to know; and as we are going to work together, and I shall have to place a good deal of reliance on you, I am anxious to know what manner of man you are. I thank you for being frank with me, and I may tell you that I am quite satisfied.'

It was close on eleven before they concluded their leisurely breakfast, and Murchison thought of other meals he had gulped down and fled from. Life lived like this was as far apart from that which was led in his brother's home as the Eskimo from the Zulu. What it was to have money, he thought with a sigh. And then it occurred to him that it was not simply a matter of cash; it was the personality of the man opposite him that was the inspiring force; he would probably have lived in much the same manner, sitting on one packing-case and eating off another in an attic, and discriminating in the brand of his margarine.

Murchison doffed his robe, put on his clumping brogues, and set off to collect his belongings from his brother's house. It seemed like coming out not only into another world, but also into another century, when he stepped out of the front door that was black mahogany on one side and grained deal on the other. He felt rather as if he were a swimmer coming to the surface for a breath of air after the exoticisms of Brangwyn's flat. He made his way over the wholesome, mundane pavements in God's good air, and took the tube for Acton. He was still a little sore at having his houri dragged to the surface, and inclined to be resentful of his employer's easy superiority, though he had to admit that it was the superiority of man over man, and not of employer over employee.

It was nearly noon when he reached his brother's house, but he was met on the steps by a slattern with a bucket and swab, who shrieked to her mistress: ''E's come back, mum!'

The mistress of the house appeared, clad in a soiled afternoon dress that did duty instead of an overall, and, not being washable, was decidedly less sanitary. She had her hair in a bun behind, and a hair-net over her fringe, for being a clergyman's wife she felt it incumbent upon her not to follow the fashions. History teaches us that the good of all ages have always been against the fashions. When men's hair was worn long, the Puritans cut theirs short; and nowadays, when men's hair is worn short, reformers and intellectuals wear theirs long. And likewise with the

31

females of the species. In Victoria's days they cut their hair short; but nowadays, valiantly declining to shingle, bob or bingle, they keep their buns as symbols of souls that rise above the things of this world.

It is curious also how seldom a religion of love sweetens the temper, and Mrs James Murchison was exceedingly acidulated in her greeting of her brother-in-law, rubbing his dignity in the char's filthy swab, as it were, while the slattern listened appreciatively.

'So you've come back at last? And did you get that post?'

Murchison thought how he would have smarted under that inquiry, with the char listening, if it were as his sister-in-law suspected it was. He had a shrewd suspicion that they had never expected him to get that post, knowing he had none of the qualifications that it had turned out to require.

'No,' he replied evenly, 'I did not get that one. In fact, the fellow was rather annoyed at my wasting his time over the interview, as he said he had made it quite clear that shorthand was essential. But I have got another, and much better job, with a fellow I knew during the War, and whom I met quite by chance, and I have come to fetch my things.'

'Fetch your things?' exclaimed his sister-in-law. 'Do you mean to say you are leaving us?'

'Yes,' said Murchison, 'I am glad to say I shall be able to take myself off your hands at last.'

It had been regularly rubbed into him that what he paid did not cover what he ate, and that they badly needed his room for their ever-expanding family; but his sister-in-law appeared to have forgotten all that, and rapped out like a defrauded boarding-house keeper:

'You can't leave without notice like that. How do you expect us to manage without your money coming in?'

'Good God,' exclaimed Murchison, 'I always understood I was accepting charity!'

This nonplussed Mrs James for the moment, and made her feel she was not doing herself justice in front of the char, on whose appreciation she was counting, and Murchison did not improve matters by turning on his heel and marching upstairs to his room and slamming the door behind him. He did not trouble to pack formally, but flung all his small gear pell-mell into his old suitcase, chucked the bulkier stuff loose into a taxi, and was gone within ten minutes of entering the house.

He had fairly burnt his boats behind him, he thought to himself with a chuckle, as he sat among his piled-up belongings in the taxi. If he were out of a job again he would have to sleep on the Embankment, Acton would have none of him. But somehow he did not think it would come to that. He ought to be able to save a bit out of five pounds a week, and he did not think that Brangwyn would see him stranded if he served him faithfully. He had a strong inner feeling, that rose again as often as he tried to curb its exuberance, that his luck had turned. He felt as if he had been caught up in the current after swirling aimlessly in a stagnant backwater.

Arrived in Cosham Street, he knocked up Luigi in his restaurant, and begged for assistance in transporting his belongings up the long stairs to Brangwyn's flat. Luigi not only turned out in person, but summoned his entire staff of affable Latins, and Murchison headed a perfect army corps, moving in single file, their arms full of oddments. He inserted in the door at the top of the stairs the latch-key his employer had given him, and the beaming procession began to enter, when from one of the deep chairs by the fireplace someone arose, who had evidently been waiting there for his arrival, and he found himself confronted by a tall, slender, dark girl, very like Brangwyn. The very girl, in fact, whose head, no bigger than an orange, had appeared at the foot of his bed in his dream. He was so startled that he stood clutching his battered old suitcase, quite unable to take the hand she held out to him or respond to her greeting. If the bull of Babylon had walked off its pedestal he could not have been more taken aback.

She smiled at his confusion.

'I am Ursula Brangwyn,' she said, 'Alick's sister. Or, rather, his half-sister. And you, I believe, are Mr. Murchison?'

Murchison recovered himself sufficiently to take and shake the hand she was still holding out to him and to admit his identity.

CHAPTER 5

It was a merciful thing that Luigi and his myrmidons were queuing up and needed attention, for although the girl was the more self-possessed of the two, as women usually are, it would have been obvious to a discerning observer that there was not much to choose between them in embarrassment.

'I had better show you your room,' she said, 'and then you can tell Luigi what to do with your things.'

She led the way up the corkscrew stairs, went along the gallery past her own apartments, and opened a door in the corner, which gave on a narrow and steep stair that had evidently been part of the original fabric of the house. At the top she opened another door, which was covered with brown baize as if to render it sound-proof, and stepped out on to a small landing lit by a glass door which gave access to a roof-garden.

'You have a little self-contained flat up here,' she said, smiling; and, looking round, he saw that open doors led into two small rooms, bedroom and sitting-room, and a third door, which was probably a bathroom.

The procession marched into the bedroom and shot everything on to the bed. Then it turned and marched down the stairs again, and they heard the door at the bottom shut after it. This did not tend to relieve the embarrassment of the two, who were thus left alone to entertain each other as best they might.

'I hope you have got everything you want,' said Miss Brangwyn, 'if not, you must ask,' falling back upon the conventional hostess's speech to prevent the formation of a silence which her companion seemed quite incapable of doing anything with.

Murchison mumbled an acquiescence, which he strove in vain to make sound decently civil, but his wits had forsaken him. All he could think of was the bull of Babylon and a girl's head no bigger than an orange that floated in the air at the foot of his bed.

Miss Brangwyn led the way out of the little sitting-room and paused on the landing.

'This is the roof-garden,' she said, opening the glass door, and he followed her out into the open air. They found themselves in an open court of some dimensions, for the roofs had been removed from all three houses, the attic walls being left standing to a height of some five feet. Leafless creepers upon the walls and leafless shrubs in tubs promised greenery in the summer, and a seat in an angle of the wall received the winter sun.

Ursula Brangwyn led the way to an embrasure in the wall and mounted a step.

'Look,' she said, pointing, and Murchison looked.

He saw, apparently quite near, the dome of St. Paul's, and in the foreground a huddle of roofs looking like the mountains of the moon. Human beings he could not see, for the near streets were too narrow. They two might have been alone in a dead world.

'The only way out here is through your flat, I am sorry to say,' said Miss Brangwyn, desperately making conversation. 'So we shall have to trespass, I am afraid.'

'Oh - er - yes,' said Murchison.

Ursula looked at him, and saw that his shyness was of such a painful intensity that she felt sorry for him, though oafishness was not usually a passport to her esteem.

'I am afraid I shall be the principal trespasser,' she said, smiling. 'And I am afraid I shall bring a gramophone with me, for I have to come out here to practise my dancing.'

'Er - yes,' said Murchison, thinking that if she wanted him for a partner he would fling himself from the parapet. She seemed to guess this, for her smile broadened, and she said:

'It is Greek dancing that I do.'

'Oh - er - do you?' said Murchison. 'That - er - must be very interesting.'

'Yes,' said Miss Brangwyn, 'it is very interesting.'

And then, mercifully, a deep-toned gong sounded in the depths below them, and she led the way down to lunch, Murchison feeling as if he could kick himself, for though he was not blessed with facile manners with women, he had never in his born days behaved like this before. He prayed that his employer would preside at the lunch table, but his prayer was not answered, and he and Miss Brangwyn settled down to a *tête à tête*. Miss Brangwyn heaved a slight sigh, and encouraged Luigi to chatter recipes.

With the discovery of the complete impossibility of Murchison, it seemed as if Miss Brangwyn's own constraint passed off, and she set herself to entertain him kindly and patiently.

Murchison realized quite clearly what was her attitude towards him, and it did not improve his state of mind. She had evidently decided that he was of weak mentality, but otherwise harmless. He would have given much to be able to inform her that she was entirely mistaken in her estimate of him; he was of perfectly normal mentality under normal circumstances, but far from harmless; in fact he would cheerfully have murdered her if he could have thought of any way of disposing of her body.

Silence fell between them after Luigi had served the coffee and disappeared; a silence which neither made any attempt to break, each having given the other up as a bad job; when a sudden exclamation from Murchison made the girl look up, startled, to find that he was staring fixedly at her breast.

'What is it? What is the matter?' she exclaimed involuntarily.

'I'm frightfully sorry,' said Murchison. 'I am afraid I am making a complete ass of myself, but the fact of the matter is I had a bit of a shock yesterday, and I'm not quite over it yet.'

'But what was it made you look at me like that?' demanded the girl, in her turn shaken out of her equanimity.

'Nothing. It was a mistake. I'm sorry.' He fixed his eyes on his plate. She raised her hand nervously to her breast. Was it possible that her clothes had fallen off her back? She could think of nothing else to account for his startled expression. Her garments proved to be intact; but as she fingered them she felt under her hand a small carved plaque of dark green jade that hung from a thin gold chain round her neck; a plaque that should have been safely bestowed out of sight under her frock, but which, in the exigencies of leaning forward to drink her soup, had slipped from the folds and escaped; and on this plaque was carved in bas-relief a winged bull of Babylon. Her fingers closed upon it convulsively.

'What do you know about my bull?' she demanded; and now there was nothing to choose between them in bewilderment and mental confusion.

'God only knows,' said Murchison, staring straight before him in acute misery. 'I don't know anything about it. I saw one like it at the British Museum yesterday. That is all!'

'That isn't all,' said Ursula Brangwyn in a low voice. 'You know more about it than that. I wish you would be frank with me.'

36

'There is nothing to be frank about,' said Murchison sulkily. 'I have told you all there is to tell. I saw a bull like that one on your locket yesterday at the British Museum. I have never seen one before, and I don't know a thing about it.'

The girl looked at him fixedly. 'I had a feeling when you saw me in the lounge that you recognized me, as if you had seen me before. Where was it you saw me? I have never seen you before to my knowledge, but I saw that you knew me.'

Murchison felt himself reddening.

'I wish you would be frank with me,' said the girl, 'you are making things very difficult for me. I don't know where I am, or what is expected of me. My brother simply sent for me. He gave no explanation. He simply said he wanted me to see that the spare rooms were got ready for a Mr. Murchison, who was stopping with him, and to look after him till he got back in the afternoon. And as soon as I saw you, I saw you knew me, and were surprised to see me here; and now I see you know my bull. I do not understand. I - I wish you would be frank with me,' she ended lamely.

Murchison saw that she was really startled and distressed, and her confusion restored his self-possession for the first time since he had set eyes on her.

'I don't understand things either,' he said slowly, squashing his cigarette-end in the saucer of his coffee cup. 'I'll tell you frankly all there is to tell, if it is any help to you. Yesterday I was at the end of my tether. Out of a job, and down on my luck, and all the rest of it. And I turned into the British Museum to kill an hour or two. And I suppose I was pretty wrought up, what with one thing and another. And I came face to face with one of those winged bulls that stand near the entrance to the Egyptian Gallery, and in the half-light - you remember how foggy it was yesterday - I thought the blessed thing was alive for a moment, and it gave me a turn. And I got into a queer mood, I don't know why, and I sort of rose up and cursed. Your brother heard me, and spoke to me. I was wandering about in the fog in the yard outside the Museum. And we found we knew each other. I had been under him during the War. And he offered me a job, for which I was truly thankful, for I was down and out, I don't mind telling you. And I suppose the whole thing upheaved me. You get upheaved when you're down and out. That's all there is to it. I don't understand it. It upheaved me beyond all reason. I am not usually the sort of idiot I am to-day.'

'I begin to understand a little,' said the girl, leaning her chin on her hand and staring at him thoughtfully. 'But you say you had never seen the bull before?'

'Never,' said Murchison. 'I was in an upheaved condition at the time, or I shouldn't have flown off the handle like I did.'

Ursula Brangwyn continued to stare, but made no comment. Finally she said, 'But you still haven't told me where it was you saw me before.'

Murchison felt himself getting as red as a turkey-cock under her scrutiny. He knew by the books on her shelves that she was a student of psychology, and felt she would put her own interpretation on his dream, and lied gamely:

'I have never seen you before.' She continued to fix him with her unblinking gaze.

'I am going to be very rude and say that I am not sure that I believe that,' she said, 'and I think it would be much simpler if we were frank with each other.'

'All right,' said Murchison. 'I don't mind, if you don't. Your brother put me to sleep in your room last night because the spare room wasn't ready; and I dreamt that a woman's head, no bigger than an orange, hung in the air at the foot of the bed. Of course, when I woke up there was nothing there, and I realized that it was a sort of female version of your brother, of whom I have always been very fond; and when I saw you I was struck by the likeness, that was all.' She must think what she pleased, if she were a Freud fan; he couldn't help it. But he was certain the scientific interpretation of that dream was pretty wide of the mark.

Ursula Brangwyn continued to stare at him fixedly without speaking. Then, to his surprise, she shut her eyes for a long moment, and then opened them and blinked like one awakening from sleep.

'Now I think I know why I have been sent for,' she said.

'I am afraid I don't,' said Murchison. 'Won't you be frank with me, as I have been with you? It was to be mutual, you know.'

She stirred the dregs of her coffee thoughtfully.

'You say you have never seen the bull before?' she said.

'Never,' said Murchison for the third time.

'Well, it is connected with an experiment my brother is doing, and that I am helping him with.'

'What sort of an experiment?'

'An experiment in psychology.'

'I am going to be just as rude as you were, Miss Brangwyn, and say that I don't believe your explanation any more than you believed mine.'

'I dare say you don't,' said the girl, 'though it is the truth as far as it goes. There is an old saying that it takes two to tell the truth, one to speak it and the other to hear it.'

'Well, I've been frank with you, and you've had a pretty good look at my immortal soul, which, believe me, it's no pleasure to me to wear on my sleeve.'

'Yes,' said the girl, 'I know you have, and I appreciate it. But it isn't easy to tell you the truth because you would probably misunderstand it if it were told you. Let me put it this way' - she looked up suddenly -'My brother thinks that there was a great deal more in the old pagan faiths than is generally realized, and he is investigating them from the psychological point of view. I have undertaken to help him' - her eyes avoided his, and a wave of colour flooded her face and neck, and even spread down her bare arms. Then she raised her eyes determinedly to his again, and looking him straight in the face, she said, 'I think he thinks you would be able to help him. And I think he sent for me so that I could see whether I would be able to work with you or not.'

'I have been engaged as secretary, Miss Brangwyn, and the engagement is only temporary, till your brother goes abroad.'

Miss Brangwyn stared into her coffee.

'My brother will not go abroad if the experiment is going on all right,' she said in a low voice.

Murchison saw in a flash the loophole that had been left for retreat if Miss Brangwyn had disapproved of him as a possible collaborator. He wondered why she had been embarrassed when he came up for inspection, and he guessed that the departure of her embarrassment had been due to the fact that she had made up her mind that he definitely would not do, and, therefore, she would not be called upon to work with him. But that since he had spoken openly she had revised her decision, and with the revision her embarrassment had returned.

The girl lifted her head and looked at him with a curious, almost frightened expression on her face.

'I had better warn you,' she said, 'that the experiment has already been tried once and - and it went wrong. And I got rather a bad shock that upset me a good deal at the time, though I think I am over it now, but it may have left me a little jumpy.'

'Of course, I don't know what my position in the matter is until I have had a talk with your brother,' said Murchison, 'but you can rely on me to do everything I can to fit in with you.'

'Thanks,' said Ursula Brangwyn, and rose from the table.

CHAPTER 6

Murchison retired upstairs to his own quarters and began to sort his meagre belongings, realizing as he did so that two-thirds of them had not been worth the trouble of transport. The task did not take long, for he was not a fastidious person, and contented himself with separating his boots from his collars and his shaving-tackle from his writing materials. This job finished, he cast about for occupation, for he did not want to engage in making push-conversation with Miss Brangwyn till tea-time, and possibly have to parry further awkward questions.

She was a queer girl. He did not know what to make of her. He wasn't sure that he liked her particularly. Still, it was necessary to keep the peace with his employer's household if he wanted to keep his job. He would have to rub along with Miss Brangwyn to the best of his ability, and the easiest way to keep the peace was to reduce intercourse to a minimum. He promised himself that she should never get through his armour again.

And then he fell to wondering what the girl herself was up to. She had reacted to him in exactly the same way that he had reacted to her. It looked as if the winged bull were a mutual friend. He recalled Brangwyn's remark about the invocation of Pan. It was an odd menage, and promised to be highly entertaining, provided he did not allow himself to be dragged in out of his depth. His role had always been as spectator of the game of life rather than participant. He must hold firmly to his role of spectator while he was in this house. It was the only safe one. If he drove his roots in too deeply there would be a nasty wrench if Brangwyn went abroad, or for any other reason terminated his engagement. Murchison's strongest instinct was to protect himself from disappointment by not expecting too much of life, an expectation which had been amply justified up to the present. Above all, he must keep the peace with Miss Brangwyn, and avoid heart to heart talks, which would probably end in friction.

He went into his sitting-room and lit the gas fire. Dashed comfortable quarters, he thought to himself, sinking into a deep, leather-covered armchair and putting his feet on the fender. The fireplace was flanked on either side by narrow bookcases, no wider than a step-ladder, and he turned in his chair and inspected the books in the one nearest to him. They were an odd assortment, and yet they did not look like chuck-outs from anybody's library. Psychology predominated, but there was a representative collection of ancient fables retold in popular style, apparently for the senior classes of schools, and finely illustrated. He selected one and began to turn over the pages, seeing Pan and the nymphs in Arcadia; Apollo driving the chariot of the sun; Aphrodite born of the sea-foam; and Dionysus with his Maenads racing over the mountains. All the lovely old myths of the childhood of man retold for children. Curious that these should appeal so much to generation after generation of mankind, while 'The Fairchild Family' and 'A Flat Iron for a Farthing' went into the discard.

He turned the page, and found himself among the animal-headed gods of Egypt, backed by the vast pylons of temples, with an indigo sky above and yellow sand beneath. Then he turned another page, and found himself face to face yet again with the winged bull. He stared at the beast, which stared back at him from the printed page.

'What in God's name are you up to?' he admonished it. 'Why do you keep on bobbing up? What's it all about? I never set eyes on you until yesterday, and now you fairly haunt me, and whenever you turn up something drastic starts to happen.'

He laid the book on the arm of the big chair, open at the picture, and considered it. The beast had a man's head, an animal's body and eagle's wings. It must have meant something to the man who made it, as the lamb with the halo and flag did to us. Curious how these symbols of forgotten faiths appealed to him while the symbols of his own faith irritated him. He had had enough of sacrifice and self-abnegation and turning the other cheek. He honestly didn't think it was sound. It was the negation of everything which appealed to his instincts as manly and honourable and self-respecting. The fruits of it that he had seen in his brother's home and his brother's church did not seem to him particularly worth while. Soured women, smug men, whom he was pretty certain weren't as good as they looked - no human being could be and keep his sanity - who all regarded him as a black sheep. And yet he honestly thought he was a better specimen of the genus homo than they were. There was a dashed sight too much of impossibly high ideals, to which no one except the unmarried females gave anything except lip-service, and a dashed sight too little of common decency. Too many haloes and

41

too few guts, was his way of putting it. His brother looked like a mediaeval saint out of a stained-glass window, very much the priest; his sister-in-law looked like a superannuated cook, and the children looked like nothing on earth, poor little brats, and there was precious little of sweetness, light or vitamins in the vicarage menage. He had had a close-up of religious life behind the scenes, and it had proved a sickener. If these were God's chosen, he did not admire God's taste.

Only cadgers throve in that atmosphere; only sycophants were tolerated at the vicarage; there was something dashed unwholesome about all those devoted spinsters who hung around his brother; it seemed to him his brother was a sort of spiritual stallion to the entire roster of Sunday-school teachers and district visitors and all the other unwanted females who help to work the parishes of the Church of England. In the old days they put a phallus up on a pole and adored it as the symbol of the fecundating principle. He rather fancied that James's surplice served much the same purpose.

The sudden ringing of a telephone bell startled him, for he had not noticed a phone in the room, and it was a moment or two before he could locate it. When he did so, he heard Brangwyn's voice at the other end:

'Will you come down to tea, Murchison?' and guessed that it was a house telephone. Brangwyn was a dashed good man at staff-work; everything in that house was thought out down to the last tin-tack.

The moment Murchison entered the lounge he knew that he had been under discussion. There was a sudden cutting-off of the conversation, a sudden seeking for superficial topics, that told him that whatever had been discussed could now be discussed no more. Ursula Brangwyn was making the tea with an electric kettle on a low tabouret beside her chair, and it was difficult to believe that this was the same beverage that arrived up from the vicarage basement in the tea-pot with the rubber spout. It was aromatic, and smelt of flowers, and the cup was no thicker than a piece of paper.

The girl looked up as he entered and their eyes met, and there was something in her expression that seemed to him to imply an understanding between them. But he did not want understandings with Ursula Brangwyn. That was the way to all sorts of trouble. So he did not speak either, and took jolly good care not to catch her eye again. He became very much the employee and only spoke when spoken to, and then governed his replies by Euclid's definition of a straight line, as being the shortest distance between two points.

Miss Brangwyn made no attempt to help anybody out, but

Brangwyn himself made push-conversation gamely. He talked of the political situation; he talked of mutual reminiscences of the War; finally he was reduced to talking of the weather.

The moment that tea was over Miss Brangwyn disappeared up the corkscrew stairs without apology, and the tension in the atmosphere appreciably relaxed. Murchison heaved a sigh of relief. Despite his stoical exterior he was acutely sensitive to atmospheres, and for anyone to attempt to deceive him with regard to their attitude towards him was a waste of energy.

They sat smoking in silence; but the silence was not uncomfortable. Brangwyn stared into the fire, and Murchison watched Brangwyn, wondering what was passing in his mind, and how it would bear upon his own affairs, which hung by so slender a thread upon his employer's grace. It might be, in fact, that they hung by an even slenderer thread, being suspended from the caprices of the temperamental Miss Brangwyn. A quick wave of resentment went over Murchison at the thought. It did not matter what loyalty, what capacity, he brought to the service of his employer if he could not placate that damned girl. Murchison doubted his capacity to placate any girl, damned or otherwise. Females had never been his strong suit.

Finally Brangwyn broke the silence.

'Let's put the cards on the table, shall we, Murchison? I don't believe in beating about the bush, do you?'

Murchison grunted, and then wondered whether he ought to address his employer as sir.

'You have been talking to my sister, I gather. How much did she tell you of my affairs?'

'She said you were interested in psychology and extinct religions.'

'Extinct religions? Mmmm,' said Brangwyn. 'That's exactly what I'm not interested in. I'm interested in some very much alive religions.'

Murchison offered neither question nor comment. Brangwyn, crushing a momentary impulse to take a hammer and drive nails into his thick head, paused to consider the best mode of approach to his unresponsive secretary.

'Has it ever occurred to you to wonder what such a symbol as the winged bull meant to the men who made it?' Murchison hesitated for a long moment. 'Yes,' he said at length. 'That was just exactly what I was wondering upstairs while I was looking at the books in my quarters.'

'Did you notice the nature of the books?'

'A mixture of ancient religions and modern psychology.'

'Precisely. And those represent my interests, as Ursula told you. And those books were put there that you might have a look at them, Murchison.'

'All right,' said Murchison, 'I'll read 'em.'

This was heavy going, thought Brangwyn, but he persevered. Murchison's outcry of 'Io Pan' in the forecourt of the British Museum; his psychism, which had enabled him to see the face of Ursula Brangwyn in his dream; and his emotion at the sight of the jade pendant all told him that his new secretary was by no means as stolid as he looked, and that his stolidity was probably his front line of defence against a world that wipes its boots on sensitiveness, wherever found. It was not an easy thing to find sensitiveness combined with a burly virility, as was the case in the somewhat rough-looking customer seated opposite to him. Brangwyn had in his mind another man, who had possessed many qualities that Murchison did not, but who had lacked the necessary alloy of honest earth. The over-tempered steel had snapped and splintered, and some of the splinters had gone into Ursula Brangwyn's heart. There had been wounds all round, and Brangwyn had not yet got the taste out of his mouth of the interview in which he had had to put hard facts in front of his sister and make her face them. Not that she had baulked at facing them. She was a thoroughbred. But her face as she did it - that was what he could not forget. And he had a shrewd suspicion that although the wound had healed on the surface, there were some splinters still lingering inside it, and it had not healed underneath. There was sepsis somewhere in Ursula Brangwyn's soul, and that sepsis had got to be got out, even if he operated on her without an anaesthetic.

He thought of the man who had caused all the trouble. He had been a remarkable personality, both physically and mentally; resembling some such swift creature as a stag, or a racehorse, or a greyhound. And his mind had had the same swift litheness. And then Brangwyn caught himself up suddenly. Why was he thinking of the fellow in the past tense as if he were dead? Of course, he wasn't dead; he was alive, God help him. It would have been a great deal better for him if he had been dead.

Brangwyn looked at the man on the other side of the fireplace. He had slipped down on the cushions in the deep chair till he was practically sitting on his shoulder-blades. His clumsily shod feet were gracelessly asprawl on the hearthrug, and his expression was sullen as he stared into the fire and gnawed the knuckles of his big, freckled hands. His rough, thick, fair hair stood up like the crest of a fretful cockatoo. His profile, seen against the dark background of the panelling, revealed a short, blunt nose, high cheekbones and a heavy jaw. A bulldog type, thought Brangwyn; thick-necked, heavy-shouldered, lumbering; but very staunch and enduring. This was a man who would never let you down, thought his employer. Once he got his teeth into a thing, he would hang on. Brangwyn had a sudden vision of a boy's face seen under a tin hat, blue eyes ablaze with the lust of battle. Murchison had always gone over the top shouting and laughing, completely berserk; appearing thoroughly to enjoy himself; charging like a bull into the thick of a bunch of Bosches.

The bull of Babylon, and all it meant - thought Brangwyn. The other fellow had been a stag. He had not fitted in with the bull symbolism. But this chap was an altogether different proposition. A creature of earth, but with volcanic fire inside him. That was how he summed him up; and that would suit his purpose very well indeed. Now, if he could only handle Murchison in just the right way, and get him where he wanted him, everything would be all right, even if he did not look a very promising specimen at the moment, sitting there gnawing his knuckles and sulking, and refusing to eat out of anybody's hand.

So he returned to the attack. 'What do you suppose it means,' he said, 'that the bull of Babylon has a man's head, a beast's body and bird's wings?'

'Haven't we all got beast's bodies?' said Murchison without looking up. 'Except, of course, my brother, who's a parson, and ends at the neck in a little pair of wings.'

Brangwyn laughed.

'I don't think that's a very practical design, do you?'

'Some very necessary functions must be difficult,' said Murchison.

'What about the eagle's wings attached to the bull's body?'

'I don't know anything about wings,' said Murchison.

'But I do,' said Brangwyn.

Murchison looked up at him under heavy, sandy brows, but did not speak. Evidently he mistrusted wings.

'When you called upon Pan in the fog, hadn't you got eagle's wings to your bull's body?'

'For the moment, yes,' said Murchison.

'Has it ever occurred to you that there might be a technique in these things? A lost and forgotten art?'

Murchison sat staring into the fire for so long that Brangwyn thought he did not mean to answer. At length he said:

'When I called on Pan in the fog out there, I touched something.'

'What was it?'

45

'I've no idea.'

'What did it feel like?'

'Like alcohol on an empty stomach.'

'Ever get that feeling in church?'

'Only once. In the school chapel, when they had a farewell service to a party of us who were joining up. A different kind of force, but it came through with a rush in just the same way. The old padre was crying while he prayed. I've never felt anything but the draught in my brother's church, though.'

'Were you under a strong emotion when you were invoking Pan in the fog?'

'Yes.'

'What was it?'

'Resentment, I think. Resentment at life in general and God in particular. I was ripe for anything when you came along. I was just about ready for crime, sir.'

'Had you said to evil, Be thou my good?'

'No, not that. I wasn't out for evil. At least not what I consider to be evil. But I reckoned that my brother and all that church crush had got hold of things by the wrong end. They reckoned I was a bad egg according to their standards, and I had always reckoned so, too. Then it suddenly came to me that I wasn't a bad egg; I was all right, and they were fools; and I reckoned I was through with Jehovah.'

'Then you deny God?'

'No, I don't deny God, but I thought I'd like a change of gods. It may sound a queer thing to say, sir, but I reckon there are more gods than one. Christianity is a lop-sided affair, and this gentle Jesus business makes me vomit. There are a lot of the younger chaps who feel as I do. I think it's in the air.'

'I think so, too,' said Brangwyn. 'The precession of the equinoxes brings a new sign of the Zodiac into function every two thousand years, and we're about due for a change.'

'We certainly could do with a change,' said Murchison. 'Civilization seems to me to have gone bad on our hands.'

CHAPTER 7

Brangwyn had begun to realize that Murchison's conversational powers resembled a car that was a poor starter, but ran well enough when the engine warmed up. There was a caution and reserve, even a surly suspiciousness about him which argued a life lived in an unsympathetic atmosphere. He wondered how much of the spontaneity of the lively young subaltern would be recovered in a congenial environment.

There was nothing to do but turn the conversational starting-handle till his companion got going.

'Murchison,' he said quietly, 'do you know why it was I offered you this job?'

'No,' said Murchison.

'As I was coming out from the British Museum reading-room yesterday I heard someone calling upon Pan as if they meant it. That is a subject which happens to be my special line of interest, and I went to the trouble to grope about in the fog until I found the person who was making the noise. At the time I had no thought of offering him, or anyone else, a job -'

'I suspected as much,' said Murchison.

'It is not my custom to pick up casual strangers and ask them to hold my pocket-book in order to prove my faith in human nature; but I was sufficiently interested in this worshipper of the old gods to wish to make his acquaintance and compare experiences. But when I found that he was a man I knew, and a man whom I had proved to possess certain qualities, among which was reliability, I modified my plans; I thought, I can do more than compare experiences - I might be able to ask him to join me in experimentation. How does the idea appeal to you?'

Murchison played his usual trick of a long silence before reply. Finally he said:

'Five pounds a week appeals to an unemployed man; naturally I'd like a job, but it's not in my power to guarantee to deliver the kind of goods you're asking for.'

'I am not asking you to guarantee anything. All I should ask you to do is to carry out certain processes in a particular way and to put your heart into the job. I'll take all responsibility for the outcome.'

'All right,' said Murchison. 'Subject to a week's notice on either side, I'm your man.' And then, as an after-thought, he added, 'Thanks very much indeed, sir, I'm very grateful for the chance.'

'I dare say you've gathered that the secretarial duties are pretty negligible,' said Brangwyn. 'But what I want you to do is to familiarize yourself with the literature of the subject as a start. When you have got the general lie of the land in your head, we can proceed to details. I also want you to keep a record of your dreams and let me do a bit of analysis on them. As long as you are undertaking this job, I want you to be absolutely frank with me in the matter of your dreams and what comes out of them. That is the chief thing I ask of you. If you mislead me in even the smallest details in that matter, you will vitiate the result of the whole experiment. Are you prepared for that, Murchison?'

'I am if you are,' said Murchison, with a short laugh, 'you've had one sample of my efforts. You needn't worry about me. I'll tilt the ash-bin while you rootle in it, if that's what you want.'

'No, not precisely. We don't want King Charles' head, or any other portion of his anatomy, cropping up in every conversation. We won't have any predestined goal in the nether regions; we'll just observe, and see what comes up under the different stimuli to which I shall subject you.'

'Oh?' said Murchison, 'so I am to be a laboratory animal, am I?'

'Yes,' said Brangwyn, 'that is just exactly what you are to be. How do you like the prospect?'

'I like it all right with you, sir, because I trust you. But I shouldn't fancy it with anyone else. I shall be selling you my immortal soul, you know, if I do this job properly.'

'I am not going to put it that way, Murchison. No one can deal in immortal souls with impunity, either buying or selling. But I am hoping that you will get interested in the experiment and really muscle in on it. No one can command that. However much I could offer, and however much you wanted the job, it wouldn't make any difference.'

'Well, anyway, you can rely on one thing, sir. I'll do my best to give you a square deal. I won't take your money and play you up. I'll tell you the truth, the whole truth, and nothing but the truth to the best of my knowledge and belief. I can't do more than that, and I won't do less.'

'That,' said Brangwyn, 'is all I require. The rest is up to me.'

He rose from his chair and went over to the cupboard, from which on the previous evening he had taken out the peacock and crimson robes, opened it, and extracted a flowing garment of dark green silk, the colour of leaves in summer.

'Will you wear this, this evening?' he said. 'The robes are part of the equipment. Tell me, when you wore the blue robe last night, did you feel anything?'

'I felt as if my inhibitions loosened up.'

'In what way?'

'Well, I felt as if I could give my imagination rein without making a fool of myself.'

Brangwyn nodded, and Murchison saw that he was well content.

Murchison experienced a keen sensation of pleasure as he discarded his heavy everyday garments and wrapped the thin silk about him. Especially did he feel pleasure in the thin, light, glove-like slippers that enabled him to move so quietly over Brangwyn's thick carpets. He felt like a kid going to a pantomime as he came down the stairs from his own quarters and opened the door on to the gallery that surrounded the lounge.

It was not until he was on to the stairs that he suddenly realized with a shock of horror that Miss Brangwyn was going to see him in his fine feathers, and, looking down, saw her standing beneath him, watching his descent. Her appearance so amazed him that he completed the rest of the descent and came towards her without knowing what he did or where he was.

She, too, was dressed in green, but in the exquisitely delicate green of the youngest buds just opening. A loosely tied girdle of heavy gold cord confined the thin silk of her robe at the waist and defined her hips; two clasps caught the robe together on her shoulders, and the loose wide sleeves fell away from her arms like wings. Murchison felt as if her outer husk had dropped off, and for the first time he saw her as she really was.

Brangwyn, from his chair, was watching the descent of the stairs. He had seen his new secretary come striding along the gallery as if he had seven-league boots, evidently full of zest for the evening's entertainment, whatever it might prove to be, and thoroughly entering into the spirit of the game, like a small boy playing Indians with his uncle.

Then he had seen the sudden check and start as Murchison caught sight of Ursula, and watched him come down the rest of the stairs like a man in a dream. The game of Indians had become the real thing for him.

'We don't feed till on towards midnight, Murchison,' said his employer. 'But there are some cocktails and biscuits over on the table.

Help yourself. We don't want you fainting by the way.'

Murchison did as he was bid, pouring himself out a glass of sherry and starting to munch a handful of small biscuits.

'What do you generally do in the matter of alcohol?' asked Brangwyn. 'I take it if it's there. I should never go out to fetch it if it wasn't. I'm afraid I don't know much about vintages. Do you want me to knock off drink while I'm on the job?' He paused with the arrested glass half-way to his lips.

'I want you to go easy on it,' said Brangwyn. 'One glass has its uses occasionally, because it loosens inhibitions. But more than one is apt to be a nuisance, because it makes you see things exaggeratedly. Distorts them just when you particularly want accuracy. There are some parts of the work when it isn't wise to risk it, because even a small amount of alcohol might lead to things getting out of hand. But we aren't on that aspect at the moment, so go ahead and enjoy your drink.'

Murchison tossed down the sherry as if it were beer, and joined them on the hearthrug.

'I think Chesterton has the right idea,' said Brangwyn. 'He says that it is all right to drink because you like it, but all wrong to drink because you need it. All right to drink to make yourself super-normal at a party, but all wrong to drink to make yourself normal for your day's work. I wouldn't in the least mind bailing you out at Bow Street occasionally, but I should hate to see you nipping.'

'Thank God you aren't a higher lifer, sir,' said Murchison. 'I should have found it very hard to bear.'

'Now,' said Brangwyn cheerfully, 'since we are all going to work together, I suggest that we have a pleasant social evening and get to know each other a bit better.' And he began to turn the handle of a cabinet gramophone.

'I wonder what you mean by getting to know each other better?' thought Murchison to himself, the sherry working valiantly inside him, as it was meant to do. 'But here goes. I'm game for anything.'

Brangwyn put in a record. 'I suggest you two have a dance together. My dancing days are over. And, in any case, I don't know the new dances.'

'I thought my dancing days were over, too,' said Murchison. 'I haven't danced since I was demobbed. I am afraid I'm not very up to date. Miss Brangwyn will have to teach me the new steps.'

'She'll do that all right,' said Brangwyn.

Murchison thought it odd that all this time Miss Brangwyn had never opened her mouth. Neither now nor during tea.

A one-step began to bray from the gramophone, and the girl rose from her chair and held out her hands. He put his arm round her, and they moved off in the rhythmic walk of modern dancing. Brangwyn switched the rugs from under their feet and sent all his wheeled furniture flying into the corners, leaving a wide expanse of polished parquetry bare for the dance.

Murchison knew at once that the girl in his arms was a beautiful dancer; he himself had a keen sense of rhythm and the muscular control and balance that athletics gives, and they went together well enough, though, as Murchison thought to himself, nothing to write home about. By the end of the record, however, they had got into each other's ways, and were a rather more than presentable couple.

'A gramophone's all right,' said Brangwyn, 'but there's no life about it. Let me get my violin and play for you.'

He took a violin from a case that lay beside the gramophone, tested it lightly, and began to play. Murchison noted that it was already tuned. He had a suspicion that the dance record on the gramophone had been a try-out, to see how he and Ursula went together, and, not having disgraced themselves, something more was about to commence.

'Ever tried following a changing rhythm?' said Brangwyn. 'It's most amusing. Change your step as I change my rhythm and tempo.'

They moved off in a slow waltz, and Murchison noted at once the difference between dancing to the living player and dancing to the mechanical instrument. He felt the girl in his arms respond also.

The tempo quickened, and they found themselves moving in the old-fashioned whirling waltz.

'Don't reverse,' called out Brangwyn, and slid into a one-step again, and they moved in a gliding walk till the incipient giddiness had worked off.

Once again Brangwyn swung them into the waltz and began to work up the tempo, always stopping them just on the verge of giddiness, and never permitting a reverse.

Murchison felt that Ursula preferred the waltz, but he liked the one-step best himself. Then the one-step gave a few lilting bars and swung into a military march, and he found himself walking sheer heel and toe, with Ursula springing lightly backwards at his side. He shifted his hand from her waist to her shoulder to give freer play.

('Come on, my lass,' he said to himself, 'you're for it now. This is my kingdom!') The fighting man had come into his own. These were the rhythms to which his heart answered. He swung Ursula round the corner in a way that would have sent anyone but a trained dancer off her feet.

Brangwyn slid into one of the old marching-songs of the War, and suddenly a deep baritone rang through the room as Murchison, all self-consciousness forgotten in the exhilaration of the dance, burst into song.

'It's a long way to Tipperary,
It's a long way to go,
But there's a girl I know in Tipperary,
A lovely girl I know.'

Murchison had had his one brief day of self-fulfilment in the War; all else had been utter repression and negation. He was the fighting man par excellence, and there was not much he had to offer a commercial world in peace-time. The old tune took him back to his halcyon days, marching with the men of his company behind him; men who trusted him absolutely, who would follow him anywhere; into whom he had managed to infuse his own joy of battle, and who believed firmly that they bore charmed lives while under his command and that no Bosche could stand against them. He had had the glorious sense of being part of a vast whole, caught up in its life, moving with its momentum. He was hardly conscious of Ursula as he swept her round the room. What she thought, what she felt, whether his employer approved of his secretary bursting into song - he neither knew nor cared. He was away in another world, his head among the stars, his feet treading upon the mountains.

'There's a long, long trail a-winding
To the land of my dreams -

Sang the violin, and the rapid toe and heel changed to a steady pacing, and then slid into waltz-rhythms based on 'Kathleen Mavourneen'. Murchison gathered Ursula closer for the waltz, and the two listeners heard a strange and moving thing - the sulky and solitary Murchison, who was anything but a lady's man, singing the song of love and longing with his whole heart, moving to its rhythm, utterly forgetful of his audience, rapt away by the simple folk-music.

Brangwyn ceased playing as the last words of the song came from Murchison's lips, and the dance ended abruptly. Murchison blinked as if suddenly awakened from deep sleep and looked down to see who his partner was, and to his surprise saw that there were tears on Ursula's cheeks. He blinked again, and then let go of her hastily. Brangwyn mixed cocktails without a word, and gave them one apiece.

Murchison sipped his glass and then stared thoughtfully at it. He would not look at Ursula, and did not know whether she was looking at him or not. As a matter of fact, she was. She was looking at him as if she had never seen him before; in the same way that he had looked at her when he saw her in her leaf-green robe, and Brangwyn, watching them, nodded to himself with inward satisfaction. The experiment had begun to move.

'It's a little earlier than our usual time, but I think we'll have a meal,' he said, knowing that food would rapidly bring them back to normal, for he did not want tensions to become too acute at the present moment, and one or the other to take fright.

Luigi, as usual, produced a meal out of his hat with the sweetest of smiles. His presence in and out of the room while it was in progress further assisted in the damping-down of the atmosphere, to Murchison's great relief, for he felt as if were skiing on unknown slopes, and did not know where he might land himself.

After the meal they returned to the lounge. The fire of logs was blazing brightly, its warm flickering light filling the room but leaving the high gallery in shadow and mystery. Brangwyn switched on a shaded reading-lamp, but left the wall lights extinguished, and in the flickering half-light Ursula Brangwyn made coffee with her electric kettle on the low tabouret at her side, and the two men lay back in their chairs and smoked, and watched her.

Brangwyn rose and fetched a portfolio, and, opening it, gave Murchison a handful of water-colour sketches. 'These may amuse you,' he said, 'they are the fruit of my travels.'

Murchison bent down to bring the portfolio within the narrow circle of light thrown by the shaded reading-lamp, and began to look through them. They were studies of Egypt, but not the vivid poster-colours of the pictures in the children's books upstairs, but Egypt seen through the haze of time that gave the imagination a chance to work. The shadowy temples, half-seen in twilight or veiled in sun-glare, caught at his imagination. The forgotten splendour of that civilization was all about him, and sorrow at its irreparable loss took him by the heart. It seemed as if they lived in a dead world to-day, and could only remember ancient glories that were no more. The shades of the prison-house had closed about them; the great gods had departed and the temples were empty and desolate. He felt he would give his soul to see Horus mount the morning with the wings of a hawk and to hear the boom of the Kephra beetle in the dusk. These things were the gods to him, and the orthodoxy of today was stale, flat and unprofitable.

'These also will interest you,' said Brangwyn, handing him another portfolio, and he recognized the strange step-temples of Yucatan, festooned with creepers and jungle-weed.

'Do you see the likeness between the two styles of architecture?' asked Brangwyn, and Murchison looked more closely and saw that the architecture of the New World seemed to be an archaic version of the architecture of ancient Egypt.

'Did you ever hear of the tradition of the lost continent of Atlantis?' said Brangwyn.

'No, I can't say that I have.'

'Plato heard of it from the Egyptian priests, and he was no fool, and neither were they. They believed that their civilisation was derived from the Lost Continent. And it is a very curious fact that there are remarkable points of resemblance between the two cultures, though there has been no communication between them within historical times. It has been one of my hobbies to trace out these points of resemblance, and the further you go, the more you see in it. At any rate, if Egypt did not get her culture from Atlantis, where did she get it from? There are no primitive Egyptian remains; it is always a full-blown culture, even from the first.'

The idea of a lost continent took hold of Murchison's imagination, as it has of that of many.

'What happened to it. How did it get lost?' he asked.

'It is supposed to have been overwhelmed by volcanic catastrophe because of its extreme wickedness in its latter days. It is a curious fact that at the exact spot that Plato gives as its site there is the Great Atlantic Deep, an enormous gash in the ocean floor, like the Grand Canyon of Colorado, and it was not discovered until modern deep-sea sounding apparatus revealed it. It is also a fact, within my personal knowledge, that the psychic atmosphere is such that it completely capsizes the crews of a cable-ship when they have to hang about there doing cable repairs. They dread going there. There are some spots on the earth's surface like that, you know, Murchison. Spots where psychic influences have been concentrated, both good and evil, and anyone who is at all sensitive feels it.'

'I went into the Polynesian Gallery at the British Museum the same time that I was mucking around with the winged bull,' said Murchison,

54

completely forgetting the silent presence of Miss Brangwyn. 'And, my goodness, I came out quicker than I went in! It fairly stank. And when I was doing my invocation in the yard it suddenly struck me that I might be raising some of the critters upstairs, and it gave me quite a turn for a moment; but I reckoned they were the fag-end of something, and not the genuine article, and, as it turned out, I was right.'

Brangwyn, although he dared not look at his sister as this confession was being made, felt her prick up her ears.

'The fag-end of anything is apt to be unpleasant,' he said, 'but I don't believe there is any such thing as innate evil, but only misplaced force. It was the same in Atlantis. It's end was evil, but its hey-day was great. There was knowledge there that we have never matched since, and that went down with the Lost Continent, save such as was preserved by the Egyptian priests. They bred for knowledge in those days, bred humans, I mean, just as we breed racehorses for speed. And they got their results. They say that it is the Atlanteans' intensive breeding that gave us the high human forehead, and that the primitive tribes tried to imitate it with the cradle-board, that squashes the heads of the babies into the aristocratic shape.'

'Dashed sensible,' said Murchison, 'the breeding, I mean. Pity we don't do the same thing nowadays - heads of colleges at stud - I beg your pardon, Miss Brangwyn, I didn't mean to say that!'

Ursula's laughter restored the blushing Murchison to composure, and the ice seemed more thoroughly broken by the little touch of smut that makes the whole world kin than it would have been by hours of high-browed exchange of views.

'It was a wise old divine who said, Why should we be ashamed to speak of what God was not ashamed to create?' said Brangwyn. 'An enormous amount of the troubles of modern civilization come from our ignorance concerning the breeding of humans. I think that the Atlanteans were absolutely right when they gave very careful thought to the matter, and the priests kept the stud-books.'

'It's the banks keep the stud-books nowadays,' said Murchison, thinking bitterly of the remoteness of any prospect of a home of his own.

Brangwyn nodded, watching him; but Ursula Brangwyn broke silence for the first time that evening.

'I am afraid I don't understand that allusion,' she said.

'Well, Miss Brangwyn,' said Murchison, 'whom you marry, when you marry, or, for the matter of that, whether you marry at all, depends entirely on how much you have in the bank. If there's family money that comes to you as soon as you're twenty-one, you get the girl you want and marry while you're still young enough to enjoy life. If there isn't, you have to wait until you're both sere and yellow, and then you produce squint-eyed kids.

'What the Government ought to do is to subsidize the breeding of humans instead of horses and cows. Give the hefty young chaps who are drawing the dole a chance to become fathers of families. It would be a dashed good national investment.'

'The trouble is,' said Ursula, 'that humans are so fastidious. They would want to marry to please themselves, not the Government. The hefty young men would probably fall in love with girls with awful ancestors and the human stud-book would go all wrong.'

'It would certainly require wisdom to arrange the matings,' said Brangwyn, 'and wisdom is one of the lost arts. I fancy it went down with Atlantis.' He rose. 'I am going to pack you two children off to bed. I have work to do.'

CHAPTER 8

Murchison went to bed in a very cheerful frame of mind. He had not enjoyed an evening so much for years. His cramped soul was uncurling itself and beginning to get the kinks out of it. He wondered what dreams he would have to produce for his employer's delectation in the morning, and whether he would be expected to dream of lost Atlantis, or a previous incarnation as a Pharaoh. He only hoped to goodness that the houris would behave themselves.

In response to his employer's questionings twelve hours later, however, he had nothing more interesting to produce than a vision of chasing a black cat round and round the flat.

'What sort of a cat was it?' asked Brangwyn, 'did you notice anything special about it?'

'It was a long-haired, fuzzy sort of beast, a Persian, I suppose,' Murchison was truly thankful to have such an innocent dream for production, at which the chastest stars might peep. Brangwyn, however, chuckled inwardly, remembering his sister's nickname of Kitten, which her aureole of wavy dark hair and small, pointed, oval face had earned her.

'I want to take this opportunity of having a few words with you before my sister appears. We can trust Ursula to be late. I have got rather a curious problem on my hands. I had trouble with your predecessor, and had to chuck him out more or less violently. There are some papers of mine that he wants to get hold of, and I do not think he would stick at very much to do it. You must keep your eyes skinned. Don't admit anybody to the flat on any pretext whatever in my absence.'

'Right you are, sir,' said Murchison cheerfully. 'Out they go, dead or alive!'

At this moment Miss Brangwyn entered, putting a stop to the conversation.

'What train are you catching, Ursula?' inquired her brother.

'The 10:57,' replied the girl.

'Ah,' said Brangwyn, 'I am afraid I shall not be able to see you off by that, but perhaps Murchison would be good enough.'

'Certainly,' said Murchison, quite amiably for him. He felt much happier with Miss Brangwyn since she had laughed at his lapse into smoking-room idiom. It seemed as if her mentality were nearer that of a man's, and therefore less incalculable than that of the average virtuous female, whom he privately considered an unnatural product of civilisation. It struck him as odd that his grenadier of a sister-in-law, who could put the fear of God into tradesmen, jobbing gardeners and hoc genus omne, and had brought nine children into the world, of whom five survived and were now reaching years of indiscretion, should be pure-minded to the verge of prudery, and the ethereal-looking Miss Brangwyn should laugh at a smoking-room jest.

Their late breakfast did not leave them much time for the train, and Brangwyn pushed them off straight from the table. Alone with Ursula in the taxi, Murchison was at a loss to know what to say to her. There were only two subjects which they had so far found in common, bulls and stallions, and he did not feel inclined to introduce either of them by the cold light of morning.

'Have you a long journey in front of you?' he asked politely.

'North Wales,' said Miss Brangwyn. 'I go as far as Llandudno junction by train, and then I have a long car-run right up into the mountains.'

Murchison opened his eyes at this information. The Brangwyns must consider his part in the forthcoming experiment of considerable importance if the girl would take such a journey as that in order to inspect him. Brangwyn must have put through a trunk call, and she must have travelled all night in order to arrive when she did.

There was neither luggage nor ticket to attend to, so they had ample time in hand at the station, thanks to Brangwyn's urgency, and Murchison sat down opposite Ursula on the wide, padded seat of the empty first-class compartment to keep her company till the train started. They had hardly settled themselves when a shadow fell across the carriage, and a man appeared in the doorway leading into the corridor.

'Well, Ursula?' he said, 'how are you?' And, without waiting for an invitation, he came in and sat down beside her. Murchison stared at him resentfully; he was just beginning to enjoy talking to Miss Brangwyn.

He saw before him a tall but slenderly built man, who was exceedingly carefully dressed, and whose perfectly regular features had a chiselled perfection that promised nonentity if it had not been for the high, narrow forehead, which relieved the face from ordinariness though it did not add to its attractiveness. Murchison thought to himself that a man with a forehead like that was sure to be a wrong 'un, though he could not have given his reasons for the impression. He felt that he did not like the man, quite apart from the fact of his intrusion; in fact, he disliked him very much indeed. The newcomer possessed personality to a marked degree; one felt it even as he stood in the doorway, and the personality he possessed was of a kind that made Murchison's hackle rise.

There was a dead silence in the carriage of such a peculiar quality that Murchison turned and looked at Ursula. She never had any colour in her cheeks, but normally they were of a creamy magnolia hue which is perfectly healthy, but as he stared he saw her gradually go the colour of ashes. The pupils of her large, dark eyes slowly dilated until there was no iris left, and they were uncanny pools of blackness. And all the while she never spoke or moved, but stared at the newcomer like a bird fascinated by a snake. He, for his part, watched this painful exhibition with evident satisfaction, and made no attempt to put her at her ease.

A wave of hot anger swept over Murchison. It was too bad for a nice girl like Ursula Brangwyn to be scared half to death by this unpleasant individual. He wasn't going to have it. Now Murchison was decidedly slow in social relationships, but he was quick enough when action was needed. He knew it was impossible to drive the newcomer out of the carriage, for he had as good a right to be there as Ursula had, so he leant forward and placed his hand on the girl's knee.

'I am afraid you're not feeling very fit,' he said. 'Would you like to come along with me to the buffet and I'll get you a drop of brandy?'

She turned her dazed eyes from the other man and gazed helplessly at Murchison without speaking. He looked her steadily in the eye and gripped her with his will, as he had done with panicking Tommies many a time out in France. He did not wait for any reply from her, but opened the door of the carriage and got out, and then leant in and lifted her out bodily, as if she had been a child, set her on her feet, holding her as she leant helplessly up against him, and said over her shoulder to the disgusted young man in the carriage:

'You keep out of the way unless you want your head punched.'

Murchison supported Ursula, who hardly seemed capable of setting one foot in front of the other, into the refreshment-room, and sat her down on a corner settee where she could lean her head back against the cushions, sent the waitress for brandy, and, diluting it with no more than its own bulk in water, took Ursula firmly by the head and poured it down her throat.

'Are you obliged to travel by this train?' he asked, 'because you are going to have your friend as a travelling companion. Why not come back to the flat and have a rest, and go on later?'

Ursula nodded acquiescence, and he led her out of the station and into a taxi, and back to the flat, sincerely hoping that Brangwyn would be at home to cope with his sister; but, as before, Brangwyn was not forthcoming when he wanted him, and he found himself with the collapsing Ursula on his hands, and not even a char in sight.

He got her out of her hat and her mink coat as if he were undressing a doll, and deposited her gently in one of the large armchairs, and sat down himself on the edge of the wide brick hearth and stared at her as she gazed into space with unseeing eyes, wondering what on earth he should do with her. He recognized that she had had a severe emotional shock; in fact, her condition reminded him vividly of shell-shock, but he could not imagine what on earth could have occurred in a civilized city to reduce her to this state. The fellow had simply looked at her, and she had gone as flat as a burst tyre. He could understand a girl getting the wind up if she had a sticky past and it suddenly rose up and smote her; he could understand her having hysterics, or something of that sort; but the kind of paralysis that had overtaken Ursula Brangwyn was beyond his comprehension. He did not think it would be much use sending for a doctor to cope with a condition of this kind, nor did he think the excitable Latins in the restaurant would prove particularly helpful. No, anything that was to be done for Ursula Brangwyn would have to be done by him, and he had better get on with it.

He bent forward and laid his hand on her knee once again.

'Look here, Miss Brangwyn,' he said, 'you have absolutely no need to be scared of that fellow. Your brother and I will send him spinning if he gives any trouble or bothers you again.'

And then, as it suddenly occurred to him that it might be fear of her brother finding out something with regard to the young exquisite that had thrown her into a panic, he added:

'Or if there is anything I can do for you on my own, you have only to say what it is and I'll do anything I can. I don't know anything about the fellow, but I have a sort of feeling he needs kicking, on general principles, if for nothing else.'

The girl slowly turned her eyes towards him. He noticed that all her movements were peculiarly slowed down.

'No,' she said in a low, toneless voice, 'there is nothing either you or Alick can do. Alick has done all he can. I am the only person who can do anything. I have got to help myself - if I can - if I can.'

'Well,' said Murchison, 'I don't know what it is that you propose to do about it, but I can tell you one thing, the longer you sit and look at it before you do it, the worse it will get.'

'There is nothing for me to do. It is just the way I feel about things.'

'There are as good fish in the sea as ever came out of it,' said Murchison.

'Yes, I know,' replied the girl. 'It isn't that. I'm not fond of him any longer. I'd be only too thankful to be rid of him. I would truly. But I can't get rid of him. I can't break the rapport between us. He still has the most awful power over me. He can make me do anything he wants.'

'Well,' said Murchison, 'he wanted to make you stop in the train and talk to him, but he didn't manage it when I hoicked you out. What's been done once can be done again.'

'It isn't just that. It's me, too. It's just like drink or drugs. A kind of craving.'

'It'll wear off with time,' said Murchison firmly, though he hadn't the faintest idea what she was talking about.

'I thought so, too,' said the girl, with a sigh, 'but it's come back as strong as ever now I've seen him again.'

Murchison suddenly remembered the girl's words concerning an experiment that had gone wrong, and which had left her considerably shaken up. He also remembered his employer's words concerning a previous secretary who had turned out badly and had to be fired hastily and was not on any pretext to be admitted to the flat; and it suddenly occurred to him that the man he had seen at the railway station might be one or other of these persons - or, more probably, one and the same person; it was unlikely there would be two separate sets of melodrama in the same family. The young man had probably been engaged as he had been engaged, got mixed up with Ursula Brangwyn, and had been slung out by her brother for some pretty drastic reason, and the girl had had the shock of a bust-up love affair, and was having a bit of a nervous breakdown in consequence. He was sorry for her, but wondered why it was she had been fool enough to fall for such a blighter; why couldn't she see that he was all wrong? Why, above all, hadn't Brangwyn seen through him earlier in the proceedings? He wondered what they had all been up to - this man, who radiated such curious personal magnetism and had such an uncanny power over the girl, Brangwyn, with his interest in queer cults and lost arts, and the girl herself, possibly badly damaged as a result of some psychological experiment that had gone wrong.

A wave of pity swept over him as he looked at the girl, sitting huddled in the big chair and staring into space with unseeing, terrified eyes. It was an ugly thing to see a human being reduced to such a condition; it seemed to derogate from the dignity of the whole human species that it was possible to reduce anyone to such a state of helplessness and subjection to the mind of another. He felt the short hairs on the nape of his neck beginning to rise. Powers were abroad that he did not understand. Anyone who had not actually seen the incident would pooh-pooh it as an hysterical girl's imagination; but he himself had felt the strange personal influence that radiated from the man; an influence that filled him, a male, with an almost irresistible desire to strike him, and that might quite well have all sorts of queer effects on a highly strung girl like Miss Brangwyn if the fellow gave his mind to getting hold of her.

Well, it was a queer business altogether. He wondered how much he was going to get mixed up with it in the course of his work for Brangwyn. The less the better, he thought, or he might be following his predecessor into the discard ignominiously. One thing was quite certain, however, he needn't get himself mixed up with Miss Brangwyn. That, at least, was optional.

To his immense relief he heard a latch-key being inserted in the door, and rose to welcome his employer. But when the door opened it was not Brangwyn who stood there, but a complete stranger, a heavily built, pock-marked mulatto, and over his shoulder Murchison caught a glimpse of the narrow, pallid face of the man he had seen at the station. A low moaning noise came from the girl huddled in the chair.

Murchison placed himself between her and the newcomers, completely hiding her from their eyes with his heavy bulk.

'Sorry, gentlemen,' he said, 'but Mr. Brangwyn's instructions are that no one is to be admitted to the flat in his absence, so I'm afraid I'll have to ask you to leave.'

The mulatto paused and surveyed him with an air of studied insolence that Murchison thought was probably assumed for the benefit of the onlookers, for he could hardly expect to browbeat a complete stranger by sheer weight of glare.

'And who might you be?'

'Mr. Brangwyn's secretary, sir; and his instructions are that no one comes into the flat in his absence, so I'd be glad if you'd go.'

'And do you know who I am?' The mulatto struck an attitude reminiscent of the late Henry Irving.

'No, sir. Don't know anything about you. I only know what my instructions are - to see that no one comes into the flat in Mr. Brangwyn's absence.'

'Do you imagine Mr. Brangwyn would have given me a key to his flat if he didn't expect me to make use of it?'

'There are other ways of getting hold of a key than having it given to you, sir. You are a stranger to me, and I don't propose to take any chances on you. If you don't go, I'm afraid I'll have to throw you out.'

The mulatto blew his chest out and looked round at his companion. They were both tall men, and the one who appeared to be the leader of the expedition looked as if he had been an athlete before time and debauchery had taken toll of him.

'Do you imagine you could throw us out?' he inquired, with an unpleasant smile.

Murchison measured them with his eye. Ursula's acquaintance was considerably younger than himself, and looked active, but had not the weight to be a formidable antagonist for a man of his bulk. The other man was both bigger and heavier, and could probably give a good account of himself for a short time, but would wind quickly, if his nose was any indicator of his way of living. Between them, however, they might take some throwing out single-handed. There would certainly be a considerable mess before they were gone. There was only one way to do it, and that was to take them by surprise. Without giving the slightest hint of his intention, Murchison charged, and with an old rugby forward's trick of the shoulder took the stranger in the chest and sent him over backwards, taking his companion with him like a ninepin, and Murchison slammed the door behind them. A series of fearful bumps told of the manner in which they were descending the stairs. It was only in the dead silence that supervened that it occurred to Murchison to wonder whether any necks had been broken.

He opened the door and looked out cautiously. The heap at the bottom of the stairs lay unpleasantly quietly upon the mat just inside the street door, which stood wide open. Murchison was too experienced a fighting man to go and examine a corpse without precautions. That was the way to get a knife in the belly. He stood debating what to do until a shadow blocked the doorway and a policeman's helmet was silhouetted against the sunshine outside.

'What's all this about, gentlemen?' he demanded, surveying the tangle at his feet, which was at last beginning to stir feebly.

'They tried to force an entry, constable,' replied Murchison from the stair head, 'and my instructions were to chuck 'em out if they wouldn't go quietly, and I've done it; but I didn't mean to chuck 'em down the stairs.'

'You seem to have done it pretty thoroughly, sir,' said the policeman, bending down and trying to disentangle the heap on the mat. Ursula's friend sat up and blinked dazedly. He looked decidedly concussed, thought Murchison. The mulatto never stirred. Murchison began to feel uneasy. Not so the policeman, who had seen alleged corpses before, and knew the symptoms. He lifted an eyelid and shoved a large thumb on the eyeball. The unconscious man sat up in a hurry and damned him heartily.

'Well, gentlemen,' said the policeman, 'as this disturbance has taken place on private premises, it's nothing to do with me unless you call me in.' And he looked inquiringly from one to the other as if to see whether anybody wanted to give anybody else in charge.

'Well, I don't quite know what to do, constable,' said Murchison. 'This isn't my house, you see. I've only been left in charge of it, so to speak. It's for my employer to say what's to be done.'

'I'd better have the names and addresses,' said the policeman, getting out his notebook, to Murchison's great satisfaction, who learnt that the younger man's name was Frank Fouldes, with an address in Chelsea, and the mulatto was Hugo Astley; whereupon Murchison pricked up his ears, for the name was not unknown to him in connection with a series of lurid revelations in one of the less reputable Sabbath journals. At the time he had paid no attention to these revelations as fact, however entertaining they might be as fiction; but now that he had seen the man himself, he reckoned that there might be something in them.

'Address, please,' said the constable, inexorable as fate.

'The Ritz,' replied the man on the mat haughtily, concentrating his attention on punching the dents out of a bowler hat.

'Which one?' demanded the law.

'Ritz Hotel!' Unutterable contempt made itself heard in the voice of the speaker, who seemed perfectly oblivious of his undignified position between the policeman's boots.

'Piccadilly or Praed Street?'

'Praed Street,' he said sulkily. The policeman's face was impassive; the trick was an old one to him. But it was a new one to Murchison, who gave a sudden ha-ha from the top of the stairs. Astley looked up at the sound, and there came into his face an expression so fiendish that Murchison's laugh was arrested in mid-career, leaving him open-mouthed. If ever the Prince of Darkness appeared in human form, he was sitting on the door-mat now. Murchison was prepared to believe anything of this man, even what the Sunday papers said of him.

'Thank you, gentlemen,' said the policeman, 'now, unless you're hurt, you'd better move along.'

They got up reluctantly and limped away, dusting themselves down as they went, the policeman watching them round the corner. Not until they were safely out of sight did he turn to Murchison and ask his name. For which piece of tact Murchison blessed him, for he judged that the less Hugo Astley knew about him, the better for his health.

CHAPTER 9

The policeman, after the manner of policemen, was non-committal; but it did not require a very shrewd observer to deduce that Hugo Astley was well known, but not well liked, in official circles. With Frank Fouldes he did not seem to be familiar, but Murchison gathered that it had not done Fouldes any good in the eyes of the law to have been found lying on the same door-mat with Hugo Astley.

Murchison returned up the stairs, a shilling having changed hands without being observed by either party. He found Ursula Brangwyn sitting up in the big chair looking considerably more normal than she had done since the incident at the station, the excitement of the fracas evidently having distracted her attention from her troubles.

Murchison grinned cheerfully at her.

'That's disposed of them,' he said. 'Second trick to us, I think.'

'Yes, that's disposed of them for the moment,' said the girl. 'But they won't leave it at that; and Hugo Astley will never forget you for having laughed at him.'

'You know him, then?' said Murchison.

'Yes, I know him.' Ursula Brangwyn shuddered.

A key sounded in the lock again, and Murchison spun round, ready to throw the next entrant down the stairs without even inquiring his business. But it was Brangwyn this time, who gave a whistle of surprise as he saw his sister sitting there, looking white and shaken.

'Hullo?' he said. 'What's Ursula doing here?'

'We've had a spot of trouble,' replied Murchison. 'A chap called Frank Fouldes turned up at the station as I was seeing Miss Brangwyn off, and made himself unpleasant; so I persuaded her to come back here and wait till the next train, instead of risking further trouble with him on the journey. And then, when we got back here, he and another chap called Hugo Astley let 'emselves in with a latch-key, and I had to chuck 'em out. And I chucked 'em out so hard they lay all in a heap on the mat at the bottom, and a bobby came along and picked 'em up and took their names and addresses. He seemed to know Astley all right.'

Brangwyn raised his eyebrows.

'What's all this you're telling me, Murchison? Let's have a few details. I must get the hang of this.'

He looked at his sister closely.

'Ursula, my child,' he said, 'run off to your own quarters. You are better out of it.' The girl rose silently and obeyed him.

Brangwyn dropped into the chair she had vacated.

'Now then, Murchison,' he said, 'let's begin at the beginning and have it slowly. You'd be a good man to write telegrams. What did Fouldes do at the station that upset Ursula?'

'He didn't exactly do anything. He just said "Hullo," and looked at her, and she conked completely out.'

'Fainted?'

'No. Came all over dazed. I saw something was up, so I hauled her out of the carriage and got her into the refreshment-room and gave her some brandy, and told him to clear out or he'd get his head punched.'

'What was your impression of the transaction?'

'Well, I don't know much about hypnotism, save what I picked up when I used to go and see one or two of our chaps in the shell-shock hospital, but it looked uncommonly like it to me. I should say he'd been in the habit of hypnotizing her, and had got her thoroughly under his thumb, so that now he's only got to look at her and off she goes. It was an ugly thing to see. I'm jolly glad to have had the privilege of chucking him down the stairs.'

'So you don't think it's all imagination and hysteria on Ursula's part?'

'No, sir, I don't. The fellow recognized the symptoms when she went all goosey, and was pleased. He was aiming at that result, and he got what he expected to get, if you ask me. She's exactly like a shell-shock case at the present moment.'

Brangwyn nodded. 'That's the best diagnosis we've had yet, and I've taken her to half Harley Street. They scout the idea of hypnosis, and want to psycho-analyse her for infantile repressions.'

'The treatment that did her most good was chucking the chap down the stairs,' said Murchison, grinning reminiscently. 'That doesn't go with infantile repressions, but it bears out the hypnotism theory.'

'How did you get her away from him at the station?'

'Picked her up bodily. Same as a kitten.'

Brangwyn laughed, remembering a certain dream.

'Was she willing?'

'Didn't ask her.'

'Caveman stuff!' said his employer, chuckling. Murchison felt himself blushing. 'What happened next?'

'I brought her back here. She wasn't fit to travel. I talked to her a bit, and she was beginning to perk up a little when I heard a key in the door, and thought it was you. But it was these two blighters, and we had a bit of a fracas because I stuck to my instructions and wouldn't let 'em in.'

'How did Ursula take it?'

'I dunno. I was busy with them.'

'What was your impression of Astley?'

'I think he's the man up higher.'

'What do you mean?'

'Well, whatever Fouldes is playing at with your sister, it's Astley who's at the bottom of it, not Fouldes, if you know what I mean. The hands are the hands of Esau, but the voice is the voice of Jacob.'

'What makes you think that?'

'I can't imagine Hugo Astley going out of his way to do a good turn to anybody, can you?'

'No, I certainly can't,' said Brangwyn.

'Then he wouldn't have bothered to come round here with Fouldes and start a row and get himself thrown downstairs if he hadn't got ends of his own to serve. I shouldn't be surprised if Fouldes is only one degree better off than your sister.'

Brangwyn looked at his new secretary sharply. 'How do you come to know all this?' he inquired.

'Just put two and two together, and used my common sense. Am I right?'

'I think you are. But I couldn't convince Harley Street. I found I'd got to handle her myself if she were to be handled at all.'

'She's easy enough to handle when you've got her on the spot,' said Murchison.

'I haven't found her so,' said Brangwyn. 'She fought me like a cat.'

'She didn't fight me,' said Murchison. 'I'd have turned her up and spanked her if she had, and I expect she knew it.'

'I expect she did,' said Brangwyn, chuckling.

Murchison suddenly realized that he was not speaking of his employer's sister in a manner that might be expected of an employee, and was smitten by alarm. But far from resenting his freedom, Brangwyn seemed highly delighted.

'There are one or two things that puzzle me, however,' said Brangwyn. 'How did Fouldes know that Ursula was travelling by that train?'

'Might be chance,' said Murchison.

'And how did he know she had come straight back to my place? It's long odds against both being chance.'

'And how did he get hold of your keys?'

'Yes, how indeed?'

'A traitor in the camp?'

'Looks like it.'

'Who served breakfast? You were discussing the matter at the breakfast table. There's a service hatch, or something, behind that curtain, isn't there?'

'Yes. If the service hatch had been left open, anyone who wanted to could have heard what was said. I'll get hold of Luigi. There'll be a murder done in the restaurant before nightfall if it's one of his people.'

'Nasty business for Miss Brangwyn.'

'Very nasty indeed, poor child. Astley's a most dangerous brute. Look what he's done to Fouldes. When I first knew Fouldes he was a decent, straight chap; a bit impressionable and apt to throw his weight about, but not an ounce of vice in him; and look at him now!'

'Do you think it's wise to leave your sister alone too long?'

'No, my dear fellow, you're quite right, it isn't. Will you go and fetch her while I phone Luigi for lunch?'

'Don't you think we ought to get a woman in to look after her?'

'What's the use of a woman? She can't pick her up like a kitten. Carry on with the good work, Murchison.'

Murchison raised his eyebrows. 'Want me to sit up with her at night?' he inquired.

'We'll manage between us,' said Brangwyn.

'Right-o,' said Murchison, 'I don't mind if she doesn't.'

He went off up the winding stairs, his heavy brogues resounding on the polished wood, and knocked on the door of Ursula Brangwyn's sitting-room. Getting no answer, he opened the door and walked in. She lay face downwards in a crumpled heap on the sofa.

'Miss Brangwyn?' he said, but there was no reply.

He walked over to her and laid a hand on her shoulder.

'Come on,' he said. 'Lunch is ready,' and shook her gently.

She gave a shudder, and burrowed deeper into the cushions. It was no use standing on ceremony, thought Murchison. In his new job as hospital orderly he had got to get on with it. He sought for an arm, laid hold of it, and began to pull.

'Come on,' he said. 'Up you get!'

Ursula Brangwyn began to slide, and to save herself from falling off the sofa, had to put out a leg. Murchison wondered whether he had gone too far, but she sat up and gazed at him quite unresentfully, and he concluded that caveman tactics suited her psychology.

'Come on,' he said, and with Ursula towing limply behind him started for the stairs. The small cold fingers in his big hand caught at his heart. It was so like a child's hand. He suddenly thought of children. Small children, running about all over a lawn, and a man coming home to them after his day's work. Brangwyn, watching them from the lounge as they went along the gallery, smiled to himself.

Murchison steered his charge safely down the winding stair and landed her in front of her brother, and let go her hand. Or rather tried to, for the small, cold fingers clung tenaciously to his, as a baby's fingers cling when they grasp something. He gently loosened them beneath her brother's watching eyes.

'Come along, Ursula,' said Brangwyn, and led the way to the dining-room. Murchison was relieved to find that they were to wait on themselves, and there was no Luigi with his intolerable chatter of menus.

Between them they got Ursula Brangwyn to take some food, and after the meal they tucked her up on a sofa at the far side of the big lounge, where she immediately seemed to fall asleep, and themselves settled down by the fire, talking in low voices so as not to disturb her.

'I think I had better explain things a bit,' said Brangwyn. 'I had not meant to do so just yet, but they have come up to a head so quickly that there is nothing else for it. Of course, you understand that all this is in strict confidence?'

Murchison nodded. There was no need to have said that. Naturally these were things one did not talk about.

Brangwyn paused, and seemed to be collecting his thoughts. He gave his companion a cigarette and lit one himself, and they smoked in silence for a short time, Murchison, out of the tail of his eye, keeping watch on the motionless, rug-covered form on the couch at the far end of the room, its face turned to the wall like Ahab.

'It's not very easy to know where to begin,' said the older man at length. 'There is so much to explain, and unless you know the ideas underlying it all you will not make head or tail of it; and I don't want to give you a lecture. You must ask questions as I go along if there is anything you don't understand.'

Murchison gave his usual taciturn grunt. Brangwyn continued:

'You know I am interested in psychology, and you also know that I

70

am interested in the old pagan religions, because I have told you as much myself. I wonder whether you realize that there must have been certain aspects of psychology that were known in those times, and are known to primitive peoples today, which Harley Street knows nothing about?'

'It had never occurred to me,' said Murchison. 'But, now you mention it, it sounds quite likely. They knew a thing or two, those old priests. Especially the Egyptians.'

'They knew several things, Murchison; some of them dangerous, like that' - he indicated the muffled form on the couch with a gesture - 'and some of them very valuable - like your invocation of Pan.'

He paused, but Murchison made no comment.

He continued.

'When I came in for some money after my mother's death I travelled in the East and elsewhere, investigating these things. And I saw some things that have to be seen to be believed. I may tell you about them some day. It is impossible to write them. One would merely be discredited.

'Most people would call them occult. I shouldn't, in the light of what I know now. That is, if you give the word occult its ordinary meaning as supernatural. In my opinion they are simply the powers of the trained human mind - and the mind side of nature.'

'What's that?' asked Murchison.

'Has it ever occurred to you that there might be an invisible reality behind appearances?'

'Yes. Always has. I've known that ever since I can remember. Nothing ever is just itself to me. During the War I could feel the soul of the German nation and the soul of the British nation contending with each other. The Kaiser was just a figurehead, poor old dud; and the German people were just a flock of sheep. They couldn't help 'emselves. It was this thing that drove 'em on. And now it's coughed up Hitler, God help 'em. It's exactly the same thing over again with different dummies. These chaps don't lead. They're shoved.'

'Did you feel the British group-soul, too?' asked Brangwyn.

'Yes, I felt it all right.' Murchison paused. 'It was that I drew on when I went over the top berserk.'

'How do you mean?'

'Difficult to describe.' Murchison pulled at his cigarette and exhaled clouds of smoke. 'It was as if imagination became real and there was tremendous pressure of life within me. I could have gone through anything. Gone through a brick wall. And you know, sir, I never had a scratch, and twice I was the only chap left alive in a dugout after a direct hit.'

Brangwyn nodded. 'You had the reputation of bearing a charmed life,' he said.

'And I could communicate - whatever it was - to the fellows under me,' Murchison continued eagerly, Ursula Brangwyn and her troubles forgotten as he re-lived his great days.

'We all saw that,' said Brangwyn. 'You were marked out for high rank if the War had gone on.'

Murchison sighed. 'I'm afraid I'm a fighting man, and nothing but a fighting man. There's not much doing for me in times of peace. I'm out of a job then. As long as you only want callers chucked down the stairs, I'm a first-class secretary. But if you want any typing or shorthand, you mayn't be quite so pleased.'

Brangwyn laughed.

'I wonder what will become of my sort if the League of Nations gets away with it,' said Murchison with a sigh.

'It won't, as long as your sort continues to be born into the world,' said Brangwyn.

They smoked for a time in silence; Murchison living over again the great days of the War, the present forgotten as something of the old magic and marvel of the battle-lust came back to him, when he had felt lifted out of himself and caught up in great tides of racial emotion and sent hurtling like a shell at the heads of the enemy. Brangwyn considered first one opening and then another, and debated as to which would be the best method of approach to inform, and explain, and carry conviction to the mind of the man opposite him, whose cooperation he so urgently needed and upon whose ability to do what was required of him the sanity of Ursula Brangwyn depended.

For Brangwyn was seriously alarmed by his sister's relapse. All the carefully built-up gain of months had been swept away by one look from the man who had caused all the trouble, and she was as bad as ever she had been. Worse, in fact; for he liked this apathy and stupor a great deal less than any amount of excitement.

It was an exceedingly difficult thing he had to do. He had counted upon teaching and training Murchison over a period of time; some weeks at least, before he asked for anything in the way of active cooperation from him. But his hand was forced by Ursula's collapse, and something had got to be done at once. He could no longer leave her safely hidden away among the Welsh mountains. Things wouldn't wait. He felt like the conductor of an orchestra who has to rely on a first violin who is sight-reading. It would take an uncommonly good man to get through the performance without letting him down.

He returned to the attack.

'When you went over the top, you experienced a kind of "divine inebriation," as the ancients called it?'

'I experienced something quite out of the ordinary, and highly enjoyable. Inebriation is as good a word as any for it. I was certainly drunk on something.'

'And you experienced another kind of influx of force when the old padre at your school chapel got worked up emotionally while he was taking a service?'

'Yes. You're right. The same sort of thing, but different.'

'And yet a third kind when you yourself got worked up and invoked Pan in front of the British Museum, of all places?'

'Yes, you're quite right. All three were different types of the same thing. I hadn't thought of that before. And, of course, they throw light on each other.'

'Can you think of any condition which was the causative factor in each case?'

'You mean what trod on the self-starter? Yes. Somebody got worked up emotionally.'

'There you have it in a nutshell. It is emotion which is the self-starter in all these cases of divine inebriation - the lifting of one out of oneself into a wider consciousness.'

'I don't know about wider consciousness,' said Murchison. 'I wasn't conscious of anything except what was going on. But I felt a tremendous increase in the pressure of life inside me, as it were; and, as I said, I could have gone through a brick wall when the power was on me.'

'Like falling, in love,' said Brangwyn watching him.

'I haven't tried that, so I couldn't say. I should describe it personally as exactly like the early stages of getting tight. I have tried that, so I know.'

'And you realize that three different kinds of emotion heralded three different kinds of experience?'

'Yes.'

'Has it ever occurred to you that there might be a technique for inducing that emotion and so producing those states of mind at will?'

'A trick, you mean?'

'No, I don't call it a trick. I mean understanding the psychology of it, so that you can bring it about and intensify and concentrate it.'

'No, it had never occurred to me that that was possible. It would be mighty interesting if it were, but rather dangerous, I should say. You would want to know what you were about.'

'Don't you need to do that with anything that has got any power behind it? You can't come to much harm pushing a pram, but you can come a mighty smash in a high-powered car; all the same, the car is the better vehicle, provided you have the nerve to handle it; if not, you are better off with the pram - or in it.' Murchison glanced across the room towards the sofa.

'Is that an example of a psychological car-smash?' he asked.

'It is,' said Brangwyn, 'and I want you to drive the breakdown lorry, if you'll be so good.'

'I'll do what I can,' said Murchison, and Brangwyn felt that there was more in those few quiet words than in most men's oaths and protestations. For, although the younger man had kept quiet and kept his head, he suspected that he had been more than a little upset by the scenes they had been through during the last few hours. He obviously was unused to any intimate relationship with women, and especially with young and attractive women. He did not know what to do with them, or how to take them. He was ill at ease and self-conscious until he forgot for a moment that they were women, and then he treated them like men, and not every woman would stand for that. Brangwyn smiled as he remembered that Murchison's immediate remedy for Ursula's distress had been to stand her a drink.

It was Murchison who broke the silence first.

'You think that Fouldes, Astley and Co. have been making use of Miss Brangwyn as part of their technique for inducing emotion, and smashed her in the process?'

'Yes, that is about it. Or, rather, it was I who smashed her, and smashed her deliberately, rather than let them finish what they were doing; on the same principle that one runs a car into a hedge and takes a minor smash when it gets out of control on a hill rather than wait for the major smash at the bottom. What I want you to do is to help get her back on to the road again, take her steadily down the hill and steer her round the bend at the bottom, and then she ought to be able to get along under her own power.'

He watched his companion closely while giving this explanation, which explained much or little according to the way it was taken.

Murchison sat silent for a while, and Brangwyn did not break the silence, letting him digest what had been given him. At length he spoke.

'What kind of emotion were they working for when the smash occurred?'

'That is a little difficult to answer briefly. I'll tell you the history of the transaction, and then you will understand it better.

'When I came back from my travels in the East, some years after my father's death, I heard that a little step-sister, whom I had never seen, was going to enter a convent, and that my consent as her trustee was necessary, as she was under age. It seemed to me a ghastly thing for a child like that to be put away for life without ever knowing what life was like. So I made it my business to stymie that transaction from the financial point of view, and when the convent found that she wasn't going to be the gilded pill they thought she was, they coughed her up quite willingly, and I had a leggy little colt of 17 on my hands to bring up as best I could.

'I found her intensely devout and intensely ignorant, but I soon cured that. I talked to her straight, man to man, plain, unbowdlerized physiology and psychology and sociology, and she took to it like a duck to water, and made all the adjustments to life she had any need to. That is why I know that psychoanalysis is not needed with her. Ursula psychoanalysed herself when given the raw material to work on in the shape of the necessary facts.

'Until this wretched business with Fouldes and Astley came along she was a singularly harmonious nature. It is on that that I base my hope of a reconstruction. We have got sound foundations to work on when once we can clear the *debris*.

'She ran round here, and at another house I had before this, and read all my books, and met all my friends, and sat curled up on that sofa she is asleep on now, and heard all their talk, and educated herself pretty rapidly; and all the enthusiasm she had previously had for religion turned on to the researches I am doing, which are really, at bottom, my religion.

'She helped me a very great deal in very many ways, for a woman's approach to these things differs somewhat to a man's, and there are some things she can do that he can't, and he has to have her help.'

'I suppose she was your pythoness,' said Murchison.

Brangwyn looked at him sharply.

'You have read along these lines a good deal already, haven't you?' he inquired.

'No, I've never read anything. I never knew they existed till you began to tell me about them. I picked up that bit from the classics at school. I only piece two and two together. All sorts of bits and scraps start coming back to you, that you never knew the meaning of before, when once you have a bit to go on. This sort of thing's all round you if you only know what to look for.'

'Yes,' Brangwyn continued. 'Ursula was a pretty high-grade pythoness till she got messed up; and a pythoness is to an ordinary medium what a medium is to ordinary mortals.

'Well, as luck would have it, young Fouldes, who was interested in these matters, used to come along for talks, and to lend a hand in the experiments, and finally became my secretary, and he and Ursula got fond of each other. It's no reflection on Ursula's taste and judgment to say that, for what he is now is very different to what he was then. I was not averse from the alliance, though I cannot say I was exactly enthusiastic over it, for I thought Ursula was capable of better things. He was not an intellectual heavyweight; but then neither is she; she is intelligent and intuitive to a high degree, but not intellectual; and because he wouldn't suit me for a life-partner, it didn't follow that he wouldn't suit her. At any rate, one has to let people please themselves in these matters.'

He paused, for his present activities belied his words. He had no intention of letting Ursula choose for herself a second time.

'I had only one thing against the boy - he had a nice disposition, was intelligent, was well-blessed with this world's goods - but, and this is one of the biggest buts in the world, Murchison, he was exceedingly impressionable. Ursula could put him round her little finger; so could I; so could anybody; so, in the end, did Astley. To be impressionable, in this wicked world, is like working in a dissecting-room with an open cut on your finger.

'There are certain things that can be done with the mind if you know how, which require a very steady nerve and considerable self-control to pull off successfully. Ursula wanted me to let Frank and her do some of these. Now I would have trusted Ursula to do the job; in fact, it was one of my hopes that she should try out that experiment for me when a suitable occasion came along; but Frank couldn't, and I wouldn't risk it, and Ursula and I had a quarrel over it. She, being in love, did not agree with my temperate estimate of Frank and his capacities.

'Frank, not being taken at his own valuation, which was never unduly low, and had gone up considerably since he had had Ursula to tell him how wonderful he was, naturally wasn't very pleased either, and ceased to regard me as guide, philosopher and friend, and took up with Hugo Astley, who is a considerably more spectacular person than I am, and both he and Ursula kept me in the dark over the matter, though I will say for Ursula that, knowing what she did about the man, she was all for keeping at a safe distance. Frank assured her that this was what he intended to do, and that he had no intention whatsoever of getting into Astley's clutches; but he who sups with the devil needs a long spoon, and the inevitable happened; Astley, having touched Frank's little finger, drew his whole body after him, and he ended up as you see him now.'

'I am a bit surprised that you think Fouldes a light-weight,' said Murchison. 'The first thing that struck me about him was the tremendous personality he had. Not pleasant, I grant you, but mighty strong of its kind.'

'That also is Astley's work. Fouldes is burning under a forced draught, and it won't last long. No constitution can stand that pressure.'

'Drugs?' queried Murchison.

'Partly. And partly certain kinds of psychological practices that Astley teaches.

'But, to continue my story, for I want to get on with it as quickly as possible, so that you may know where you are before the next move takes place, as it will before long, if I'm not very much mistaken.

'Astley took Fouldes in hand, and developed him hand over fist in a way I would never have risked doing with a man of Frank's make-up.'

'Then there are other people as well as you working along these lines?' interrupted Murchison.

Brangwyn hesitated for a moment, and then decided on frankness.

'Ever heard of the occult fraternities?'

'I've heard of the Rosicrucians.'

'We'll name no names; but, anyway, you know that people do organize for the study of the kind of thing I'm interested in, and that there is a secret tradition and a lot of unpublished manuscripts on the subject?'

'I know now you've told me. I didn't know before. Oh, yes, I did, though. The *Sunday Herald* had a whole lot about it, but I didn't believe a word. I thought all that sort of thing was extinct, like the Comte de St. Germain and Paracelsus.'

'It is very far from being extinct. London, Paris, New York, Berlin - are full of all sorts and conditions of organizations experimenting and researching, and playing about generally with the Unseen. Mostly they are just mutual admiration societies, and the only credentials required are credulity and a vivid imagination. But some are like the one run by Hugo Astley, and that is an altogether different pair of boots.'

'What do they go in for? Blackmail? Drugs? A spot of loose living?'

'All those, and more, with a dash of subversive politics thrown in sometimes. But that is not peculiar to them; there are very few night-clubs that wouldn't answer to that description. No, the thing that entitles organizations like Astley's to our consideration, if not our respect, is their knowledge of certain of the rarer powers of the human mind. And that knowledge is genuine, Murchison. There is no fake about it. I'll tell you what it is, and I'll show you how it's done if you work with me.'

'Are you planning an expose?'

'What's the use? Astley's been exposed over and over again. Exposure is what he thrives on. So much free advertisement. No one who mixes up with Astley nowadays can plead ignorance of what they are doing. Besides, an exposure would only drag Ursula's name in the mud. No, I mean to fight him with his own weapons, get Ursula away from him, anyway, and lay him out once and for all if I can.'

'Isn't Miss Brangwyn away from him, then?'

They both glanced involuntarily at the motionless form on the sofa at the far side of the room, vaguely outlined under the folds of the heavy fur rug, for, warm as the flat was, Ursula had complained of being cold.

'Ursula is here all right, as you see, so far as her body is concerned. But you know the old song:

"My heart's in the Highlands, my heart is not here;
My Heart's in the Highlands a-chasing the deer;
Chasing the wild deer, and following the roe,
My heart's in the Highlands wherever I go."

'That's why Ursula's so dazed. She isn't here at all. She's off with Hugo Astley and Fouldes. She wants to do nothing but lie in a kind of day-dream and think of them.'

'Can't we walk her up and down and flick her with a wet towel or something?'

'That,' said Brangwyn, 'is patching at symptoms while you leave the disease untouched. No, we've got to do more than that for Ursula, and that's what I'm coming to presently.

'Where was I? O yes, I had told you how Astley got hold of Fouldes, and, through Fouldes, of Ursula.'

'You had told me he had done so, but you didn't tell me how he had managed it. Do you want me to know that? I don't want to, if you don't.'

'I want you to know all there is to know, my dear fellow, so that you can help me effectually. Astley, who is as cute as a waggon-load of monkeys, got hold of Fouldes through his vanity as easy as kiss hands. He forgot all he'd ever heard about Astley, and took the line that he was one of the world's misunderstood geniuses and a suffering martyr. He's a genius, all right, but he's not misunderstood. They understand him perfectly at Scotland Yard, though they can't catch him out, much as they'd like to; and he'll be a martyr too, one of these days, if my luck holds.

'Astley couldn't get hold of Ursula direct, I'll say that for her. But he taught Fouldes some Voodoo tricks that he got from his negro grandmother, and Fouldes tried them out, and pretty soon he had Ursula on a string, and then Astley pulled the end of that string, and Ursula was in his hands.'

'What did he want her for? The usual?'

'Yes, and no. No, not quite the usual, though I have no doubt that would not have been entirely overlooked. Ever heard of the Black Mass?'

'Gosh, yes! Was that the game? But what exactly is the Black Mass? They desecrate the Host, don't they? What had she got to do with it?'

'Know what the altar is in a Black Mass?'

'No, what is it?'

'The body of a woman.'

'Jerusalem!' said Murchison, 'and what happens to the woman?'

'Astley's wife is in an asylum.'

'So I should imagine. And glad to be there, I dare say.'

'So you will naturally understand I was not anxious for Ursula to participate in any Black Masses, and as soon as I tumbled to what was afoot, and I tumbled to it early in the proceedings fortunately, for I knew the symptoms, I tackled the situation, horse, foot and artillery. I got Astley out of England by the simple expedient of putting a debt-collector on to buy up a selection of his debts and keep on county-courting him, and hoped I had settled the whole business, for Fouldes went with Astley. But things had been done to Ursula's soul that couldn't be dealt with quite so simply.

'You remember what I told you about those down-rushes of power in the divine inebriation. Well, Ursula had been used for that purpose, and used pretty roughly, too, not in the way it should be done. Now, when you are doing a thing like that, you have to be in circuit, in the same way that an electric light is in circuit. It always has two wires, you notice. It won't light up if there's only one. For instance, when you had a divine inebriation with the spirit of Mars as you went berserk over the top, you earthed on to the Germans. When there weren't any Germans for you to earth on to, you were a bit of a handful, you know, Murchison.'

'Who did I earth on to when I got in circuit with Pan outside the British Museum?'

'You earthed on to me, because I happen to be a good conductor of that particular kind of force.'

'What would have happened if you hadn't been about? Would I have blown a fuse?'

Brangwyn looked at him for a moment. 'If I hadn't been about, it wouldn't have happened. I was in the Museum library for the purpose of looking up certain old formulae known in medieval times that are in the manuscripts there. My mind was on it, and, like the old padre at your school, I was emotionally worked up, for I am very fond of Ursula; she is like my own child to me, rather than a step-relation, and it was exactly a year ago that day that she and Frank had come to me for my blessing on their engagement.

'I was wanting someone to complete the circuit so that I could get Ursula on to her feet again, and it was exceedingly difficult to find exactly what I wanted: and all the time I was copying out the old symbols, and the names of power, and the words of evocation, my mind was questing back and forth over this person and that person, and piecing together a sort of ideal person out of this quality and that quality, a highly magical operation, of course, and, hey presto, I picked up you, who had exactly the qualities I wanted, as surely as a big gun picks up an invisible target.'

'So this is magic, is it?' said Murchison quietly, his face an expressionless mask.

'Do you define magic as mumbo-jumbo?'

'I always have.'

'I define it as the practical application of a knowledge of the little-understood powers of the human mind.'

'Is this the technique you spoke of?'

'Yes, Murchison, it is. Do you dislike the idea?'

Murchison thought it over for the best part of a cigarette.

'Can't say I like it,' he said at length.

This was a setback for Brangwyn, and a serious one.

'There is nothing but the use of these little-understood powers that will put Ursula on her feet.'

'Maybe; but she ought never to have got into this condition.'

'She never would have if she had stuck to me and steered clear of Astley. If a drug is active enough to do any good, it is always capable of doing damage in an overdose. Don't you differentiate between Black Magic and White Magic?'

'Afraid I don't. It all seems pretty murky to me.'

'You said once you trusted me, Murchison. Would you say I was a bad man?'

'No, I've always thought you were the best chap I've ever met.'

'Well, such as I am, it was the practice of these little-understood things that have made me what I am. You can judge a tree by its fruits.'

'The same tree sprouted Astley.'

'No, that is just exactly what it didn't do, Murchison. He is working on an entirely different formula.'

'What do you mean by that?'

'I am trying to get in touch with the spiritual forces that built the universe so that I may be part of evolving life; he is trying to use them for his own ends. Working on his formula, Frank swells up like a bullfrog and Ursula is like a sucked orange. Working on my formula, they would have been the positive and negative poles of a battery, generating current.'

'What sort of current?'

'An intensification of life on all its levels.'

'I see. And Fouldes goes and plugs in with the wrong voltage and shorts the whole caboodle?'

'Something like that.'

'And what do you want me to do?'

'I want to go back and repeat the experiment up to the point it went wrong, and so get Ursula back in circuit with cosmic force again, so that she can charge up, for at the moment she is like a run-down battery.'

'You mean you want to work the Black Mass?'

'Good God, no, my dear fellow, what do you take me for? No, I should like to teach you the technique I would have taught Fouldes if he'd been any use, and let you and Ursula work together. If she once gets interested again, she'll soon pick up.'

He hoped he might be forgiven this Machiavellianism. After all, the experiment, once started, possessed a perfectly self-regulating mechanism. If it wasn't going on all right it would speedily come to an end. To explain in detail was hopeless at the present juncture. How could the fellow be expected to understand? And if he only half understood, he might shy at cooperating. It was best to run him in blinkers for the present. If the dream of the black cat were a reliable indicator, he would run in the desired direction. Black cats were reputed lucky, thought Brangwyn with a chuckle. 'Are you game for the experiment?' he asked.

'Well, sir,' said the cautious Murchison, 'I'm game for it as far as I can see it. I can't say more than that, can I? Now what is it exactly that you want me to do?'

'For the moment I only want you to get into sympathetic rapport with Ursula.'

'How do I do that?'

'How were you feeling towards her when you pulled her out of the train at the station?'

'I felt frightfully sorry for her; and I'd have loved to have kicked her pal for his own sweet sake, quite apart from her. There was something about that fellow that got my goat at the very first sight.'

'Go on feeling sorry for her. Feel as sorry as you can, for, God knows, she needs it. Imagine yourself standing between her and these blighters. Resist them mentally, and hang on to her for all you're worth. You will soon pick up a rapport with her if you do that.'

'I may pick up a rapport with her all right. In fact, I fancy I've done so already. But will she pick up one with me? I don't fancy she has very much use for me.'

'She soon will have, if you give her a sense of protection.' Brangwyn prayed that he might be forgiven this half-truth.

'I can give her that all right. I'm big enough and ugly enough to protect anything. And she'll know she's safe with me. I'm not interested in Black Masses. I don't see where the fun comes in with that sort of thing.'

CHAPTER 10

Ursula Brangwyn continued in the same drowsy, dazed condition throughout the evening, and could not be persuaded to eat. Brangwyn sent Murchison off to bed early.

'Get some sleep while you can,' he said, 'we may have trouble before morning.'

'What sort of trouble?'

'Ever heard of telepathy?'

'Yes.'

'Well, Fouldes and Astley may try to come through to Ursula telepathically, and there will be the devil to pay if they do. That is when I shall want you to lend me a hand.'

Murchison acquiesced, though it seemed odd to him that Brangwyn could not hold his sister down single-handed.

To go to bed was one thing, but to go to sleep after all the happenings of the day proved to be quite another matter, and Murchison lay awake and smoked cigarette after cigarette.

The business in which he had become involved was a decidedly odd one, and it was only his complete trust in his employer which made him willing to lend himself to it. Brangwyn had struck the right note when he had asked Murchison if he trusted him. To Murchison he represented the ideal of perfect manhood, developed and balanced in all its parts. He could imagine no higher aim than to be like Brangwyn. Just as he had worshipped him as a boy, so he respected him as a man. He congratulated himself on his extraordinary luck in having such a man as Brangwyn to work under. This business with Miss Brangwyn was a queer one. He did not pretend to understand it.

He saw that it was something a good deal more than the shock of a broken engagement, as he had at first supposed. He had a shrewd suspicion that Brangwyn had not put quite all the cards on the table. Especially with regard to the part for which he himself was cast in the transaction, but that was hardly to be expected. Several points in the narrative had struck him as odd. It is not usually considered a desirable

83

thing for an employee to get into sympathetic rapport with his employer's womenfolk, and he wondered that that aspect of the thing had not struck Brangwyn, who was quite as much a man of the world as a student of strange sciences. He wondered whether he was designed for the role of sucked orange while Miss Brangwyn swelled up like a bull-frog in her turn, and judged that his five pounds a week would be dearly earned if he were. He also wondered what would happen when the time came to sever the rapport, which he judged as being used as a temporary scaffolding during the rebuilding of Ursula Brangwyn. He felt that he would be wise to look out for himself, and not get too deeply involved in the business.

Finally he came to the end of his cigarettes, and reluctantly turned out the light and settled down to sleep.

It seemed to him that he had hardly turned over when he was aroused by the ringing of the telephone bell in the next room. He leaped out of bed and answered it.

'I'd be glad if you'd come down and lend me a hand,' came Brangwyn's voice at the other end. 'The expected has happened.'

The poverty-stricken Murchison did not own a dressing-gown, so he pulled on his old trench-coat over his shoulders, and, because his brogues would make an unholy clatter in the silence of the night, went down bare-footed. To his horror, the first person he encountered at the foot of the stairs was Miss Brangwyn, as wide awake as she had previously been drowsy.

She was in a dressing-gown of deep rose-pink silk, the same colour as her eiderdown, he remembered, and her hair hung in two long plaits down her back. Murchison had never seen a girl with long hair before in these cropped days, and it startled him. It made her seem so much more feminine. Brangwyn was fully dressed, and had apparently not been to bed.

'We're going to have a bit of supper,' said Brangwyn, 'and we thought you might like to join us.'

'Yes, rather,' said Murchison, wondering what was afoot, and waiting for his cue. He saw a saucepan of milk warming on an electric hot-plate in the hearth, and bread broken up in a basin beside it. Evidently Miss Brangwyn was going to be fed.

'Keep an eye on the milk, will you, Murchison?' said Brangwyn, and disappeared into the dining-room.

The embarrassed Murchison, knowing that it was more than the milk that he was expected to keep an eye on, wrapped the trench-coat round him and strapped the belt securely. He saw Miss Brangwyn watching him.

'I'm frightfully sorry you've been let in for all this,' she said, and Murchison heaved a sigh of relief to find that she was in her right mind.

'Don't you worry about that,' he answered. 'I'm only too glad to do anything I can.'

At that moment the milk came to the boil, and he hastily snatched it off the hot-plate. Slowly and clumsily he poured the milk on to the bread, his huge hands seeming far too big for anything they got hold of.

'Won't you let me tuck you up on the sofa again?' he said to the girl. 'You'll get cold, wandering about the room like that.'

Meekly she lay down on the big chesterfield in front of the fire, and he put the rug over her. She was evidently not going to play him up, as she had been doing with her brother.

He was just reaching out his hand towards the bowl of bread and milk, to give it to her, when he felt a sudden cold draught of air stirring in the room, as though a door had opened somewhere, and at the same time there came upon his soul a sense of panic fear, as if in the presence of intense but intangible evil. He felt the short hairs on his neck beginning to rise.

'My God, what's that,' he exclaimed involuntarily.

He saw that Ursula Brangwyn was sitting upright on the sofa, looking about her with terrified eyes.

He recognized intuitively that the evil was of the same kind, only infinitely stronger, as the unpleasant personal magnetism that had radiated from Fouldes as he stood in the door of the railway carriage looking at Ursula. He remembered Brangwyn's words about a telepathic attack which was to be expected, and reckoned that this was it.

He reached out his hand to the girl.

'Come on,' he said. 'We meet this standing up.'

She rose instantly from the couch and together they faced in the direction from which the force appeared to be emanating. The influence seemed to be coming in waves, with pulsations within the wave, dying down for a moment between them, and then coming up again with renewed vigour. Unconsciously Murchison had gripped the girl by her shoulders and turned her to face the force that was coming at them, and they stood thus, staring in the direction from which the invisible influence radiated, stiffening to each successive wave of force, like swimmers clinging to a half-tide rock. It was so tangible that it was difficult to believe that there was nothing physical about it.

85

Gradually the influence weakened, became uncertain, and then faded altogether; they relaxed their tenseness, and Ursula dropped down on the sofa. Murchison sat down beside her feet, and, without realizing what he did, took her hand in his, and they sat thus staring at each other without speaking.

'You felt it, too?' said the girl at length.

'I should think I did! Good Lord, whatever was it?'

'I think that it was Hugo Astley; telepathing, you know. It was much, much too strong for Frank.'

Whatever it was, it was damed unpleasant. Well, anyway, let's shove it behind us. The less you think about that sort of thing, the better. Eat your bread and milk and forget about it.'

'I couldn't eat anything. I couldn't really.'

'Now, come on you must just try. You'll be all right when you get started.'

He placed the small tray on her knees, and held it there, steadying it with his hand, and Ursula meekly began to eat her bread and milk. When Brangwyn returned he found them thus. The girl, with the loosened plaits of her dark hair straying over the soft folds of the rose-pink silk that fell across her breast. The man, with his thick fair hair standing up in every direction, his dirty old trench-coat girt about him over his pyjamas, and his bare, sinewy feet planted on the parquet. Ursula, he thought, looked slightly self-conscious, but Murchison was serenely fatherly, and reminded him of a St. Bernard with a kitten. He rose at his employer's entrance, but sat down again beside the girl's feet, and Brangwyn, who was watching closely, noticed that Ursula made no motion to draw them aside.

Brangwyn had a tray in his hands, and he and Murchison settled down to sandwiches and sherry, while Ursula finished her bread and milk. They chatted quietly of anything and everything but the recent disturbances, and Brangwyn observed that Ursula looked much more normal and Murchison seemed almost jolly, which was something decidedly new in his usually rather glum employee. Things were beginning to move, he concluded.

He was just thinking of suggesting a general return to their respective beds when he saw Murchison suddenly cock his ears, as it were, and stare into space over Ursula's head. The girl gazed at him, startled, for a moment, and then she, too, turned her head and looked in the same direction. Then Brangwyn also caught it, and felt the waves of evil influence come rolling in, banked and double-banked.

He was experienced in dealing with such things, and the waves divided and swept past him like the tide round a pier. But there was nothing he could do for the other two. This was not the time to give instructions that might be half-understood, and therefore muddled. It was best to leave Murchison to his unaided wits. The girl he could do nothing for. She had passed out of his reach on the tides of the force as if water had whirled her away. Her face had taken on the unnatural calmness of the face of the dead, all the moulding that gives character even to an unlined face being smoothed out; it was almost the face of an imbecile - utterly mindless. What possible chance was there that he - Murchison - or anyone - could reach her and touch her in that condition?

She rose slowly from the couch, Murchison staring helplessly at her. Brangwyn saw at once that the strong rapport that had been between them earlier in the evening had broken and that Ursula had gone from Murchison just as much as she had gone from him.

Murchison turned and looked at him helplessly, as if asking for instructions. But that was not what he wanted. He wanted Murchison to act from intuition. For there was only one thing to do with the girl, and if it were not done spontaneously, it was worth very little.

But Murchison, alas, would not do things on his own initiative in his employer's presence, thus forcing Brangwyn to take the lead. Brangwyn, feeling rather like Alice playing croquet with flamingoes for mallets, which turned and looked at her whenever she tried to hit a ball with them, started his secretary off with a push and hoped that Nature would do the rest.

'Go after her,' he said, 'and see she does not bump into anything and hurt herself. She is sleep-walking.'

Obediently Murchison rose and set off after Ursula; but the girl's smooth, gliding walk was covering the ground faster than he had realized, and before he could reach her she had walked straight into one of the pillars supporting the gallery, the crack of her head on the sharp-edged wood resounding through the room. She recoiled dazed, her hand pressed to her bruised face and an expression of bewildered pain in her eyes, and Murchison, without realizing what he did, caught her in his arms, cursing himself for the inaptitude that had allowed this mishap to occur. She looked up into his face with the startled expression of a child waking from sleep on unfamiliar surroundings.

'It's all right. It's all right,' said Murchison, stroking her shoulder, oblivious of the silent watcher on the hearthrug. The girl gazed up at him dreamily out of her dilated eyes, her attention apparently distracted from what had previously held it with a hypnotic fascination; but gradually the other influence re-asserted itself, and she began to turn sideways in his arms and look over her shoulder; her hand clutched the folds of his trench coat in a convulsive grasp as she peered behind her, and she clung to him as if she had suddenly found herself on the edge of a precipice.

Murchison found himself staring in the same direction, but there was nothing to be seen. Ursula Brangwyn was looking into another dimension. The grandfather clock in the corner ticked and ticked as they stood thus, motionless, the silk and swansdown dressing-gown against the grimy khaki of the trench coat. Brangwyn began to wonder if the man also were succumbing to the influence of the hypnotic force that was being used so effectually on the girl.

Slowly Ursula began to disengage herself from his arms, and the spell was broken.

'No, you don't!' said Murchison, tightening his grip upon her. She began to struggle in a half-hearted fashion, and naturally made no impression on the big and powerful man, who held her gently enough, but without the slightest intention of letting her go. She looked up into his face with a surprised expression, as if inquiring what he were about.

'You're not going,' he said, smiling down at her.

She shuddered, and pressed closer to him, looking apprehensively over her shoulder. Then, all of a sudden, she shrieked and jumped as if red-hot iron had touched her, and began to struggle like a mad thing. Murchison hung on to her relentlessly, crushing her into immobility against him till she could do no more than quiver. Brangwyn watched them, never stirring, and saw a curious change come over the man's face, the change he had seen come as zero hour approached, and he got ready to take his men over the top. Murchison's eyes grew bleak and blue and wide in the inhuman glare of the berserker, and Brangwyn's imagination pictured a winged helmet on the shaggy fair hair. He wondered what was happening at the other end of the telepathic wire, and reckoned that something was coming over that had not been reckoned on. Murchison was in a towering rage, that was obvious; the blind, blazing eyes were seeing something pictured in the imagination, and a stream of rending, tearing hate, as destructive as dynamite, was being poured out on to it. If Fouldes and Astley were *en rapport* at the other end of the telepathic wire, they were getting it in the neck. Brangwyn wondered how his sister was faring in the midst of this furious strafe. Murchison, oblivious of everything save the vision before his mind's eye, appeared to be squashing her absolutely flat.

Then suddenly, a change came over the atmosphere of the room. The strange, evil power that had been pouring in as steadily as waves beating into a bay, broke and starred like a smashed mirror, running in every direction like spilled quicksilver, and in another moment the room was empty.

'Phew!' said Brangwyn, relaxing with a sigh of relief. He saw Murchison let go of Ursula and stare at her as if he had never seen her before. Ursula was panting, evidently having had all the breath squeezed out of her. They both looked perfectly normal, and very surprised and self-conscious, and with one accord they turned and gazed at him apprehensively. He, for his part, would have liked to have embraced and blessed the pair of them. The operation was going according to plan.

Ursula, recovering her self-possession first, as females usually do, turned and led the way back to the fireside, Murchison following.

'Well,' said Brangwyn, breaking the embarrassing silence, 'so that's that.'

'Yes,' replied Murchison, dropping into a chair as if exhausted. 'That is very much that.'

Ursula Brangwyn stared at him without speaking, a strange expression on her face, as if she had suddenly perceived all manner of unsuspected potentialities.

CHAPTER 11

Murchison had no difficulty whatever in getting to sleep when he retired to bed for the second time that night. He was as completely exhausted by his strafe as if he had done a long cross-country run. As soon as his head touched the pillow he was off, and knew nothing more till he felt himself being shaken, and looked up to see the grinning Luigi standing over him in broad daylight.

'Mistaire Brangwyn, he ring zhe telephone, but you hear noting. He send me ask whether you 'live or dead?'

'Tell him I'm alive, will you, Luigi?' said Murchison, rolling out of bed. But as soon as be began to move about he was not quite so sure. He felt as if he were getting up for the first time after a long illness. Virtue had gone out of him with a vengeance.

When he arrived down in the dining-room after a hasty toilet, he found Brangwyn and his sister lingering over the after-breakfast cigarettes, and began to apologize for his tardiness. This was not the sort of thing that is expected of an employee.

'How are you feeling, Murchison?' inquired Brangwyn.

'So-so. A bit as if I'd had a night on the tiles. To tell you the honest truth, I'm feeling rather cheap,' was the reply.

'Rather like a Leyden jar that has discharged its spark?'

'Yes, exactly.'

'I thought you would. That is because you are not in circuit. If you had been in circuit with Ursula, you would have been all right. I must show you that trick before we have any more of these doings.'

'Oh lor!' said Murchison, 'are we likely to have 'em regularly?' and he gazed in anguish at Miss Brangwyn, wondering whether it were to be his mission in life to clutch her to his bosom periodically.

'I am afraid we are likely to have one or two more attempts before they give it up as a bad job,' said Brangwyn, trying to speak casually. 'So we may as well get the circuit in working order so as to be prepared for all eventualities. Go on, Ursula, you little vamp, charge him up again.'

Ursula flushed scarlet, and flashed an angry look at her brother.

'I'm afraid I can't,' she said. 'I don't feel like it.'

'Go on, my child. It's the least you can do. He's run himself out for you.'

The girl rose reluctantly and advanced towards the embarrassed Murchison, who wondered what in the world was going to be done to him.

'Put the palms of your hands against hers and enter into it imaginatively. Take what she is going to give you,' commanded Brangwyn.

Murchison, looking about as receptive as a shying horse, did as he was bid. He felt a pair of small, cold palms pressing against his. Nothing happened. Ursula Brangwyn looked so cross and uncomfortable that he forgot his own embarrassment in feeling sorry for her. He thought he felt a faint tingling warmth coming into the palms, but before he could be sure it was not his imagination, she withdrew them.

'It's no good, I can't do it. My hands are cold,' she said, and walked out of the room.

Brangwyn made no comment on her going, but lit another cigarette and sat down to chat to Murchison while he ate his breakfast.

'Well, you've seen something of our goings-on. What do you make of them?'

'I dunno. Not much, I'm afraid,' said Murchison, who felt half dead, and was praying that the hot coffee would put sufficient life into him to enable him to get through his day's work.

Brangwyn looked at him sharply. 'You'll be all right shortly,' he said, 'don't worry about it. Take life easily till you pick up. There's nothing much to do at the moment.'

Murchison smiled a sickly smile. 'Am I a psychological car-smash?' he inquired.

'Good Lord, no, my dear lad. Your battery's run down, that's all that's the matter with you. You'll be all right as soon as you get going again.'

'Well,' said Murchison, rising limply from the table, 'someone will have to swing my starting-handle for me, for devil a spark can I get out of myself.'

He went languidly up to his own quarters, and found there a char bumping about with a sweeper; he turned and went out on to the roof-garden and dropped on to a seat in the angle of the walls like a sick cat crawling into a patch of sunlight.

The pale winter sun was doing its best, and there was quite appreciable warmth in the angle of the walls, open to the south and sheltered from the wind. He turned his face up to it, shutting his eyes against the bright light, and let the sunshine beat upon his skin, feeling instinctively that this was the one thing that could restore his drained vitality.

He did not know that he was being observed through the glass door that led out on to the roof-garden, nor that Ursula Brangwyn, obeying the same instinct as himself, had come up, seeking the sunlight. Neither did he hear the door opened quietly, and the girl cross the leads on tiptoe and stand beside him, an expression of resolution on her face, as if she had at last made up her mind to some irrevocable plunge.

But she did not put her resolution into action at once, but stood looking down at the oblivious man on the seat, considering him. Murchison, believing himself to be alone and under no necessity of keeping up appearances, had abandoned himself to his exhaustion, and lay back in the corner of the seat looking utterly worn out, his head against the rough brickwork of the wall, the pitiless sunlight beating down on his face and revealing all the lines in it, and his frayed collar, and every crease and threadbare patch in his shabby clothes. The girl, gazing down at him critically, had a sudden revulsion of feeling for this man who looked like a tramp, and her resolution wavered.

She could not go through with this thing. It was impossible. Her whole fastidious soul rose in revolt. And then she bethought herself of what her position would be if she did not go through with it. She heard her brother's voice saying, 'Give it a fair trial, Ursula. It can't hurt you to give it a fair trial. I won't ask you to do more than that. If it doesn't come off, there's no harm done; and if it does, it will be all right. You needn't worry about that. I know what I am talking about. If it comes off on these lines it will be a much bigger thing than ever it was with Frank.'

And she had replied. 'I suppose you fancy you are one of those old priest-kings of Atlantis?'

And he had answered, 'I was once, my child; or so I think.'

A strange thing, reincarnation, mused the girl, gazing down at the face of the man in front of her, who seemed to have dropped off to sleep. What had this man been in past lives? Had he ever had any connection with her? She thought not. There was no responsive stirring of memory within her at his approach. It was not like Frank, whom she had known at once. They had rushed together like twin souls. For once she doubted her brother's wisdom when he said that this thing, if it came off, would be far bigger than the thing with Fouldes could ever have been. He looked a pretty hopeless proposition, this rough, trampish individual who had shaved exceedingly sketchily, whose tie was like a bootlace, and whose hair badly wanted cutting.

But her brother's voice came back to her, saying, 'I only ask you to give it a fair trial, Ursula.' If she tried to pick up a rapport with Murchison, and failed to do so, nothing would happen and no harm would be done. But if she tried and succeeded - what then? Titania and Bottom? Ursula was not particularly anxious to succeed, desperate as her situation was if something could not be done to break the evil influence that had got her so completely under its sway.

She stood looking down at the man, studying his face and hesitating. Alick had said he was thirty-two, five years older than herself; but he looked much older than that. She had thought before that his expression was sulky and bad-tempered, but it did not look like that now. He simply looked very weary, and melancholy almost to hopelessness. She remembered he had said that he had been out of a job and at the end of his resources when he had obtained this engagement with her brother, and the anger rose up within her that a man with his fine War record should have been reduced to that. She thought of Frank Fouldes. He was younger than Murchison, and had just missed the War; and, in any case, he was most emphatically not a fighting man, declaring that nothing would induce him to bear arms in the event of another war, and lend himself to the inhuman folly of slaughter. Ursula pondered which was the better man, the simple-souled fighter, who had armed and marched at the first call of his country, or the intellectual, who had set his face against war? Reason was on the side of Fouldes; but a deep-seated and stubborn instinct answered to Murchison. Ursula found herself wishing that there had been something of Murchison in Frank Fouldes; if there had been, she felt, the debacle with Astley would never have occurred, and she would have been happily married by now. She recognized the tougher fibre of the rough-looking individual in front of her, and she had had a searing experience of 'the brittle intellectuals, who snap beneath a strain'; nevertheless, a bullock is a poor exchange for a stag.

Ursula Brangwyn felt bitter and disillusioned at that moment and very disinclined to go on with the experiment, especially as the man on the seat slumped down into an untidy heap as his sleep became deeper, and looked less attractive than ever. She gazed with repugnance at the grime of the old trench-coat he was wearing; evidently a relic of the War. How grubby it was! Fancy not sending it to the cleaners! She wondered how he had managed to get those curious streaks of dirt on the shoulders, and suddenly realized that those must be the marks made by the straps of a haversack. She had been old enough to remember the War days vividly, and there came back to her a scene at a railway station, with men clad just like this one lying asleep on benches, and something in her esteemed very highly these men who had stood between her and destruction. Murchison was forgiven his unsightliness. Just so did war-worn men sleep when they came out of the trenches.

As Ursula stood musing before him, Murchison slid yet lower on the seat, and cracked his neck at an angle that awakened even him; and opening his eyes as he heaved himself up on his hard couch, he saw the girl standing before him. He looked at her in surprise for a moment, and then got clumsily to his feet, stiff from sleeping in a constrained position.

Ursula plunged without more ado.

'I was so sorry I couldn't magnetize you just now,' she said, speaking quickly and nervously, 'it just wouldn't work. I don't know why. One has to feel in the mood for those things. But I'll do you now, if you like.'

Murchison looked down at her quizzically.

'What is it you propose to do to me, Miss Brangwyn?'

'Don't you understand these things?'

'I'm afraid I don't. They're all Greek to me.'

'But Alick said you knew a lot about them?'

'I'd never heard of 'em when I came to the flat a couple of days ago.'

The girl, who had been holding out her hands towards him, expecting him to press his palms against them, dropped her arms to her sides and stared at him in perplexity.

'Then - then you haven't had things explained to you?'

'No, Miss Brangwyn, I've had nothing explained to me. I am not paid to ask questions. I'm paid to do as I'm told.'

The girl went scarlet to the roots of her hair, and he wondered why. His remark had seemed to him innocent enough. He had evidently uttered some sort of double entendre without knowing it, and had better make haste to explain himself.

'Your brother told me that you had had a psychological car-smash over these blighters, and asked me if I'd bring the breakdown van out to you, where you were ditched. He gave me to understand that you and he and Fouldes had been doing some sort of psychological experiment, when Astley buffed in and shunted you off the rails, and he wants to repeat the experiment with me in the place of Fouldes, up to the point where it ran off the line, so that he can get you back on the rails, as it were. That's all

I know about it. I don't want to pry into your affairs. I know Brangwyn, and I trust him. His word is good enough for me.'

Ursula Brangwyn looked at him with a strange expression on her face, which he could not fathom.

'And what do you suppose will be the next move after I am back on the rails?'

'I've no idea. Brangwyn said he would help me to get another job when he no longer needed me.'

The girl laughed a sudden, nervous laugh that had no mirth in it.

'Do you realize that if we do this experiment, and it - it comes off, you will never get rid of me? Never - never - never.'

'Good Lord, what do you mean?'

'That - that if we establish the magnetic circuit that Alick wants us to establish, it can't be broken - that is, not easily.'

'I understood that he intended to use me as a kind of scaffolding while you were rebuilding, and that when the job was done I should be taken down and carted away.'

'Did he say that?'

'Well, no, not exactly. That was how I worked it out.'

'Then you worked it out wrong. You will be built into the structure if this goes through.'

'I don't know what you mean, Miss Brangwyn. This is all beyond me. I wish you'd speak plainly.'

The girl looked at him silently for a moment.

'You'd better ask my brother,' she said, and turned on her heel and walked off.

But when she got to the glass door leading back into the house, she did not pass through it, but seemed to change her mind, hesitated, and then turned and walked towards the embrasure where she had stood with Murchison the previous day, showing him the view, and leant there, with her elbows on the brickwork and her chin in her hands, staring out over London.

She remained there for a considerable time, Murchison watching her in perplexity, puzzling over her words and trying to make out their significance, piecing two and two together in the light of what he already knew, but not getting very far.

Suddenly she turned and came towards him, and he rose to meet her.

'Do you realize,' she said, 'that the experiment is already well under way, and it is too late to back out, even if we want to?'

'I am afraid I don't know anything about it, Miss Brangwyn, and my brain's completely addled this morning.'

'How are you feeling?'

'A bit limp.'

'You're feeling more than a bit limp. You're feeling rotten.'

'How do you know?'

'I know what's been done to you.'

'And what may that be?'

'You took what was meant for me and short-circuited it.'

'I am afraid I'm none the wiser.'

She looked at him in silence.

'Alick is perfectly right. There is only one thing to do for you, and there is only one thing to do for me. Hold out your hands. No, like that, fingers up. Now press your palms against mine.'

He did as he was bid. There was no need to bid him enter into the experiment imaginatively now. The girl's feelings were evidently deeply stirred, strive as she would to hide them, and her emotion infected him. He felt her hands trembling as she pressed her palms hard against his, but they were no longer cold, but burnt with a kind of dry, electric heat that pricked and tingled against his flesh as if an electric current were coming through them.

He felt himself take a deep breath involuntarily, and then everything faded out except the girl's face, with its great dark eyes fixed on his.

He was aware of nothing save the tingling in his palms and a sense of glowing warmth that was spreading slowly all over him. It was like taking an anaesthetic. How long it lasted, he never knew, but at length the girl stepped back, panting, withdrawing her palms from his, and the spell was broken. He found himself standing in the roof-garden in the pale winter sunlight facing a girl whose cheeks were flushed and her eyes bright and starry, and a curious smile on her lips. Something had been done to him; something very definite had been done to him, but he did not know what.

But, whatever it was, it had restored him to normal. He no longer felt that terrible drained sensation, as if he had had a bad haemorrhage.

'Thanks very much,' he said. 'I'm awfully grateful to you. I feel pounds better.'

At that moment the glass door opened, and Brangwyn came out on to the roof.

'Well, Murchison?' he said, 'Feeling better?'

'Yes, sir, pounds better, thanks very much.'

Brangwyn looked at Ursula, and smiled. She coloured up, and her eyes dropped.

'I'm going out,' she said. 'I've got some shopping to do,' and she vanished through the glass door.

'Is it wise for her to go alone?' asked Murchison.

'No, by jove, Murchison, it isn't.'

And Brangwyn vanished precipitately on the heels of his sister, leaving Murchison alone to his meditations.

CHAPTER 12

Left to his own devices, Murchison lit a cigarette and cogitated. What in the name of heaven was it all about? Brangwyn and Hugo Astley both dabbled in strange sciences, in what was, he supposed, called the occult. Only Brangwyn denied that it was occult; or, rather, he defined the occult in a way that Murchison had never heard it defined before. Hugo Astley had made a most unholy mess of Ursula Brangwyn, if her brother were to be believed, and, wild as it all appeared to be, Murchison felt that he was to be believed; he himself had seen enough to set him thinking.

'A stone's throw out on either hand
From that well-ordered road we tread,
And all the world is wild and strange:-
For we have reached the Oldest Land
Wherein the Powers of Darkness range.'

Murchison stared at the little fleecy clouds that sailed in the pale winter blue over the haze of London, and wondered where in the world he was going, now that he had left the well-ordered road of everyday life. Unquestionably it was the Oldest Land he was coming to. He was raising things that had been forgotten since the childhood of the race.

It was too cold to stop out on the roof-garden any longer, for the little clouds were gathering over the face of the sun, and it was evident that the best of the day was over. Murchison returned to his sitting-room and lit the gas fire, and as the asbestos gathered heat and glowed incandescent, took from the small bookshelf beside his chair the story-book of ancient tales, and turned over the pages till he came to the winged bull.

The great beast stood on his plinth exactly as had done his brother in the British Museum. Bull-foot advanced as if moving at a steady walking pace, unhurried, unpausing. Behind him was a vast pylon, and above its sculptured pediment was the dark blue of the night sky sown with stars.

Firelight appeared to play upon the bull, illuminating his great flanks and throwing shadows across his mighty wings, folded back into darkness. The beast was all the more impressive for being but half seen.

Murchison stared at him as if he would penetrate his secret by sheer force of staring.

'What the devil do you mean, you great brute?' he demanded aloud. 'You mean something, I know that, because you stir me so tremendously; but what is it you mean? Man-headed? Beast-bodied? Bird-winged? What is the answer to your riddle? Are you the soul? I suppose that's what all these symbols really are. They all refer to the soul in some way or other. Well, we've all got beasts' bodies all right. That's an easy one. But are we winged? Blowed if I know. Never saw any signs of it myself. And what about the human head? I've got a human head same as you; and I've got the body of a beast, the same as you - and don't I know it! But have I got wings? Might have. It's possible. No good denying possibilities. It remains to be seen. I certainly have had for brief minutes once or twice. Going over the top. And when I called on Pan. And when I held Ursula in my arms and strafed Astley. My God, I mustn't think of her as Ursula! I shall call her that to her face if I do! And then there'll be all the fat in the fire.

'What is Brangwyn playing at? Why is he chucking me at his blinking sister in the way he is doing? It's simply asking for trouble. I don't end at the neck like a cherub, whatever she may do. It isn't fair. Dammed if I hug that girl again! Throw her down and sit on her. Or shove a sofa cushion over her face. But paw her I don't, and damned if she shall paw me!'

The ringing of the telephone bell, and Brangwyn's voice summoning him to lunch, interrupted his meditations, and he went downstairs, pulling himself together to face Miss Brangwyn.

But he need not have worried. She was full of her shopping, and was arguing with her brother as to whether they really had carried some particular colour correctly in their heads, and would the shop change it if they hadn't? Miss Brangwyn in this mood was quite manageable. He had merely to eat his food and keep his eyes to himself. Nothing was being asked of him, and he had ample opportunity to contemplate the vast and unbridgeable gulf that safely separated him from his employer's sister.

When they gathered round the fire in the lounge for coffee Brangwyn evidently considered that his secretary was being neglected, and ought to be drawn into the conversation, but Murchison plunged about like a dray-horse on a slippery day, and they soon let him alone. He noticed that Miss Brangwyn made no attempt to help to draw him into the conversation, and had not, in fact, glanced at him, save for one brief moment when their eyes had met as he entered the room, and both had looked away again hastily. He resented that. After all, he was a gentleman by birth and education. Why should he be treated like a waiter? But then he recalled to himself that it simplified matters for him a great deal if Miss Brangwyn were a little distant, and he had better be grateful for small mercies, for the situation, in his opinion, might easily get out of hand.

'Now listen, you two children,' said Brangwyn at last, breaking in upon Ursula's nervous flow of trivialities. 'Neither of you had much sleep last night, and I particularly want you to be in good form this evening, for we have some work to do; so I suggest that you take an afternoon nap. Don't drink any more of that coffee, Murchison, or you won't sleep.'

Murchison saw Ursula's hands suddenly clench themselves together as they lay in her lap, but she uttered no word. She evidently knew what was before them, and it inspired her with dread. Or so he interpreted it. He gazed steadily at his employer under his heavy, sandy brows, and his eyes had the peculiar cold gleam of blue eyes when they are unfriendly. Why shouldn't he ask questions if he wanted to? Why should he be driven like a sheep because he was paid a salary? Brangwyn had not bought his immortal soul for five pounds a week. There were some things that were not included in the bargain, and he wanted to make sure that the evening's transaction was not among them. If it included hanging on to Ursula Brangwyn any more, he was off.

'What is it we are doing tonight?' he asked in level tones.

'We are doing a tentative experiment,' said Brangwyn, picking his words carefully and watching the other, 'to see whether you are really suitable for the job we have in mind. I think you are, and so does Ursula.'

'I never said that!' Ursula interrupted hastily and angrily. 'I said I was willing to give him a trial.'

'If you go into it in that spirit, it certainly won't work,' said her brother.

'I can't help the spirit in which I go into it. That's up to him. It's for him to make me go into it in the right spirit.'

'I think you are asking too much, Ursula. Remember he is new to these things. If you start throwing cold water about at the start, nothing can possibly come of it.'

Ursula twisted her hands together and looked sulky and upset.

'You had better ask yourself what alternatives you have before you start making difficulties,' said her brother.

Murchison suddenly rose from the chair.

'If I am the difficulty,' he said quietly, 'I am quite willing to withdraw. I don't want to be forced on Miss Brangwyn any more than she wants to have me forced on her.'

He suddenly felt a hand on his shoulder.

'You mustn't do that,' said Brangwyn in a low voice in his ear. 'If you back out now we shall have the most appalling mess. Ursula has got to work with you. You have got to make her work with you. For God's sake don't let me down, Murchison, you're my only hope. If this doesn't come off, Ursula will spend the rest of her life behind asylum bars.'

Murchison stared helplessly at the girl's white, rebellious face. He thought she looked nauseated, but he was too sorry for her to feel insulted. He went and sat down on the edge of the wide brick hearth beside her knee.

'What's the trouble?' he said. 'Won't you tell me what the difficulty is, and see if we can't straighten it out?'

The girl put her hands over her face.

'It's rotten!' she said. 'Rotten for you, and rotten for me.'

'What's rotten?' said Murchison in the same low voice.

'Oh, I don't know. I can't explain. You wouldn't understand.'

He turned to Brangwyn.

'Can't you tell me a bit more, sir? I'm working in the dark, and it makes things very difficult. I could be a lot more useful to you if I knew a bit more.'

'Difficult, Murchison, very difficult. You see, the test is that you spot the thing for yourself. If I told you point-blank, it would invalidate the whole business. Trust your instincts and intuitions. Go ahead and never mind convention.'

'Um,' said Murchison. 'Conventions have a way of coming home to roost. Mrs. Grundy is a sound old dame. She knows human nature. I'd sooner not play her up, if you don't mind.'

'Unless you are prepared to take a certain amount of risk, Murchison the thing can't go through. Won't you take a chance on Mrs Grundy? I'll accept full responsibility for the consequences.'

'I'm afraid of letting you down, Brangwyn.'

'What would you consider to be letting me down?'

'Oh, God, need we go into this?'

'Ursula, my child, run off and get your rest.'

The girl rose, white as a sheet, and stood hesitating, looking from one to the other of the two agitated men. Then she turned to Murchison.

'I'm awfully sorry,' she said in a broken voice. 'I'm awfully sorry to be such a beast. It isn't that I don't like you. I just can't help it. I'm very grateful to you, and I'd be truly thankful for your help if you can put up with me. I need it so awfully badly,' and she turned ran out of the room.

'Well, there you are!' said Brangwyn, plunging his hands into his trouser pockets, and taking a turn or two up and down the room. 'I don't know how to put it to you, Murchison. One would have to explain so much before it became comprehensible. And a half-explanation would be worse than none at all, because it would send you off on the wrong track. Look here, will you be content to run in blinkers for a bit longer, and let me steer you?'

'Well, now, sir, I'll tell you just how I'm placed. I've got no one belonging to me, and my life is no particular catch. I am perfectly willing to take risks, provided I know what they are. What I don't fancy is barging along in the dark; not because I'm afraid of what I may run into, but because I don't want to let you down. I know my own limitations a great deal better than you do. There are some things it is not in me to do; and some things at which I would definitely draw the line, whatever you offered me. All I want is to make sure that what you are planning doesn't include any of these things, so that I shan't find myself having to back out at a critical moment. It isn't that I'm shirking or funking, but I don't want to bite off more than I can chew. I can't go on blindfold any more, sir. I am doing nothing but put my foot in it.'

Brangwyn took another turn across the big room before replying.

'If you insisted on having the differential calculus explained to you, would you give an undertaking that you would understand the explanation?'

'I couldn't give an undertaking to understand all of it, but I reckon I should understand enough of it to follow the drift; and, at least, I could assure myself that it didn't contain anything I didn't fancy.'

'Very well, then, Murchison, I will do my best, and all that I ask is that you will not be hasty in forming a judgment, but will give the thing a chance. I am afraid I shall have to be rather crude, but, put briefly, the thing is this, I am hoping that you will be able to cut out Frank Fouldes with Ursula.'

'Good God, sir, what do you mean?'

'Just exactly that, Murchison. There has been some very queer in and out running, for which you must take my word at present; you may understand more later, when you see how we go to work ourselves.

Ursula has been worked upon by means of the rare knowledge of which I have told you; it is impossible for me to get her right simply by cutting her off from Fouldes; there is a curious, subtle link between them; there are also other things, which are not personal, little-understood natural forces, of which you know nothing at present; Ursula and Fouldes have been made to form a kind of circuit which carries these forces. If I break that circuit I destroy Ursula; therefore I cannot break it. All I can do is to replace Fouldes with someone else, someone clean and straight, who won't do Ursula any harm and will treat her decently.'

'Well, that's a plain statement, at any rate,' said Murchison. 'But you haven't told me how you propose to do the trick.'

'I want to get these natural forces, psychic forces, but no less natural because they are psychic, to flow in circuit through you and Ursula. If that comes off, Fouldes is automatically shunted and we shall have no more trouble with him. Any further fuss he may make will only be of the kind that a lawyer can deal with. But these subtle forces, Murchison - these are things a lawyer cannot deal with; nor can a doctor, more's the pity.'

'And what is the exact mechanics of the job?'

'It will be done by means of ritual. Are you any the wiser?'

'Not a scrap.'

'Well, you will be after tonight, for I propose to try it out on a small scale. A very small ritual, I promise you that, Murchison, just enough to see whether the power will flow between you and Ursula or not.'

'I know nothing about these things, sir, but if I am any judge, it won't flow. She has no use for me, and I have no use for her, save as part of my job.'

'You know a good deal about these things, Murchison, if you can tell whether power is flowing or not. I admit it is not flowing at the present moment, because Ursula is panicking, and you are hanging back in the collar. But you can't deny that there have been moments when it has flowed, when you have been in sympathy with each other. It is on this that I am banking.

'On this, and my knowledge of your respective characters, which tells me that you ought not to be uncongenial to each other.'

'Well, now, granted that I do get into sympathy with your sister, where do you expect it all to end?'

'Need it end, Murchison?'

'What do you mean?'

'Well, you're a bachelor and she's a spinster.'

'Yes, but damn it all, man, I've got no visible means of support!' Murchison entirely forgot the respect due to an employer in his agitation at the prospect opening before him with such breath-taking rapidity.

'You've got a good job with me, Murchison. The fiver a week is only your starting-price, and Ursula has means of her own.'

'But, look here, Brangwyn, this is out of the question. I never set eyes on the girl till a couple of days ago, and she has made it very plain that she doesn't fancy me. She wouldn't be willing, even if I were. No wonder the poor girl's jibbing!'

'Well, Murchison, do you fancy her?'

'To tell you the honest truth, sir, I don't.'

This was a facer for Brangwyn, who, watching closely, had come to the conclusion that his secretary was highly susceptible in that quarter.

'Anyone else you fancy?'

'No, sir, nobody. Never has been. I have never been in a position to even think of marriage. I've had my fair share of sordid adventures, but fewer than most, and more sordid than most, because I hadn't the cash to finance them adequately. When I was in the army, and had cash, I had ideals, and wouldn't look at 'em. Later, since life has knocked the ideals out of me, I haven't had the cash even to buy milk, let alone keep a cow. I don't care about stale pastry, so I cut all that sort of thing out.'

'I had an idea,' said Brangwyn quietly, 'that you were - er - susceptible to my sister.'

'Damn it all, sir, placed as I am, I'm susceptible to any woman who isn't an absolute char! I'm like that bull of Babylon your sister uses as a book-plate. I've got a beast's body, I admit it; but, thank God, I've got a human head! Because I've got impulses it doesn't follow that I give way to them. Why shouldn't I have impulses? I'm not ashamed of them. It's normal. There would be something wrong with me if I hadn't. It's circumstances that are wrong. The country as a whole. If it hadn't been for the War I wouldn't be in this pickle. I try to be as decent as I can under the circumstances, but I don't pretend to be a saint. I've no wish to go loopy.'

Murchison stopped for sheer lack of breath, the veins standing out on his forehead.

Brangwyn looked at him steadily, a slight smile on his lips.

'Has it ever occurred to you,' he said, 'that the bull has wings?'

Murchison passed his hand wearily across his eyes. 'Yes, I know it has, but I could never make anything of that.'

'It is the winged side of the bull that I want to develop between you

104

and Ursula. I have knowledge of these matters, Murchison, unusual knowledge. The woman I would have worked with died during the influenza epidemic that followed the War. I want to pass on my knowledge. I had hoped to pass it on to Ursula, if she had married the right sort of man; I wouldn't pass it on to Fouldes, and that was what all the trouble was about. He tried to get it from Astley, for Astley also has knowledge; but he has got hold of it by the wrong end. The result we know. Ursula knows that if she wants that knowledge she has got to be prepared to work with the right kind of man. I think you would be the right kind of man.'

Murchison suddenly found himself as dead tired as he had been earlier in the day. Virtue had gone out of him during his moments of excitement and self-revelation.

'I'll work with her, if that's what you both want,' he said wearily. 'But I won't marry her, and that's final.'

Brangwyn studied him closely.

'Will you tell me exactly how you feel about my sister?'

Murchison shifted uneasily in his chair. The truth probably meant the loss of his job.

'To be perfectly candid with you, I don't particularly like her, though I'm very sorry for her. There's something about her that rubs me up the wrong way and makes me feel on the defensive, if you know what I mean. An inferiority complex, I suppose. She's smart, and I'm uncouth. She's conscious of it, too; my uncouthness, I mean; she wouldn't care to have me as an escort if she were going anywhere, and I don't blame her. She's no use for me, and I've no use for her - but I'll tell you frankly, sir, when she did that magnetizing stunt she played Old Harry with me. I find her - since that - what the film posters call glamorous; but I don't like her any better on that account. That's a plain statement of how I feel; you must make what you can of it, for I can't make much of it myself.'

'That's a very honest, and a very observant statement, Murchison, and I'm grateful to you for the confidence you have placed in me. Now I am going to put one more probing question to you. Supposing you were well off and could meet Ursula on the level, how would you feel about her?'

'I don't think I should like her any better than I do now, sir. That's my honest belief. We have nothing in common.

'But I don't deny that if she chose she could have me on a string - but then, so could any woman.' He gave a short and bitter laugh. 'But it would only be for a time. I'd soon get over it. You will eat garbage when

105

you're starving. I know, for I've done it. But you won't include garbage in your daily menu once you're in Easy Street. That's why, although I know I'm susceptible, I'm not such a damn fool as to yield to it. I don't mind being gigolo to your sister, but I'm damned if I'm going to marry her. I should be knocking her about at the end of a month.'

Brangwyn studied him closely, and wondered how much of this was pride and how much was genuine. Murchison was exceptionally sensitive. He had followed every move in Ursula's mind with perfect accuracy. It was useless to try and throw dust in his eyes. Ursula was reluctant, and for the exact reasons that he had divined. Her brother's choice did not appeal to her.

He debated whether he should take the responsibility of acting on his strange knowledge, and forcing the inclinations of these two people. He asked himself, what was the alternative, and what might be the possible consequences? The alternative - an asylum for Ursula. The worst possible consequence, a divorce. He did not hesitate.

'Look here, Murchison, you know I have studied these things pretty deeply. Will you believe me if I tell you that if this experiment succeeds, things will come all right between you and Ursula? If it doesn't succeed, you will be no worse off than you are now, and no harm done. If you will give it a fair trial, and it doesn't work, I will see you get a decent job. And if it does work, I will see you through.

'I have got a bad heart. My hold on life is precarious. If I go out, who is there to stand between Ursula and perdition? The one thing I would like above all others is to see her married to some decent chap. I will make a will leaving my money equally between you and her if you will marry her. I don't want to put you in your wife's pocket. That's an intolerable position for any decent man.'

Murchison sat silent for a long time. At length he spoke.

'What do you mean by saying things would come straight between me and Ursula if the experiment went all right?'

Brangwyn noted the use for the first time of his sister's Christian name by his secretary, and smiled inwardly.

'I mean that if the cosmic forces get in circuit between you, you would get very fond of each other.'

'Why so?'

'Because it is the circuiting of certain forces between two people which makes them get fond of each other. These things are going on all the time, only we don't understand them. Their liking for each other puts them in circuit, and then the cosmic forces flow through. But it is possible to put them in circuit with each other, and then the fondness follows, provided, of course, they are not too incompatible; in which case one would not be able to set up a circuit. But the current keeps on jumping between you and Ursula spontaneously, and therefore I reckon that you will not only be able to form a circuit, but will carry a very high voltage when you get going. That is what I want to test tonight. I want to see whether we can get a low voltage definitely to travel between you and Ursula. I have no doubt whatever as to the outcome of the experiment, provided neither of you deliberately inhibit.'

'What do you want me to do? I haven't a notion about these things. I shall be like a bull in a china-shop.'

'I simply want you to carry out the instructions I shall give. This is not a set ritual, in which you would have to know your part like an actor in a play. But a spontaneous ritual, in which I shall have the general plan in my head, and shall direct you, but you yourself will have to do spontaneously whatever occurs to you under the circumstances in which I shall place you. It is a kind of acted psychoanalysis. It enables your subconscious mind to come up to the surface, and there are some strange powers in the subconsciousness, believe me, Murchison.'

Murchison scratched his head. 'Supposing my subconscious mind delivers the goods and you don't like 'em?'

'We must chance that. I've a pretty good notion of the sort of goods it will deliver on this occasion. Besides, we don't just up-end the ash-bin at random, as you so graphically put it on a previous occasion; we order the goods we want, and if they are in stock it is these that are delivered, and no others. All I want to do is to place a small order, and find out whether they are in stock or not. I think they are, but I can't be sure. I also want to make a start with the job. This will be a definite start if it goes all right.'

Murchison rubbed his nose. 'If I follow my spontaneous inclinations, I may end up by kissing your sister.'

'Splendid!' said Brangwyn. 'There's nothing I should like better.'

'But there may be things she'd like better. A pretty long list, too, by the looks of her.'

'Don't you worry about that. If it works for you, it will work for her. And, honestly, Murchison, it's her only chance. If you can't cut out Fouldes with her, she's done for.'

'All right,' said Murchison, 'I'll do what I can, within certain specified limits. If she wants a gigolo, I don't mind gigoloing - within reason, that is. But I won't marry the girl, sir, and that's my last word.'

And with that Brangwyn had to rest content.

CHAPTER 13

Murchison was awakened from his afternoon nap by the usual telephone bell, and heard Brangwyn's voice summoning him to an early meal before the doings of the evening.

'Had a good sleep, Murchison?' came the voice over the telephone.

'Yes, thanks. I'm in first-rate fettle. Ready for anything.'

'Dream at all?'

'Yes, I dreamt I was at the Zoo, and someone let the black panther out.'

There was a sound like a chuckle at the other end of the line as Brangwyn rang off. So the black kitten was growing up and becoming formidable? No longer a creature to be chased, but one to be fled from?

Murchison was not a person who did things by halves. He made up his mind that he would take Ursula Brangwyn on, flirt with her outrageously, take her mind off Fouldes, and ask Brangwyn to get him the promised job when he had made the place too hot to hold him. He did not think this would take very long. He had never thought of himself as a gigolo; and, however low he had fallen, had always held that gigolos were one degree lower. But he saw clearly in this case that he would be doing the girl a good turn. Once her infatuation for Fouldes was broken up she would have a chance. At present she had none. He had seen that for himself. He felt genuinely sorry for her, and was very glad to be able to help her. He would put his heart into the job. All he hoped was that he would be able to pull up without skidding. He had a vision of Brangwyn insisting on his making an honest woman of his sister.

When he arrived down in the firelit lounge, he found Ursula Brangwyn alone, lying back languidly in one of the big armchairs. He took a firm grip on himself and sat down on the edge of the wide brick hearth at her feet, folding his arms round his knees, thus bringing his head on a level with hers so that he could look straight into her eyes.

He was a Yorkshireman, and there is no finesse in the Yorkshire heritage. 'I want to talk to you,' he said.

Ursula Brangwyn gazed at him without speaking.

108

'Your brother has put the cards on the table at last. I didn't know what he was driving at before. I give you my word I didn't. You know the ins and outs of the thing just as well as I do, probably better, so I may as well speak plainly. It will be less embarrassing for both of us. I'd like you to think of me as if I were a doctor. Doctors have to do all sorts of intimate jobs for people, and they do them impersonally. It's all in the day's work to them. That's the way we've got to look at it. I'm the doctor and you're the patient, and that's how I shall think of you. I wish I could give you an anaesthetic,' he smiled, but no answering smile stirred the pale lips of the girl. 'I am afraid that's not practicable. But I swear to you that when the job's done I'll clear out and not bother you any more. I said I regarded myself as scaffolding, to be taken down and carted away when the job was done. You thought I might have to be built permanently into the structure, but I pointed out to your brother that that wasn't possible. It wouldn't suit either of us. We both know that. This is a job of work that's got to be put through. There's no possibility of an anaesthetic, so you've just got to stick it, same as having a tooth drilled, and I'll do all I can to minimize the discomfort.'

He ceased, and looked at the girl, awaiting her reply to his advances.

It came at length. 'I'm very grateful to you,' she said in a low voice, but looking him straight in the eyes. 'I don't know how in the world it's going to turn out. I am just trusting my brother. I feel as if my mind had gone completely into abeyance, and I simply can't think or plan, or anything. I know it's just as bad for you as it is for me. I should think you'd want a - a deodorizer, or something.'

Murchison laughed. 'Do you know the story of the butler who gave notice to his noble employer and then withdrew it, and when asked why, he said, "I've made up my mind, my lord, that you are my cross, and I've got to bear you." '

They were both laughing when Brangwyn came into the room and summoned them to dinner.

Luigi was in great form, having discovered a new way of cooking veal; and Murchison realized that there were times when it was a great advantage to have the loquacious Italian to turn on and off like a tap.

Brangwyn left them alone again after the meal, alleging he had some telephoning to do. Murchison had his doubts of this, and wondered whether Ursula had them too. He took his seat on the edge of the hearth and watched her make the coffee. In for a penny, in for a pound.

'Will you let me call you Ursula?' he said abruptly, and without any preamble. 'You see, I think it will kind of make it difficult for us to work together if I have to call you Miss Brangwyn. Recall us to earth, as it were, whenever we get going.'

'There is magic in a name,' said the girl in a low voice, trying to gather up scattered coffee-grains from the tray where her nervous hand had spilled them.

'Yes, that's what I felt, only I didn't exactly know how to put it. Now about me. My misguided parents called me Edward when I was christened, but no one has ever called me that since. I have always been Ted to my friends.'

He paused, but there was no reply from the girl. This was heavy going, but all the safer for that. The thing that would have really made him skid was a rapturous response. However, he could not imagine the fastidious Miss Brangwyn being really rapturous over anything.

'Now look here,' he said, plodding along flat-footed with the same steady pace as the bull of Babylon, 'there's one thing I've observed in my dealings with you. It's no use talking to you. That makes no impression whatever. There's only one way to get at you, and that's to touch you. Mind if I do?' and he laid his hand over hers and looked her straight in the eyes. To his amazement he saw them fill with tears.

'What's the matter?' he asked, his hand tightening on hers involuntarily.

'You're so awfully sweet to me, and I'm such a pig to you,' answered the girl in a broken voice.

'That's all right. Don't you worry about that.' He patted her hand gently, and they sat together silently in the firelight, the girl's slender hand in his, the coffee forgotten as they stared into the fire, each busy with their own thoughts.

Murchison was amazed that, whereas he had expected to have to fight a battle for self-control every step of the way, he found himself rifled with the profoundest peace as he sat with the girl's hand in his. There was no accounting for it. It was a peace that passed all understanding. And through the peace there flowed a sense of the most intense compassion. He had always been a man who, for all his roughness, was quick to pity; but he had never realized before that it was possible to feel compassion such as this.

'Don't worry,' he said huskily. 'I'll see you through.' He suddenly wondered whether his present state of mind would serve Brangwyn's purpose. He had no doubt whatsoever, in fact, Brangwyn had left no room for doubt, that his employer deliberately intended to trade on the sex side of things in order to bring about his sister's recovery. But there was no sex in this feeling that was between them. With the first touch, which he had expected to arouse it, the whole thing had vanished, leaving instead this intense sympathy. Was this the wings of the bull, that raised him, a kind of bovine Pegasus, into the higher air?

He had gone into the thing entirely selflessly, hoping to do the girl a good turn; expecting to get nothing out of it for himself save a lot of worry and nervous wear and tear. And, instead of the strain he had anticipated, there was this great peace. He had stumbled through the Labyrinth into the presence of the Minotaur; and, instead of a monster, there was the Virgin. He remembered having read of the Witches' Sabbath, and how the postulants for that dark initiation were led up to the altar to kiss the latter end of the Goat of Mendes, and, when they got there, it was the beautiful calm face of the priestess of Isis that their lips touched.

He was so absorbed in his thoughts that Brangwyn came into the room and discovered them thus, and it was not until he found himself blinking in the glare of the electric lights switched on by his employer that it occurred to him to remove his hand, and then he did so without any particular haste or the least embarrassment.

Brangwyn heaved a sigh of relief as he sensed the change in the atmosphere.

'If you are ready,' he said, 'we will go downstairs.'

They followed him through a door in the panelling that Murchison had not realized existed, and found themselves on a continuation of the spiral staircase that led downwards and was evidently walled off from a corner of the second-hand book-shop, which was the next-door neighbour to Luigi's restaurant, and also part of Brangwyn's property.

But their downward way continued so long that Murchison realized that they must have passed below the book-shop and would ultimately come out in the basement. A door closed the bottom of the staircase, and as Brangwyn switched on the light as they passed through it, Murchison realized that the basement was very far from being in its pristine state, but was got up as are few basements in that part of London.

They found themselves in a room of modest dimensions entirely surrounded by cupboards, the whole place warm almost to suffocation with central heating. Brangwyn opened one of the cupboards and took out a diaphanous robe of palest green; it was exceedingly thin, but exceedingly voluminous; dozens of yards of material must have gone to the making of it. He handed this to his sister.

'Go and get dressed,' he said, and she vanished through a door in the

111

corner, which evidently led to a dressing-room, for Murchison got a glimpse of a mirror.

'Don't come back until we send for you,' Brangwyn called after her.

He opened another cupboard and took out a straight-hanging, sleeveless garment of heavy gold tissue. 'This is for you,' he said, handing it to Murchison. 'I am afraid you will have to strip. It doesn't do to have winter woollies appearing in the middle of a ceremony.'

Murchison saw the sense of this, and though he would dearly have loved to have clung to his pants, did as he was bid, letting Brangwyn lace golden sandals on to his bare feet and bind a golden fillet about his shaggy fair hair, which stuck out in a veritable sun-god's halo all round it. A broad band round the hips, like the sash on the cassock of a priest, completed the outfit.

Murchison surveyed himself in a long mirror, and perceived a startling figure. He saw at once that his kit was cut on the lines of the tunic of an Egyptian priest, save that it was all gold from head to heel instead of bleached linen. It was absolutely plain save for the rayed golden sun-disk embroidered on the breast. Murchison realized now why the room was so warm. It had to be if one were to disport oneself thus scantily clad. He also realized, however, that with the shedding of his everyday garments he had also shed his everyday personality. The man that looked back at him from the mirror was not himself; it was someone from the Oldest Land that had risen to the surface from the depths of his unconscious mind. Someone that he himself might have been in a previous incarnation. He remembered what Brangwyn had said about the Lost Continent and its forgotten wisdom, and wondered whether the form of the garment he wore was older than Egypt. Was he clad as were the priests of lost Atlantis? Something in him replied that he was; that even so had he been clad once before. It was as if he were recalling the memories of a dream of overnight which had been forgotten on waking. He felt a curious change coming over his personality, as if something greater than his thwarted, bewildered daily self were coming into action. He had put off his inhibitions with the drab garments of civilization. With the pagan robe he had put on the pagan outlook free, self-assertive, near to Nature. He felt Brangwyn watching him, and knew that his employer had observed the change in him and was well pleased.

Brangwyn rapped on the door of the dressing-room. 'Are you ready, Ursula?' he called. The door opened, and Ursula Brangwyn came out.

She was clad in a filmy, flowing green robe that billowed around her in a cloud. It hung from a narrow band of gold about the breast, but no

112

girdle confined it at the waist, and it flowed as she moved like wind-blown smoke. A gold fillet bound the dark hair that had been released from its plaits, and golden sandals similar to his own were upon her bare feet.

She, too, was not Ursula Brangwyn, but someone else, someone who also came from the Oldest Land.

Brangwyn still clad in a lounge suit, addressed them, and so potent was the man's personality that it overflowed the modern garments so that they did not seem incongruous.

'Now listen, you two. Go in and sit down while I robe. I shall come in presently and do my part, during which you remain seated; I shall chant, and invoke, and play my violin. When the spirit moves you, you start to perform your parts. You take the initiative, Murchison, at least, I expect you will. Now bear this in mind, and picture it in your imagination - Ursula represents the earth in spring. You are the sun-god gathering strength as the days lengthen. My music and my chanting, if I do my part properly, ought to cause images to rise in your imagination; accept those images as if they were real, and live in your imagination while the rite goes on. That is the aim of it - to stir the imagination. This is a kind of psychology the schools know nothing about. You will know something about it, though, before you have finished, and you will see how extraordinarily effectual it is.

'When you get really into it, and feel as if it were real, but not before - don't budge before it becomes real to you, Murchison, or it will be a fiasco, and worse than useless - act out the play as you feel it. I don't know what will come to you, and I shall be very interested to see.'

Murchison followed Ursula through a felt-covered door, evidently designed to prevent the leakage of sound, and found himself in a spacious, candle-lit apartment. There were only half a dozen candles in high ecclesiastic candlesticks ranged in a circle round the room, but walls, ceiling, floor and every article of furniture was painted in a shining golden hue, and the light of the candles reflected back again and again till the very air of the room seemed to glow with golden light. Murchison checked and halted, amazed, his breath held like that of a diver into deep water. So completely did this golden room take him away from everyday things into a new and wider life that he could hardly draw breath for a moment in its rarefied atmosphere; he was like a mountaineer who climbs to great heights too swiftly; his mechanism would not adapt itself to the new conditions for a moment.

Ursula made her way across the golden floor with soundless steps.

Murchison judged the flooring to be of cork lino with a coat of gold paint, and it gave out no sound to the tread of their sandals. She took her seat on a throne-like chair of carved and gilded wood at one side of the room and, without speaking, motioned Murchison to take his seat on a similar chair placed opposite, the breadth of the room away. Towards the far end of the room, an equal distance from both their seats, and forming an equilateral triangle with them, was a small, square altar, also of bright gold, and on it was, somewhat incongruously, a rough pitcher of unglazed earthenware with a shaggy mass of pine boughs in it, their resinous needles smelling aromatically in the warmth of the room. Surrounding the rude pitcher were ranged a cup of curious shape, three parts full of a very dark wine; a platter of broken bread, and a small dish of coarse salt. The shape of the cup put Murchison in mind of the famous cup of the ancient king that had been moulded from the breast of Helen of Troy.

At the end of the room at which they had entered was a raised, curtained platform, reached by three steps, which acted as an effectual screen to the door and enabled anyone to enter and reach the dais unobserved by those already within the room.

Ursula Brangwyn had assumed the posture of the ancient Egyptian gods; sitting bolt upright, knees and feet together, hands along thighs. Murchison imitated her, taking the opportunity to have a good look at her, as her eyes were fast shut.

He had never considered her in detail before. His rather shy and shamefaced glances had only conveyed to him a general impression.

He saw that she was tall and long-limbed, and that slender, olive-skinned hands lay along her thighs. She was thin almost to emaciation, and it marred her looks; but, apart from that, she was very beautiful in a strange and unusual way. He could imagine that everyone would admire her, but not everyone would like her. Her head was rather small, and the hair seemed heavy on it, like the hair of Lady Hamilton in Romney's portrait of her as a nymph. In fact, Ursula Brangwyn was rather like Nelson's beloved. But her expression was different. Her whole temperament was different. Aloof fastidiousness was written in every line of her body, from the thrown-back poise of her head, with its close-held mouth, to the way she placed her narrow feet side by side on the golden floor. Murchison felt sorry for the man who should marry her. She was a creature quite unsuitable for human nature's daily food.

Murchison suddenly found himself disliking her. Something primitively male in him resented the aloof untouchability of her.

'All right, you bitch,' he found himself saying under his breath. 'I'll rub your nose in it for you, and that'll larn you!'

Ursula Brangwyn, knocked off her pedestal by a hearty hand and well and soundly rolled in mother earth, might wake up a much saner and more normal creature than she was at present. A zest for the job welled up in him. He forgot all about his sympathy and compassion in a satyric mirth and mischief entirely foreign to his normal nature. He was the goat-god after the nymph for a moment. And then he pulled himself together. This wouldn't do. She was his employer's sister, and he would lose his job if he went too far. The glamour of the room fell away from him, and he saw no longer the green-clad dryad of the trees, but Miss Brangwyn, her diaphanous draperies only redeemed from indecency by what looked like a bathing-dress to match worn underneath. He appraised the room and its fittings, and decided that they were painted plywood, and the draperies the ordinary stock-in-trade of the upholsterer. The golden thrones he judged to be Tottenham Court Road Jacobean, with the varnish pickled off and replaced by a coat of gold paint. He noted the wires strung from the ceiling that supported the corners of the curtain-poles on the dais, and chuckled like the child who sees into the wings at the pantomime. He would play his part, and have a bit of fun out of Ursula Brangwyn into the bargain. It was what he was paid for, and the bitch should have good value. His eyes narrowed to slanting slits like those of a goat.

He heard a slight rustling on the dais, and reckoned his employer had got into his glad rags and was arriving. He glanced at his opposite number, and thought that she looked tense and apprehensive, and suddenly felt sorry for her again; the goat-mood vanished, and he became a decent human being, anxious to lend the girl a hand. It suddenly occurred to him that the great gross bull had achieved a human head; it remained to be seen whether it could sprout wings, and if so, what form they would take. He felt an inner excitement of curiosity rise within him, and gave himself up to the glamour of the adventure.

A single clear bell-note rang out from the curtained dais, and the amazingly resonant voice of Brangwyn filled the room.

'Hekas, Hekas, este bibeloi!'

A classical education is not supposed to be of very much use in a competitive world, but Murchison had found it coming in handy since he had thrown in his lot with Brangwyn and his strange sciences, and he recognized the warning cry of the Dionysiac Mysteries which bid the profane to flee from the path of the divinely inebriated revellers lest they be torn to pieces by the frenzied worshippers.

It startled him; and the faint thrill of fear went through him which is the surest presage of a successful psychic experiment. Ursula Brangwyn's eyes remained fast shut, but his were open, darting here and there about the golden room as if expecting to see the gods appear at any moment. He was rapt away out of himself, his imagination enthralled as it had sometimes been at the pictures, and for the time the pasteboard scene was real and he himself another man, a creature of dream and wish-fulfilment, come back from the Oldest Land at the evocation of the imagination.

Then the violin spoke, and he gave himself up to the music.

At first it rippled and ran like purling water, or the wind in spring woods that are in bare leaf, and he thought of Ursula Brangwyn's diaphanous green robe. Then it deepened and strengthened, and he thought of the summer woods in deep leaf and full of bird-song: and then began a rushing, circling fire-music that made him think of the sun's corona of towering flame, each licking tongue thousands of miles in height. The golden room seemed to turn to red-gold flame, and he could feel the heat and excitement of it upon his face. He found it extraordinarily hard to keep his seat and keep quiet.

The music ceased, and with a faint rattle of rings on rods the curtains parted, and a strange and startling figure appeared on the topmost of the three steps of the dais. It was Brangwyn, clad in a great golden cope shot with salmon-pink; on his head, and adding a foot and a half to his already considerable height, was the headdress of united Egypt with the Uraeus-serpent reared before it.

Brangwyn stretched out his hands, and without a word spoken, called the two of them to their feet as a conductor gathers up his orchestra. Murchison wondered how the girl, with her tightly closed eyes, caught this soundless cue. Then he saw that she was in a sleep-walking, hypnoidal state, and wondered what Svengali act was about to be performed.

Brangwyn caught his eye and held it, and, holding up his hand for attention, began to intone in his sonorous voice, to the intense surprise of his hearer, the words of a modern poet.

'Years have risen and fallen in darkness or in twilight,
Ages waxed and waned that knew not thee or thine
While the world sought light by night and sought not thy light,
Since the last sad pilgrim left thy dark mid-shrine.

116

Dark the shrine and dumb the fount of song thence welling,
Save for words more sad than tears of blood, that said;
"Tell the king, on earth has fallen the glorious dwelling,
And the water-springs that spake are quenched and dead."

Murchison felt the misery and frustration of the world flowing over him like salt tides of darkness; it seemed to him that the candles flickered and grew dim, and in that obscurity he felt his own misery and frustration sweeping on with the tide, caught up in its movement and made part of the vast whole. It was no longer a thing personal to him, but a vast movement of life that had found a channel through him. He lost the thread of the words for a moment, and when he recovered them again the rhythm had changed from strophe to anti-strophe.

'And he bowed down his hopeless head
In the drift of the wild world's tide. And dying,
"Thou has conquered," he said,
"Galilean"; he said it, and died.'

Murchison thought of that great pagan, Julian the Apostate, striving to make head against the set of the tide.

When his wits returned to the mundane plane he found that the key of the chant had changed again, a note of furtive triumph was creeping into it; and he thought of the secret, guarded meetings of the witches' sabbaths, waking the old gods and breaking through the repressions of the priest-ridden walled towns of the Middle Ages.

'Yea, not yet we see thee, father, as they saw thee,
They that worshipped when the world was theirs and thine,
They whose words had power by thine own power to draw thee
Down from heaven till earth seemed more than heaven divine.'

Who was this unnamed god who was thus being evoked with such magnificent rhythm and imagery, and whose power was already filling the room with a strange excitement? Murchison was on the alert for the name to come; but somehow it eluded him, for the gorgeous imagery filled his imagination like clouds of golden smoke, shutting out sense and hearing in waves and only permitting him glimpses of his surroundings at intervals.

'To the likeness of one God their dreams enthralled thee,
Who wast greater than all gods that waned and grew;
Son of God the shining Son of Time they called Thee,
Who wast older, O our father, than they knew.'

Murchison saw before his eyes such scenery as might be in the moon, and amid it, 'grey-haired Saturn, quiet as a stone.' The vision was fleeting, and sped before he could grasp it, but he knew that he had once again missed the actual words of evocation.

'Old and younger gods are buried and forgotten
From uprising to downsetting of thy sun,
Risen from eastward, fallen to westward and forgotten,
And their births are many, but their end is one.
Divers births of godheads find one death appointed,
As the soul whence each was born makes room for each;
God by God goes out, discrowned and disanointed,
But the soul stands fast that gave them life and speech.'

The words struck Murchison like a knife-thrust. Here was the key for which he had always been searching! The key to the mystery of faith. The faith that would persist in believing, despite all disillusionment, that round the next corner it would find the Real and the Good. The gods of men's worship were not things in themselves, but the creations of the created - the forms under which man represented to himself his ineffable Creator and Sustainer, the form changing as man's power of understanding increased. The forms did not matter; peppery old Jehovah with his long white beard and golden crown could go into the discard without anybody being damned; and, equally, those who liked him could go on worshipping him still, without being damned either. You could help yourself to the kind of god that suited you, so long as you realized that he was only a dramatization. The real thing was behind all the gods, and no man had ever dramatized it. On your head be it if you made yourself a nasty god that liked blood-sacrifices; or a silly god, who wanted to make a pink sugar confectioner's heaven of this tough old earth. The nearer you got to the facts in your conception of God, the better for you, but no man's concept had ever been the truth, the whole truth, and nothing but the truth, nor ever would be. When he reached that stage he would just quietly pass out and go free. God was the Absolute, whatever that might mean. Murchison shrewdly suspected it meant nothing. Anyway, it was no use to the average human brain, which needed bulk to work on, same as the intestines. It had to have images and a story. God and the gods. That was it. God was many-sided, you couldn't see every side at once; and the gods were the facets of the One. Christianity was a facet. Voodoo was a facet. The Tao was a facet. God was as many-sided as the soul of man.

And the trouble with Christianity was that it was so damned lop-sided. Good, and jolly good, as far as it went, but you couldn't stretch it clean round the circle of experience because it just wouldn't go. What it was originally, nobody knew, save that it must have been something mighty potent. All we knew of it was what was left of it after those two crusty old bachelors, Paul and Augustine, had finished with it.

And then came the heresy-hunters and gave it a final curry-combing, taking infinite pains to get rid of everything that it had inherited from older faiths. And they had been like the modern miller, who refines all the vitamins out of the bread and gives half of the population rickets. That was what was the matter with civilization, it had spiritual rickets because its spiritual food was too refined. Man can't get on without a dash of paganism; and, for the most part, he doesn't try to. He leaves that to women and parsons.

'Day by day Thy shadow shines in heaven beholden,
Even the sun, the shining shadow of Thy face;
King, the ways of heaven before Thy feet grow golden;
God, the soul of heaven is kindled with Thy grace.'

Murchison pricked up his ears and gave his attention to the resonant, intoning voice. He felt certain that the actual words of invocation were on their way now, for the voice was gathering power as a horse gathers itself together for the jump.

'As they knew Thy name of old time could we know it,
Healer called of sickness, slayer invoked of wrong,
Light of eyes that saw Thy light, God, king, priest, poet,
Song should bring Thee back to heal us with Thy song.
For Thy Kingdom is passed not away,
Nor Thy power from the place therefore hurled;
Out of heaven they shall cast not the day,
They shall cast not out song from the world,
By the song and the light they give

We know Thy works that they live;
With the gift Thou hast given us of speech

We praise, we adore, we beseech,
We arise at Thy bidding and follow,
We cry to Thee, answer, appear,
O Father of all of us, Paian, Apollo,
Destroyer and healer, hear!'

So the secret was out! It was an invocation to the sun-god that was going on, hence the golden room and the golden robes. Brangwyn, in his rose-gold cope, was unquestionably the Priest of the Sun, but what was he, Murchison? In some manner the servitor of the sun-god, that was quite certain, but in what manner? That was not yet made plain. He must wait and see. At any rate, they had got steam up properly, and he would not have long to wait. It was a glorious experience, and he abandoned himself to it with an unbelievable zest. He had never known it was possible to enjoy himself so wholeheartedly, all thought of the consequences was lost. He was pulling lustily with the tide.

The curtains on the dais fell back into place with a soft rattle of rings, and the music began again. Wild music, Tzigany music, sliding in and out of even more barbarous rhythms as Africa and its syncopations were laid under contribution. Murchison found himself beginning to wonder where it was all going to end. This stuff got into one's blood and let all sorts of things loose. But he had a feeling that Brangwyn had the situation well in hand, and that there would be no crash. He suspected that the music was being used to whip him up for that last tremendous fence that he must take at full gallop if he were to take it at all. He began to breathe deeply and rhythmically, in time to the music; and as he did so he felt a kind of tide beginning to flow in and out of him, energy waxing and waning with a curious, pulsating rhythm.

Then the music, with no break in its sequence, slid into the tremendous pealing of the chant;

'O all ye works of the Lord, bless ye the Lord: praise Him and magnify Him for ever!'

'Sun, moon and stars, bless ye the Lord; praise Him and magnify Him for ever!'

Brangwyn was steadying him for the fence.

The room became quiet, and very still; yet with the stillness of supreme pressure, like something that is about to burst. Then there came on that quiet air a slow and limpid tune, rhythmless, not unlike a Gregorian chant, exceedingly archaic, and Murchison felt a curious glow of warmth envelop him. He felt something behind him, overshadowing him, as if with a pair of vast hawk's wings. He felt a sudden deep trilling in his throat, like the humming of the strings of a double-bass in a kind of pizzicato, and then a voice such as he had never heard in his life burst from him:

'Ra! Ra! Ra!'

Then there was a dead silence, and he felt himself break out in perspiration all over. Enough wits were left to him to realize that this was mediumship, with a god for control! A curious sense of helplessness came over him, and slight fear.

He felt the humming gather strength in his throat again, and once more the Voice broke forth;

'I am Horus, god of the morning; I mount the sky on eagle's wings. I am Ra in mid-heaven; I am the sun in splendour. I am Toum of the downsetting. I am also Kephra at midnight. Thus spake the priest with the mask of Osiris.'

The power slackened and passed as the last words died away, and Murchison found himself back again in waking consciousness, with the sight of the room before him where previously there had been nothing but golden fire-mist. But he had come back with a difference. Everything that was Ted Murchison had been swept away and he had thrown back to some deep, primeval level of consciousness. He was in the Oldest Land. He was of a forgotten race. And he had knowledge.

This golden temple was consecrated to the sun-god, the lord and giver of life. He knew that. Knowledge welled up within him, coming back as memories come back when one returns to the scenes of one's earliest childhood. As each fresh object in that consecrated temple caught his eye its meaning came back to him.

He himself was about to play his part in the great sun-rite which brings life and fertility to the earth and inspiration to the heart of man. He looked up at the dais where the high priest stood, awaiting his cue.

The rose-gold cope shimmered and fell into heavy folds as the hands of invocation were raised.

'Helios, Helios, Helios!' came the deep voice of the high priest. This was the cue, and he rose from his seat and took three steps towards the earth-priestess opposite. She rose, and took three steps towards him, and the rite began.

He had no very clear remembrance of that rite, either at the time or afterwards. He knew they waltzed together to slow rhythms, which he presumed Brangwyn played on his violin. He knew they came up to the altar and drank together from the cup of dark, resinous-tasting wine, and ate together of the broken bread dipped in the coarse salt, for he felt the tang of it on his lips for long after. Together they inhaled the waiting fragrance of the pine-branches with their little dark cones. Then they danced again.

That was all there was of it upon the physical plane. But inwardly much more was going on. But they were not two individuals. He was not doing something to Ursula Brangwyn, nor she to him. They were two forces, not two persons. He was the sun in heaven bringing life to the earth. She was the earth, absorbing it hungrily, drawing it from him to satisfy her crying needs. And the more she drew from him, the more flowed into him.

He felt himself all brightness, as if he were compact of shining gold. And he felt the woman in his arms gradually light up like the earth at dawn as the sun steals over the fine of the eastern hills. Finally she, too, was all brightness, and they were made as one as they circled in the slow rhythms of the waltz.

Then twilight began to fall. The music moved slower, and finally there was silence. Together they stood before the altar with its pine-boughs, its bread, wine and salt. The hands of blessing were extended over them, and consciousness came back to normal.

Ursula Brangwyn disappeared behind the dais, and he heard the door softly opened and shut. A gesture from Brangwyn stayed him from following. They remained silently facing one another across the small, cubical altar; two big men in their shining robes, the one crowned with the towering tiara of Egypt, the other with his own shaggy fair hair bound by a Grecian fillet. Murchison noted that the cubical altar was exactly the height of the navel of a six-foot man.

Finally Brangwyn turned, and beckoning Murchison to follow him, left the shimmering golden room that had been the scene of this mysterious rite. Without a word they began to unrobe in the outer chamber, Murchison peeling off his narrow golden tunic as if it were a sweater. Silently they got into the clothes of convention, struggling with their collars and tying their ties without word spoken. It was not easy to return to civilization.

Murchison did not see Ursula Brangwyn again that night.

CHAPTER 14

When Murchison awoke in the morning he knew that something had been done to him. What it was he could not have said. It was as if tight cords that bound him body and soul had been released. There was a joyousness and freedom in the air instead of the despondency and isolation that usually beset him. He sat up in bed and asked himself what it was all about. The events of the previous evening had an unreality about them. They were more like a vivid dream clearly remembered than actual happenings. He felt that they belonged to some other kind of reality than the things of normal life. That they were valid, and had a reality of their own, though if weighed up by ordinary standards they were such stuff as dreams are made of. All the same, whether they were dream or wake, they had left their mark behind them, and he felt that he would never go back to be quite the same man he was before he had danced the dance of the sun in the golden room with the green-robed figure that was the earth in spring. It was all mad, exceedingly mad, but, all the same, he believed it to be wholesome. There was upon him a new zest for life, and he leapt out of bed and sang in his bath in a way he had not done since the Kaiser retired to Doorn and the world had no longer any need of fighting men.

He arrived down to breakfast very fresh and pink-cheeked from his tub, and Brangwyn, glancing up from the paper at his entrance, thought of Norse myth and legend and the ancient sagas. He, too, saw that this was not the same man as the sulky, heavy-footed, clumsy-moving Murchison of overnight. This was a man who could leap along the reeling decks of the longships and be first over the bulwarks when they grappled. Brangwyn stared at him. He had expected that the previous night's experience would make a difference, but not as much difference as this. He was exceedingly sorry now that he had sent his sister away. He would have liked her to have seen this entry.

Murchison took his seat at the table, unfurled his napkin, glanced round, and noted that the table was only laid for two.

'Miss Brangwyn all right?' he enquired.

'Quite all right, thanks,' replied his employer. 'I packed her off back to Wales by the night mail. She is better out of the way for the next stage of the proceedings.'

Murchison raised his eyebrows in query.

'Last night was not to be taken as a precedent,' said Brangwyn. 'It was a try-out, as it were. Now you have got to settle down and put in some solid work, and that young woman is a distracting influence. She would encourage you to lick off all the jam and leave the plain bread and butter underneath.'

Murchison was conscious of a sudden rush of resentment. Brangwyn had no right to interfere between him and Ursula. He wouldn't have it. Then he pulled himself up. This was ridiculous. What claim had he got on the girl? He wasn't her husband, or ever likely to be. He could hardly claim any rights over her on the strength of having danced with her. All the same, something in him resented this obvious common sense. There was a bond between them, a very definite bond. He couldn't define it, but he knew it was there. Brangwyn had got to take a back seat from now on, though it wouldn't do to let him suspect it. It was he, Murchison, who stood nearest to the girl now. Then he realized that his employer was watching him closely, and wondered whether his face had betrayed his thoughts, and hastily grasped the porridge-ladle and slopped some porridge on to his plate and began to eat without noticing that he had neither milk, sugar nor salt. Brangwyn, watching the savourless mess going down scalding hot, smiled to himself, and concluded that Murchison had got it badly.

'Any dreams last night, Murchison?' he asked suddenly. Murchison paused with the porridge-spoon half-way to his mouth, and eyed him suspiciously.

'Yes,' he said at length. 'Any amount, but I can't remember the half of them at the moment.'

'Let's have some bits and scraps to be going on with,' said his employer affably.

Now Murchison remembered a certain dream particularly well, but it had been such a wonderful experience that he was reluctant to speak of it and so spoil it by exposing it to the light of common day. He could still feel the glorious sensation of that dream, the sense of swift movement and flight. Then he remembered the bargain his employer had made with him, that instead of the monotonous drudgery of clerking he should merely be required to be frank about his dreams, and pulled himself together to fulfil his duty as a laboratory animal.

'I dreamt I was riding,' he said, 'riding a remarkably fine beast and travelling at a great rate. I was riding over downs, or sand-dunes, near the sea. It was grey twilight, and everything was bare and grey and kind of formless, save for numbers of scattered thorn-trees. That's all I can tell you. There wasn't much to the dream in the way of incident, simply the sensation of riding and movement, and the landscape sliding by, and the sea not far off.'

'What manner of horse was it you were riding?'

'A magnificent beast, a thoroughbred all right. I could tell that by its gait. Very springy and smooth. A tremendous stride. It was like riding a race, only I was all by myself.'

'What colour was the horse?' asked Brangwyn slyly.

'Black, jet-black. I can see its neck now. A magnificent beast.'

'Mare or stallion?'

'Oh, I dunno. I didn't go into those anatomical details. It was a magnificent beast. That is all I know. The thing that chiefly struck me was the sense of movement. Flight through space. It was a glorious sensation. Like being set free. I can't describe it. I bet there would be a lot in that dream if one came to analyse it.'

'Analyse it now. I'm interested in dreams.'

'Oh lor, I dunno. I want my breakfast.'

'All right. Get your breakfast. No one's stopping you. But tell me this. Did you notice anything special about the horse?'

'No, nothing, except that it was black, and had a lovely gait. I don't remember mounting, or dismounting, only riding; and one doesn't see much of a horse when one is on it.'

'Well, what about black? What associations have you with black?'

An association with black instantly leapt to Murchison's mind - Ursula Brangwyn's long black hair. He felt himself going the colour of a peony. That is one of the disadvantages of a fair skin. Dissimulation is a hopeless undertaking. And he had promised entire frankness in the matter of dreams. He forced himself to look his employer in the eye, his face burning like fire.

'I think of your sister's hair,' he said, and Brangwyn watching his victim closely, was thankful the bread-knife was out of reach lest he should suddenly have found it planted in his vitals.

He looked away, to give Murchison time to recover himself, and when he looked back again was surprised to see that he had gone dead white.

'Don't you think we are playing with fire, sir?' he said.

'We are kindling a fire, but not playing with it, my boy. We are getting up steam in the boiler, to be precise. Don't be afraid of it, Murchison. We are on to a very big thing if we have the nerve to see it through.'

'Yes, that's the problem,' replied Murchison. 'Have we? Or rather, have I?'

'You will have, when you are trained,' said Brangwyn. 'That was why I packed Ursula off. You mayn't have now, but when you are trained it will be a different story.'

Murchison sat silent, staring into space, his hands gripping the edge of the table hard. What sort of asceticism was going to be demanded of him that he should stifle his natural instincts that were being called forth so strongly? What sort of sacrifices would he be required to make? Did Brangwyn realize what all this business was beginning to mean to him?

'I won't run you up a blind alley, if that is what you are worrying about, Murchison,' came his employer's voice. Then in pranced Luigi with a special brew of kidneys, and the spell was broken.

It was not until they were smoking their after-breakfast cigarettes, and Murchison had simmered down, that Brangwyn reopened the subject that was in both their minds.

'I expect you are beginning to get the hang of things a bit now, aren't you, Murchison?'

Murchison grunted.

'You see how we use a ritual to work up a particular emotional state, and while you are in that state how something magnetic flows between you and Ursula?'

Murchison grunted again.

'Well, yesterday was just a trial run, but it showed you the possibilities, and that if you were trained as Ursula has been trained, there could be a great deal more in it than there was last night.'

'There was as much in it as I knew what to do with,' said Murchison.

Brangwyn repressed a desire to kick him.

Murchison suddenly looked up at his employer from under his heavy sandy brows.

'What was it that spoke through me at one point in the proceedings?'

'Ah, what indeed? If we knew that we should know a good deal. We don't know what these things are, Murchison. At least, I don't, though there are some people who think they do, but "I hae ma doots." We don't know what they are, my dear chap, we only know they are immensely

126

powerful. It might be your subconscious; it might be telepathic suggestion from Ursula and me, for we were visualizing for all we were worth. Or it might be what it purported to be, though I think myself that that is unlikely. My belief is that it is a mixture of all these. A great natural force, dramatized by your subconscious mind, just as Freud says repressed emotion is dramatized by dreams. It's only one remove from dreams to hallucinations, wherein a lunatic objectifies them and acts them out. These things are all first cousins to each other. If we knew all about one of them, we'd be able to explain the lot. But, as it is, we only know a little about all of them, and can explain nothing.

'But although we can't explain it, we can use it. We can't explain electricity, but we know how it is generated, and how conducted, and how to put it to work for heating, lighting and power. That temple is a generating station; the ritual, the dynamo; your imagination, the electric motor at the other end of the circuit; your larynx, the wheels of the tram that are turned by the motor. That's the best description I can give you. I can tell you what this thing does, but I cannot tell you what it is. By their fruits ye shall know them. Are not the fruits fullness of life?'

'They certainly are,' said Murchison. 'I nearly burst.'

Silence fell between them again, to be broken at length by the younger man, who removed his cigarette from his lips and said, *a propos* of nothing, 'What are the gods?'

'The gods, my dear boy, are lenses that wise men have made through which to focus the great natural forces.'

'What have they made them out of.'

'Thought-stuff, my lad, thought-stuff. Are you any the wiser?'

'No, not much. And yet I am, though. I have an idea what you mean, though I can't put it into words.'

'I think Swinburne had, a bit more than an inkling when he said:

"For no thought of man made Gods to love and honour
Ere the song within the silent soul began,
Nor might earth in dream or deed take heaven upon her
Till the word was clothed with speech by lips of man."'

'Was that Swinburne you were reciting last night?'

'Yes. "The Last Oracle." Swinburne thought, as Nietzsche thought, that the old gods are not without significance, and that we lose a lot by neglecting them.'

'What do you reckon we lose, sir?'

'We lose the use of the subconscious mind, Murchison.'

Murchison pondered this for the best part of a cigarette. At length he spoke, 'And what happens if we wake up the old gods again?'

'We recover the use of the subconscious mind, and we get into touch with great natural forces from which civilization has cut us off.'

'And where do you place Christianity in this show?'

'It has its place, Murchison, it has its place. It sweetened life when paganism had become corrupt. We lack something if we get too much of it. It isn't true to life if you take it neat.'

'After my experience of it in my brother's church I find it difficult not to cough it up and spit it out.'

'You will make a mistake if you do that, Murchison. You will lack something. Take it as a contribution to spiritual thought; there is no need to discard it, lock, stock and barrel, because you can't make it the whole of life.'

'I'll have to let it alone for the present because I've been reduced to a state where I heave at the sight of it.'

'Then, let it alone, my dear fellow, if you feel like that about it, and take your ethics from the Buddha.'

'I thought there was only one Name under heaven whereby we might be saved?'

'That, Murchison, together with all the more bigoted bits of the Gospels, are not of the same age as the rest of the text.'

'What do you mean?' The question was sharply asked.

'I mean that modern scholarship knocks the stuffing out of churchianity and gives you a chance to have a look at Christianity, which is a very different matter.'

'So far as I can see,' said Murchison, '"you pays yer money and you takes yer choice" when it comes to reading the Bible. It's a case of Jack Spratt and his wife. One denomination picks out all the hell-fire literature, and another picks out all the light and love, and so the Bible suits everybody, and they can all call 'emselves Christians and damn the other feller heartily. It's a most accommodating book.'

'It isn't a book, Murchison, it's a collection of literature and folk-lore ranging over a thousand years. It is as if you bound up Chaucer and Shakespeare and Mallory and Bunyan and Pope, together with a few excerpts from the Restoration dramatists, and took them all literally except the latter, and you had a spiritual interpretation of those, because it was the only way of rendering them digestible.'

'Then why bother with it?'

'Because it is great spiritual literature; because it is part of our racial heritage, and we need to learn what it has to teach us. And we need to learn what Buddha has to teach us, too, and Confucius.'

'I have often wondered what was the meaning of that text, "In my Father's house are many mansions."'

'That is a thing which you will learn something about if you work with us, Murchison.'

CHAPTER 15

Brangwyn had great belief in hygienic living as the only basis of efficiency, and insisted that Murchison should take a brisk constitutional after his breakfast as the best start for the day's work. Murchison, who was taking his role as laboratory animal literally, took his hat, nothing loath, and set off for Regent's Park as instructed, truly thankful that this should be his task rather than the hated quill-driving.

As he let himself out of the front door he collided with a large wooden shutter that was in process of detaching itself from the facade of the second-hand book-shop. Out from under the shutter, like a wood-louse from under a brick, came a smallish, ferrety-faced son of the people, an obvious Cockney, who stared at him sharply.

'Sorry,' said Murchison, though it was no fault of his that the collision had taken place.

'Didn't know you was there. No damage done, I 'ope?' said the small man, continuing to eye him sharply.

'None at all, thanks,' said Murchison, rubbing the dirt off his slouch hat, to which it had not made much difference.

As he went down the street he had the feeling that the sharp, beady eyes of the small man were observing every step he took, and, taking the opportunity to glance over his shoulder as he rounded the corner, he found that he had not been mistaken. The man stood with the shutter still in his arms, gazing after him fixedly.

Instead of bearing north for Regent's Park as instructed, Murchison turned left at the end of the block, and then left again, thus bringing himself back into the far end of the road from which he had started. No one was outside the second-hand book-shop now, and Murchison passed silent-footed in front of it and turned in at the door. A large cat sat washing itself on the mat; he took a long stride over it and found himself alone among the musty piles of dog-eared literature.

He looked round for the ferrety man, but there was no sign of him. Then, in the silence, there came a sound that explained his absence, the faint creaking of a telephone being dialled. Then came a Cockney voice.

130

'That Mr. Astley? Monks speaking sir. E's just gorn out. Yes, sir, thank you, sir, I will,' followed by the sound of the receiver being hung up.

Murchison took one stride over the abluting cat and was gone. It would not do for Monks, if that was the name of Brangwyn's manager, to know that he had been overheard. Moreover, he had learnt all that he needed to know.

He opened and shut the door of Brangwyn's maisonette as quietly as he could, and prayed that the creaking of the stairs under his bulk would not convey any intelligence to the prick-ears next door.

As he opened the door into the lounge, Brangwyn, who was sitting over the fire with a cigarette, glanced up in surprise from his paper.

'Hullo, Murchison!' he said, 'don't tell me you've been round Regent's Park in this time!'

'No,' said Murchison, 'I've not been in Regent's Park, but I've been somewhere a dashed sight more useful. I say, sir, you know that corkscrew staircase of yours, leading down to the nether regions where you have your performances, does it lead down through the book-shop or the restaurant?'

'It leads down through the book-shop, hidden behind the shelves. But why do you ask?'

'I think I've solved the problem as to how information leaks out of the dining-room.'

'How?'

'The fellow in the book-shop is a wrong'un.'

'What makes you think that, Murchison?'

'Well, sir, I collided with him and his shutter as I came out of your front door, and I didn't like the way he looked at me. I thought he was a dashed sight more interested in me and my doings than he had any need to be. So, instead of going straight ahead at the corner, I swung round the block and took him in the rear. And he was busy telephoning our pal Astley to tell him I'd just gone out.'

'But, good Lord, Murchison, are you sure? There isn't a telephone in the shop. I never saw any occasion to put one in.'

'Well, he has, if you haven't. There's one there now.'

'That explains a good many things that have puzzled me,' said Brangwyn thoughtfully. 'But I should have thought that Monks, of all men, had reason to be loyal to me.'

'Is he under an obligation to you?'

'Yes, Murchison, a very great obligation.'

'Then that's probably the cause of the trouble. Gratitude disagrees very actively with some people, sir, and that little cock-sparrow, as sharp as a needle and as common as mud, is sure to have an inferiority complex. I'd as soon have a warmed-up serpent in my bosom as a fellow with an inferiority complex who's under an obligation to me.'

'And Astley, who is a very great deal shrewder than I am, has worked on that inferiority complex. I'm not shrewd, Murchison, and no one knows it better than I do. If I had been shrewder, Ursula would never have got into her trouble.'

'No, sir, you aren't a bit shrewd. It's amazed me, sometimes, how a fellow who knows as much as you do should see so little. You need a secretary, sir, and I'm glad you do, for I shan't feel so much as if I were taking your money under false pretences.'

'I suppose we all tend to judge others by ourselves, Murchison, and it never occurs to me that people will act the way they do.'

'That's right, sir, that's your trouble. But you let me judge 'em for you, and I'll tell you how they'll act all right, because but for the grace of God, that's how I'd act.'

Brangwyn looked curiously at the man standing over him in his filthy trench coat, cheerfully accepting all the sins in the decalogue as his natural heritage, and compared him with the idealistic Fouldes, who would not eat meat for humanitarian reasons.

'What shall we do with Monks, Murchison? My instinct is to chuck him out and sow the place with salt.'

'Don't you do that, sir. You let him bide. He may come in very handy.'

'But I don't like the feeling that I'm being spied on. How can we talk in comfort if we never know when he's listening in? And, good God, how much does he know already?'

'That's what I'm wondering, sir. Do you think he's got a private entrance on to your corkscrew stair?'

'Might have. It's only matchboarding. Good God, what a fool I've been!'

'Are those special papers you told me of all right. The ones you said Fouldes wanted to get hold of so badly?'

'Yes, they're all right. They're in a safe. I'm not worried about them. The thing that's worrying me is the amount of information they've got hold of about our doings with Ursula. If they know about last night, the fat's in the fire properly.'

'Well, if the fat's in the fire, you'll soon hear it sputtering. Personally,

I don't think Astley would be interested in my comings and goings if bigger game were up.'

'Let's hope you're right. I'm not ready to come to grips yet.'

'I suppose you mean that I haven't come into line yet?'

'Well, yes, frankly, Murchison, that is about it.'

'You needn't worry about that, sir. I mayn't know much, but my intentions are all right. I may back and sidle a bit, and be a bit coy, as you might say, but I won't let you down. There's nothing I'd like so much as to wipe that brute Astley in the eye. I've never seen anybody I've disliked so much.'

'Well, my dear lad, I'll have to take you at your word, for we shall be in the dickens of a hole if this thing blows up prematurely.'

'I suppose your sister is well looked after? She's in safe hands, is she?'

'She's right up on the flank of Snowdon, in a shepherd's cottage. No one knows she's there.'

'By herself?'

'By herself in the cottage, but only a few hundred yards from the farm, and the only way to the cottage is through the farmyard, unless you're a first-class rock climber.'

'And the farm people?'

'Good old God-fearing Welsh. Do anything for you if they like you, and anything to you if they don't. Yes, I'd trust them, and I think you would, too.'

'Well, I suppose you know your business best, but I shouldn't have left her alone.'

'She won't have anyone with her.'

'She can't have everything she wants in this wicked world.'

Brangwyn smiled inwardly.

'Do you know what I think, sir?' said Murchison. 'I think that they're planning to do something while I'm out. Planning to raid you, or something. Else why does Astley want to be told when I go out?'

'But they can't raid me in broad daylight, my dear fellow. Luigi's got about fifteen nephews in the room underneath, and they've all got knives. They'd make mincemeat of anybody who raided me. Fouldes knows the ways of the house, and he'd never risk it.'

'Well, sir, when I go out for my constitutional tomorrow, you have all the fifteen up to keep you company. And another thing I should do, if I were you. I should put the heater out of action in the dining-room, and then Luigi will shift the dinner-table in here of his own accord, and no suspicions will be raised if we change our feeding-place. It will be an awful bore to have to make push-conversation all through meals for Monks's benefit.'

Murchison removed his trench-coat and hung it over the banister at the stair-foot, and perched his hat on the newel-post. Then he came and sat himself down in his usual chair, fished a packet of gaspers out of his pocket and lit up. Brangwyn watched him closely. Hitherto his attitude had been that of a rather grudging deference, variegated by sudden flashes of alternating resentment and loyalty. To anyone who could not look beneath the surface Murchison was an unprepossessing specimen; difficult to work with, owing to his uncertain temper, and not promising overmuch efficiency owing to lack of natural aptitude and indifferent training. But a curious change had taken place since the previous evening. He was like a man who has changed from tight boots into easy shoes. There was still the deference of the younger man to the older man; but the leadership of the expedition had passed unobserved into Murchison's hands. The practical man had taken the philosopher under his wing, and the philosopher was truly thankful to have it so.

There was no Ursula to brew coffee, so Brangwyn pulled up a tea-trolley and made tea with the ubiquitous electric kettle. It was no use putting his secretary on to such a job as that. The enormous red hands were only fit to handle weapons and tools. Murchison, who would drink whatever was given him at any hour of the twenty-four, poured three large cups down his throat one after the other with great satisfaction, just as he had tossed off the rare sherry. Brangwyn realized a little dubiously that this hearty Philistine would take a good deal of fitting into Ursula's elegant sophistications, and was struck by a sudden qualm as to the wisdom of his choice. He wished it were possible to avail himself of his secretary's shrewdness of judgment upon this point, but realized that circumstances forbade it. As a matter of fact, Murchison had already expressed his opinion pretty uncompromisingly.

So Brangwyn put the matter aside, and got to business. 'Now, Murchison,' he said, 'I am going to tell you what I want you to do as your part of the work. I want you to go into training as sedulously as if I were putting up a purse for you at a prize-fight.'

'Right you are, sir. Nothing I'd like better. What I hate is hanging about and feeling I'm not earning my keep.'

'You've got a working knowledge of psychology, haven't you?'

'I shouldn't care to call it that. It has always interested me. My brother had got various books on the subject, which he understood about as much as the cat, and I used to read 'em.'

'Very good, then, we'll take that for granted. Now the thing I really want you to get up is mythology. You'll see why later. You will find a pretty representative selection of books in your quarters. Browse among them, and tell me which appeals to you most.'

'I can tell you that right away. Thor and Odin, and all that crowd, and, after them, the Egyptians.'

'Do you care for the Greek?'

'Not particularly.'

'Or the Keltic fairy lore?'

'Don't know anything about it. Shouldn't imagine I would. I could never stick stories when I was a kid. I like something with a kick to it.'

'Well, sample it, anyway, and see what you make of it. Or, to be more accurate, what it makes of you. Then the next thing I want you to do is to practise meditation. Can you visualize clearly?'

' Yes, awfully clearly. Always could. When I was a kid I hardly knew fact from fancy.'

'Thank goodness. That will cut out a lot of time in your training. You can go straight ahead with the composition of place.'

'What's that?'

'It is the way Ignatius Loyola trained his Jesuits. Only we apply it to other ends. The Jesuits visualize New Testament scenes, and work up an extraordinary religious pressure. We visualize the old myths, and work up pressures of quite a different kind.'

'What kind?'

'It depends on the myth visualized.'

'Supposing I meditate on Aphrodite rising from the foam, what happens then?'

'You wait till you're legally married for that, my lad. I don't want a scandal. I'll tell you what to meditate on.'

'If I meditated on Bacchus and his crew, would I get drunk free of charge?'

'If you were sufficiently highly trained you could produce a very curious kind of inebriation. If you were not so highly trained, you would probably find you were getting in with a drinking set and taking more than was good for you.'

'The feller I keep on meditating on without meaning to is my old bull.'

'What in the world's that?'

'Didn't I tell you? Oh, no. It was Miss Brangwyn I told. When I was in the British Museum the day you found me, I had a most extraordinary

135

experience with one of those winged bulls of Babylon near the entrance. It was very foggy, and the light was funny, and I thought the brute was alive. In fact, we kind of palled on. I saw his old face in the dusk, and thought he was human, and was just going to speak to him when I saw he was an exhibit, and that I'd been had. And yet I hadn't been had. There was something there, and I can't tell you what it was. But it was real, and I touched it. And it was from that that all the fun began.'

'So that explains it. Good God! What an extraordinary story.'

'Explains what, sir?'

'I've been working on the winged bull formula with Ursula all the time.'

'I'm afraid I'm none the wiser.'

'No, my dear boy, you can't be expected to be. But let me put it as clearly as I can. All these animal gods are psychological formulae just as H_2O is a chemical formula. In the old myths the bull is always a phallic symbol, meaning crude sexual force. The eagle's wings are spiritual aspiration - the flight to the sun. The human head is human intelligence. Put the three together, and how does the formula read? The powerful bull form of the natural instincts soaring on eagle's wings of spiritual aspirations, with consciousness poised between them.'

'What the psychologists call sublimation?'

'No, my dear boy, that is just exactly what it isn't. The symbol of sublimation is the white-winged angel of no particular sex, so dear to the Sunday-school illustrators.'

'Then what is the symbol of repression?'

'The dear little cherub who ends at the neck, whom you have already quoted to me.'

'Oh, that constipated little beast? He's no use to anybody. But tell me, what does my bull stand for?'

'For full function on all levels of consciousness.'

'In other words, for holy matrimony?'

'Yes, Murchison, that is exactly what it does stand for, absolutely literally. Only not, perhaps, as understood by the prayer-book, which plainly indicates that it regards matrimony as *faute de mieux*.'

'The less there is of matrimony in it, the more there is of holy, or so I've always understood.'

'And the more there is of holy, the less there is of wholesomeness, as you may have observed. No, Murchison, we keep our elemental bull, and we don't let the wings and the head go soaring off as a cherub, who is bound, as you say, to be constipated, having an intake, but no output.'

'Yes, I think we'll stick to my bull. He's a decent old beast, though a trifle broad in the beam. Funny, isn't it, that ever since I made his acquaintance he keeps on bobbing up?'

'How so?'

'Well, as soon as ever I start to take a look around my quarters, I open a book, and there he is, as affable as you please. And as soon as I sit down to a meal with your sister, he pops out of her frock. But he goes back a jolly sight quicker than he came out, I'll admit that.'

'What's all this? Ursula has never told me a word about it.'

'There was nothing much to tell. She has him for a book-plate, too, hasn't she, now I come to think of it? By Jove, the place is stiff with bulls. What does it all mean?'

'What did you say when you saw Ursula's Gnostic gem?'

'I didn't say anything. I've got that much manners. But I'm afraid I stared at it rather hard, and she asked me what about it, so I told her what I've just told you, and she seemed rather interested, but I couldn't get much out of her, and I didn't like to pump her.'

'Yes, I dare say she was interested! But the little puss never told me a word.'

'I say, sir, what does the cow symbolism mean?'

'The cow-goddess is Hathor, the lower form of Isis, the moon-goddess. She is the Mighty Mother, the all-fertile.'

'In other words, the earth in spring?'

'Yes, Murchison, the earth in spring.'

'And you want my bull for your cow?'

'No, Murchison, I do not want the bull god Apis for the cow Hathor. I want the winged bull of the sun for the moon-goddess Isis, in whom the cow-horns have become the lunar crescent on her brow. Do you understand the symbolism?'

'Not altogether.'

'You will if you don't let me down.'

CHAPTER 16

Brangwyn and Murchison ate their breakfast next morning to a running accompaniment of loud grumblings at the cold, guaranteed to be clearly audible through whatever spy-hole the faithless Monks had established; and when Murchison departed for his constitutional he left Brangwyn safely guarded by the presence of two active young Italians who were wrestling with the heater without much success; for a heater that has been cut off from its source presents insuperable difficulties.

Murchison felt eyes following him from behind the serried ranks of volumes in the book-shop windows, and was pretty sure that the telephone was being dialled before he turned the corner.

He took a 'bus to Regent's Park and started to circumambulate the Outer Circle at a good round pace, as bidden. He had gone, perhaps, a quarter way round, when he heard himself accosted, and, fuming sharply, found himself face to face with Astley, who was smiling affably and apparently bore no ill-will for his recent rough handling. So it was he himself who was the quarry, not Brangwyn in an empty flat?

'I hope you will allow me to explain and apologize, Mr. Murchison?'

('How the devil do you know my name?' thought Murchison to himself. 'I bet that's Monks's handiwork. But I suppose I shall learn more if I am civil than if you get what you deserve.')

'I think the apologies are due from me,' he said aloud, despising more than ever a man who could apologize for being kicked downstairs. 'I had my instructions, however, and I had to abide by 'em. And I think you'll admit I gave you fair warning.'

'Couldn't have been fairer,' said Astley. 'Shall we have a drink on it and call it all square?'

'Right you are,' said Murchison. 'Where shall we go?' He wondered whether he was being decoyed away somewhere as a preliminary to kidnapping, and was thankful he had got his favourite stick in his hand, a mighty ash-plant, like a young alpenstock, and shod with an iron spike, an ugly weapon in such hands as his.

'There's a little pub just outside the next gate. I dare say we might

138

not appreciate its clientele when business is in full swing, but it will be quiet enough at this time of the morning. Shall we drop in there?'

'Right you are,' said Murchison. 'My motto is the same as Tommie's, "There's no bad beer, though some beer's better than others."'

Murchison set a brisk pace, for he wanted to find out in what sort of physical condition his companion was, in case it came to a scrap, and had the satisfaction of hearing him begin to wheeze by the second lamp-post. The magnificent physique was probably a hollow shell, rotted out by whisky, or even less desirable dope.

The pub was soon reached, and proved to be a humble little place frequented mainly by taxi-drivers and carmen. The tiny saloon-bar was empty, but there were sounds of a disgruntled coster coming from the public bar. The upholstered divinity behind the beer-engines demanded their pleasure with a more than professional smile, for they were not her usual type of customer. Murchison chose a light lager, for he wished to have his wits about him, but Astley had a double whisky.

They took their drinks to a little marble-topped table set in the corner angle of a red plush settee that ran round two sides of the room, and settled down for what Astley evidently intended to be a careful bit of diplomacy. He opened the ball by comparing English pubs with Parisian cafes. Murchison grunted. He went on to compare them with Spanish ventas. Murchison grunted again. From Spain it was only a step to South America and voodoo, and from thence to Tibet and the Lamas. Murchison suddenly woke up to the fact that he was being impressed, and tried to make his grunts sound awestruck.

'Queer old bird, your revered employer,' said Astley reminiscently. 'Did he ever tell you how he met me in the middle of a glacier on the road to Lhasa?'

Murchison's grunt indicated a negative, and he lent a bored ear to a long account of the encounter. He was beginning to wonder whether he had been mistaken in thinking that he was the object of interest, and whether it might not be that he was merely being kept out of the way while something was being done at the flat, and was contemplating the advisability of bidding Astley goodbye and leaping into a taxi, when Astley suddenly came to business.

'Are you at all interested in Brangwyn's researches?' he inquired with disarming casualness.

'Don't know anything about 'em,' said Murchison, burying his nose in the tankard of light lager, which had lasted out three double whiskies consumed by his companion.

139

'Oh, don't you?' Astley was obviously surprised by this information. 'We quite understood that you were there to help with his experiments.' The double whiskies were getting in their work, Murchison noted, and Astley was losing his normal caution. He judged the time had come to give him a lead.

'If you want to know what I'm there for,' he said, 'I'm there as chucker-out.'

Astley chuckled. He evidently did not lack a sense of humour, even at his own expense. 'So I gathered,' he said. 'How did you get to know Brangwyn?'

'I was under him during the War, and ran into him again accidentally a few days ago, and he offered me a job, and I took it.'

'Are you fixed up with him permanently?'

'No, only till he goes abroad, whenever that may be. He doesn't know himself yet.'

'And then you will be out of a job?'

'Looks like it, doesn't it?'

'Want a job?'

'Well, naturally.'

'Like a job with me?'

'What do you want doing?'

'Same as with Brangwyn.'

'Chucker-out?'

'Yes, and make yourself generally useful.'

'What's the pay?'

'What are you getting now?'

'Five quid a week.'

Astley opened his eyes.

'Pretty good pay, that. What are your qualifications?'

'Well, I don't mind making myself generally useful.'

Murchison was pretty certain that Astley was feeling for his complexes in order that he might work upon them as he had with Fouldes and Monks, and contrive some sort of treachery against Brangwyn, and he judged that if he appeared responsive, he might learn a good deal.

Astley smiled unpleasantly. 'In other words, you aren't particular what you do?'

'You wouldn't be particular if you'd been out of work as much as I have.'

Astley cast an appraising glance over his shabby outfit, and smiled again, and any scruples that might have lingered in Murchison's mind took their departure.

'All right, you come to me when Brangwyn gives you notice, and I'll find you something. And meanwhile, would you like to make a bit for yourself?'

'Shouldn't mind, so long as it wasn't too risky.'

'Large profits and quick returns can't be got without risks, my dear fellow. Say, have a whisky?'

'No thanks, never mix my drinks, but I'll have another lager if you like.'

The drink being duly supplied, Murchison having watched, not without apprehension, a fourth double whisky making its way down Astley's throat, they got down to business.

'You know the safe in the corner of Brangwyn's bedroom?'

'No, can't say I do. Never been in there.'

Astley looked rather taken aback. 'Well, there is one, anyway, you can take my word for it. And the key to it is on Brangwyn's key-chain that he always has fastened to his braces' button. There are some papers in that safe that belong to me, and I can't get them out of Brangwyn. I don't want to have to take him to court; beastly expensive job. If you like to retrieve those papers for me, I'll pay you handsomely. You'll cost me less than counsel and all the rest of it. Brangwyn can't say anything because they aren't his papers, see?'

'I see prison bars in front of me if I slip up on a job like that. What do you call handsome payment?'

'Fifty?'

'Not on your life. I'd get penal servitude if I were caught out. Make it one hundred.'

'Can't be done. Cheaper to take him to court.'

'Not a bit of it, if it's a High Court case.'

'Oh, well, will you do it for seventy-five?'

'I'll have a shot at it for seventy-five, but, of course, I can't guarantee anything.'

'No results, no payment.'

'All right. Cash on delivery. Where am I to find you?'

Astley handed him a very superior card, but Murchison, who knew the street, noted that it did not bear a very superior address.

'I had better be getting along,' he said, stowing the card away carefully in a shabby and bursting old pocket-book. 'I'm supposed to be taking a constitutional in the park for the good of my health. One of my boss's fads. He's a bit of a freak, but harmless.'

'He's a freak, all right, but I'm not so sure that he's harmless,' said Astley, with more asperity than the occasion appeared to call for.

Murchison, a wide grin on his face, flung down the superior bit of pasteboard in front of his employer.

'I done a deal,' he said.

'Good Lord, Murchison, what's all this about? What sort of deal have you done?'

'Undertaken to steal the papers out of your safe. Astley offered fifty for the job. I asked one hundred, and we closed at seventy-five, and when you give me the sack I can have a job with him. So if ever you want a little inside information concerning the old gent, you give me that sack, and I'll take him on and play a few of Monks's tricks on him.'

At that moment Murchison's bulging old pocket-book bulged still wider, and out of a gaping seam shed a couple of pawn-tickets. Murchison picked them up, examined them, and flung them in the fire. Brangwyn, watching him, looked him all over as Astley had done, but in a different spirit, and marvelled at the morale of a man in his position who treated an offer of seventy-five as a practical joke. He said no word, but took fountain-pen and cheque-book from his pocket, wrote out a cheque for seventy-five, and handed it to Murchison.

'I want you to accept this, my lad, because I like your spirit. Now don't look at it like that. It won't bite. Don't be silly, Murchison. Take it in the spirit in which it is given.'

Murchison twiddled the cheque helplessly between finger and thumb; then he stowed it away in the old pocket-book without a word; cast a worried look at his employer, and finally managed to blurt out, 'Thanks very much, sir, I'm very much obliged to you.'

That afternoon Murchison did a little shopping. He went to a certain tailor who had represented the height of ambition to young officers in days when promotion was brisk, and irresponsible youths were drawing pay and allowances meant for family men. There he ordered a smart, double-breasted blue serge suit. The tailor looked at the old grey flannel trousers, cheap ready-made sports jacket, and the trench-coat with the stains of Flanders mud still faintly discernible under the London grime, and wished that his new customer could be photographed as 'Before' and 'After' for his advertising brochure.

Having chosen the material for his suit, after much consideration and fingering, for a Yorkshireman considers that he has a vested interest in woollens, Murchison gazed thoughtfully round the shop at the studies of enormously elongated young men on the walls, and the experienced shopman knew that his customer was meditating a second suit, and waited patiently. He watched Murchison's eyes dwell on a design for a dinner-jacket, and to his surprise saw a sudden look of annoyance cross his face, and with an impatient shrug Murchison demanded curtly to be shown designs for plus fours. How was he to know that Murchison would be damned if he'd pamper the fastidiousness of Ursula Brangwyn?

CHAPTER 17

Day followed day uneventfully in the maisonette tucked away in the Bloomsbury slum. Murchison was sent out daily for the constitutional that health demanded, and always pursued the same route at the same time, so that Astley could find him readily if he wanted him; but nothing happened.

But if nothing were happening in the outer world, there was plenty going on in the subjective realm of the spirit, which is the happy hunting-ground of those who traffic in strange arts. Murchison read as bidden the tales of the childhood of man, when the clouds of glory were still trailing about him and every common bush afire with God; and, as he read, he seemed to drift further and further away into the land of faery, so that it became as real to him as the wake-world, and it was only by an effort he could recall his attention to mundane affairs. Brangwyn had bidden him spend half an hour twice a day in meditation, going over the myths in day-dream and imagining himself in the Egyptian temples or on the slopes of Mount Olympus. But Murchison soon found that the myths formed a continual running background to his daily life, as if he were all the time standing with his back to a kinematograph screen.

Brangwyn took a great interest in these day-dreams, and even more so in the stories that wove themselves into Murchison's dreams at night; time and again he dreamt of the exploits of the heroes, himself sharing in their adventures. Brangwyn, patiently waiting for his pupil to begin to dream of the gods themselves, began to wonder if Murchison's subconscious mind contained any ideas unconnected with war and hunting, and how long it would take his inferiority complex to exhaust its interest in the exploits of heroes. But the interest was so persistent, appearing morning after morning in the dreams related by Murchison as they ate their belated breakfast over the fire in the lounge, safe from the prying ears of Monks, that Brangwyn recognized that something more than doughty deeds must be interesting Murchison. He noticed a curious recurrent emotional tone that appeared in dream after dream in some form or other. Always Murchison seemed to consider himself invulnerable save to attack from the rear; and through all the dreams ran a curious undercurrent of disgruntlement and sulkiness. Brangwyn began to wonder whether there were a smouldering resentment directed against himself, and whether he would in the end be treated by Murchison as he had been treated by Monks, but found it difficult to believe this in face of the attitude of father and son into which they had gradually slipped, almost without realizing it.

He pondered deeply upon the symbolism presented night after night by the dramatizing subconsciousness of his pseudo-secretary. What was this Achilles-heel that he feared? And with the question came the clue. Achilles had a vulnerable heel, and Achilles also suffered from sulks. Deprived of his beloved Briseis, he sulked in his tent and refused to fight until the death of his friend called him to action and revenge, and his supreme heroism led to the restoration of his lost mistress.

Brangwyn looked across the table at the man opposite him, who, blissfully unconscious of what was passing in his employer's mind, was engaged in consuming a large plate of porridge.

('So you are sulking in your tent, are you?' thought Brangwyn to himself, 'and you will not fight until Briseis is restored to you? In other words, you will not magnetize Ursula because she does not respond to you; and she won't respond to you because you do not magnetize her. How the devil is one to break the vicious circle?')

Murchison, having disposed of his usual ample breakfast, went out to walk it off. As he approached the gate that lay a third of the way round the circuit of the park, he saw a bulky figure hanging about, and guessed that Astley was getting tired of waiting, and had come to inquire about the fulfilment of his order.

The greeting was affable to brotherliness on both sides, and, without need for word spoken, they headed for the pub.

'My turn this time,' said Murchison. 'Couple of double whiskies, please, miss.'

They repaired to their corner table with the drinks, and by some curious sleight of hand the full and the empty whisky glasses changed places, and when they were replenished, changed places again. In fact, Astley's glass was like the Magic Cauldron, which, however much was taken from it, was never empty. Murchison did some hasty mental arithmetic, computing how much money he had on him, for it would not be a cheap matter to make as seasoned a toper as Astley tight.

'No luck at all. No flies on Brangwyn.'

'What can one do with a fellow who neither drinks nor womanises?'

145

grumbled Astley, who seemed to feel that Brangwyn was taking an unfair advantage in leading a godly, righteous and sober life.

'What indeed?' said Murchison, edging Astley's glass away by inches and sliding his own forward with almost unperceptible movements. Astley absent-mindedly took up the full glass that stood so invitingly to his hand, and tossed down its contents. Murchison nodded to the barmaid, and the long tumblers were once more replenished.

'What do you think of the girl?' inquired Astley conversationally. 'Not much,' said Murchison. 'Long, narrow strip of swank. Not my style.'

Astley chuckled. 'Not my style, either. But there's no accounting for tastes. Where's she got to, by the way? When did she leave your place?'

'She left about ten days ago. I've no idea where she is. I shoved her on the Irish boat-train at Euston the time I tried to see her off and she didn't go.'

Astley winked. 'She's not in Ireland. Don't you worry. The Irish boat-train stops at Llandudno junction and picks up the mails from the north. Your little friend drops off there and goes up to a shack Brangwyn has in the mountains.'

'I don't care if she drops off where it doesn't stop,' said Murchison, 'so long as she doesn't hang around the flat.'

Astley looked at him sharply. 'You don't seem to fancy her much,' he commented.

'I don't mind her,' said Murchison, 'but it's a nuisance having her hanging about the flat.'

'Bit of a misogynist, aren't you?' said Astley, continuing to eye him.

'No, I'm not. A girl's all right if you can have a bit of fun with her, but when there's nothing doing and she wants a lot of waiting on and fussing after, well, I prefer her room to her company, that's all.'

'Do you know what I think?' said Astley. 'I think that they've got designs on you, Brangwyn and that Morgan le Fay sister of his.'

'What d'you mean?' said Murchison sharply, startled by Astley's shrewdness.

'Brangwyn dabbles in some pretty queer quarters of some pretty queer arts, and, as for that sister of his, she's a first-class vampire. Literally, I mean, not just metaphorically. They mean to feed her on you, I think, and as she bucks up, you'll go downhill.'

'You needn't worry about that. She's got no use for me, cooked or raw.'

'And have you got no use for her?' asked Astley, continuing to watch

Murchison with a scrutiny under which he felt his fair skin beginning to burn uncomfortably.

'No, sir, no use at all, not on your life. I don't need any chaperoning in that quarter.'

'I shouldn't be too sure of that, if I were you. If I wanted to work the Mass of the Bull with Ursula Brangwyn, you're the exact type I'd choose, and I'll bet Brangwyn spotted it.'

'What d'you mean?' said Murchison, trying to look curious, but not too curious, and feeling a growing sense of uneasiness.

'Know what the Mass of the Bull is, that they used to celebrate in Crete? The origin of the Minotaur legend?'

'No, 'fraid I don't.'

Astley told him, and he did not mince his words. Murchison opened his mouth indignantly to repudiate Astley's conception, and then shut it again hastily. He must play his part of ignorance and unscrupulousness.

'Talk about lounge-lizards!' he said, 'well, I'm blowed! All the same,' he added, 'I honestly think you're wrong. I dare say I may be there to see that nobody meddles with Miss Brangwyn, or any of Brangwyn's other valuables; but I am pretty certain that nothing would induce the girl to have any truck with me. Anything she fancied would have to come out of the top drawer, and no mistake. To be perfectly frank with you, Mr. Astley, she treats me as if I were a waiter.'

Astley's ear was quick to catch the note of resentment that had crept into Murchison's voice unawares.

'If I were in your shoes, my lad, I'd soon disillusion her. But you can say what you like, I bet I've spotted Brangwyn's game. They tried it on once before, you know, with young Fouldes. But he couldn't hold her. Too much of a Nancy-boy. Now you're just the right type.'

'I should have thought that Fouldes was just her fighting weight.'

'No. That's where you're wrong. A very vital woman, if she has ideals, invariably goes in for ultra-refinement; if she hasn't got ideals, she goes on the variety stage and makes a big hit with the gallery. If you take a woman like the Brangwyn girl at her face value, and treat her to ideals and refinement, you miss the mark. What she wants is sheiking. That's what Brangwyn knows. He's cute. And he's picked you out for the job. Look at your type. People are always attracted by opposites. There's Ursula Brangwyn, dark as midnight; touch of the Kelt. They're a Shropshire family, I believe. Then there's you, a blond beast, as we used to say during the War. Couldn't be a more perfect pair. You're for it all right, Murchison. Believe one who knows. Sure the girl doesn't attract you? She ought to, by all the rules of the game.'

Murchison felt himself growing the colour of a beet. 'I can't stand the damned girl!' he snarled.

Astley guffawed shamelessly. 'And are you quite sure you don't attract the girl?'

'Absolutely sure. Haven't I told you she treats me like a waiter?'

Astley's ha-ha's brought the barmaid from the public bar in hopes of sharing the joke.

'What more do you want? This isn't leap year! The Ursula Brangwyn who ought to be on the variety stage is taking it out of the Ursula Brangwyn who ought to be in a stained-glass window, and she's passing the kick on to you.'

'I dunno what you mean,' said Murchison, outwardly sulky and insulted, but inwardly experiencing a strange warmth and glow. 'I've got other fish to fry,' he added hastily, hoping they would prove to be red herrings.

'That's a pity,' said Astley, looking genuinely disappointed. 'I should have liked to have seen that experiment come off, even if I didn't have a hand in it. Look here, I'm going to let you into the know. I've taken a fancy to you.'

('And so you ought,' thought Murchison, 'after the number of my double whiskies you've put away!')

'It was all fixed up for Ursula and Fouldes to work the Mass of the Bull, when old Brangwyn poked a stick into the works and dished everything. Now, I've been helping Fouldes, teaching him a thing or two, and I think we'll be able to land that girl in the near future. Now, look here, you'd be a much better partner for her in the Mass than Fouldes; if I give Fouldes the push will you take it on? You'll have an exceedingly interesting experience, and you'll land a girl with money.'

'I dunno about that. I've other fish to fry. It'll have to be made worth my while.'

'I can make it worth your while all right,' said Astley.

('Oh, can you,' thought Murchison. 'Then why do you live in a slum?) What do you propose to do?' he asked aloud.

'Drop in on the girl unexpectedly when she's alone, and use force if necessary. She'll be amenable enough when once she's broken in.'

'How'll you manage to get her alone? Her brother looks after her like a cat at a mousehole.'

Astley winked. 'She's a young woman who's fond of being alone. Goes for long walks, and all that. As a matter of fact' - he dropped his voice to a whisper - 'Fouldes is up in Wales now, watching his chance. He'll do your dirty work for you, and as soon as he brings her back to my house I'll give him the push and send for you. I'll make it worth your while, you needn't worry about that. And, anyway, you'll have a bit of fun.'

('I'll have a bit of fun, all right, you spotted black swine!' thought Murchison, 'and I know who I'll have it with, too!')

'It might be rather a lark,' he said aloud. 'But I don't want the girl for keeps. I've got other fish to fry, as I told you.' He rose.

'Must you be going?' said Astley, looking longingly at his empty glass. '

'Fraid so. Must do a bit of work sometimes.'

Brangwyn, glancing up from his desk, found his secretary standing over him, looking like a storm-god, and saw that something had struck him on the raw and roused him from his Achilles-sulks. In a few curt words Murchison told his news. Brangwyn, staring at him, saw he was simmering like a kettle coming to the boil.

'This is an ugly business,' said Brangwyn.

'Ugly, do you call it?' cried Murchison, and supplied an amended version that came straight from the trenches.

'What are you going to do about it?' he demanded at length, when he had recovered his breath, and Brangwyn had stopped blinking.

'The first thing I am going to do,' said Brangwyn quietly, looking at his enraged lieutenant, 'is to sit down and think it out. This is a problem that requires strategy, not force, and we have got to lay out our plan of campaign very carefully, because Ursula is not to be relied on. For two twos she would go over to the enemy.'

'What do you mean? Go to Fouldes? She's scared to death of him. She'd run a mile at the sight of him.'

'Are you sure of that, Murchison? Did she run at the sight of him, or did she cower down helplessly?'

'She cowered all right. She went absolutely flat. But I should have said that nothing would have induced her to look at the fellow of her own free will.'

'Murchison, if there were only Fouldes to reckon with I would not worry, but Fouldes has Astley behind him, and Astley knows more about the rarer aspects of hypnosis than any man in Europe. I know a good deal about it, but I can't hold a candle to Astley. And I don't know that I particularly want to. There is a price that has to be paid for certain

149

aspects of that knowledge that I am not sure that I should care to pay. Give Fouldes half a chance, and I believe Astley was quite right, he could land Ursula.'

'Well, what do you propose to do about it? Sit down and let him land her?' Murchison looked so truculent that Brangwyn began to fear that if he did not take action forthwith he would get his own head punched.

'Look here, Murchison, sit down and write Astley a letter pretending to play into his hands. That, and his reply, may be a piece of evidence that will be useful to us. Moreover, it will give you a foothold in his precious establishment that may come in handy. He planted Monks on me; good God, why shouldn't I plant you on him?'

'Right you are, sir, what'll I say?' Murchison took a Woolworth fountain-pen out of his pocket. Brangwyn produced heavy, embossed notepaper from a cabinet. Murchison, his knees clapped together to form a table, and his large feet wound round the legs of his chair, prepared to take dictation. Brangwyn looked at him, and thought he had never in his life seen anything more clumsy. The huge, overgrown schoolboy, with the cheap little pen grasped in his red fist, and his shock hair standing up on end all over his head, was the most unlikely private secretary that anybody ever had.

'Dear Mr. Astley,' dictated Brangwyn, and Murchison laboriously scrawled it down in sprawling, unformed longhand.

'I have been thinking over our talk this morning, and although I don't see much chance of getting hold of the papers you want while B is at the flat, I may be able to do so if he is away for a bit, and I believe he is going away shortly. If you can wait till then I will have a shot at it. £75 being the price.'

Murchison raised his head. 'There's a little nobbly bit might go in there that will give a realistic touch to the outfit. I bargained like a Sheeny with him because rogues never trust each other. Let's put the result of my bargaining in. Shall I say, "No results, no pay, but cash on delivery"?'

'Right you are,' said Brangwyn, and Murchison scrawled it down.

'With regard to the girl,' continued Brangwyn, 'I'm game for anything I'm paid for, except to actually marry her, and I can't do that because - What was it you said to him, Murchison?'

'Because I have other fish to fry,' said Murchison.

'That's right, put that in. You haven't really got other fish to fry, have you, Murchison?'

'Me? Good Lord, no! Do I look like it? That was a red herring, that fish. What next, sir?'

'Your usual signature, and whatever ending you feel to be appropriate. You know what terms you are on with him.'

'"Yours affectionately," I think!' said Murchison, concluding his scrawl.

'Now then,' said Brangwyn, 'make a copy of that, and get it off to him.'

Murchison scribbled a copy in pencil on another sheet of Brangwyn's best notepaper. 'There,' he said, 'I can read that, even if no one else can.'

Brangwyn thanked his stars that there was no serious secretarial work to be got through with the help of his most inept assistant.

'Now then,' said Murchison, 'what are we to do about Ursula?'

'There's only one thing to do, get down to her as quickly as possible.'

'Why not wire her to be careful?'

'Unwise. She would only panic. Her nerve is completely gone.'

'How do the trains go?'

'We've missed the morning one. There isn't one till the afternoon now, which will get us in about eight at the junction. Then we've got twenty miles over mountain roads in a hired car. I think the best way would be to use my car. It's pretty high-powered, and it's all main-road running till you get into the mountains. We can't expect to get in before dark, but we have got powerful headlights, and in any case we shall be no later than the train, and will have the car for use at the other end, and we may be very glad of it if we want to get Ursula away quietly and quickly.'

'Right you are, sir, but I haven't got a licence.'

'I have, and once we are out of London the bobbies aren't to know which of us is which. I have got the car in the mews behind this house, will you go round and fetch it while I put a few things into a suitcase?'

'No, sir, not on your life. You shove your shaving tackle into one pocket and your pyjamas into another, and come as you are. We don't want to advertise to Monks that we are off on an expedition. If you want a clean collar, you can buy one.'

Brangwyn meekly acquiesced, and Murchison went off to his own quarters to collect the needful.

On a chair in a corner stood a pile of cardboard boxes. His trousseau had begun to arrive. He cut the string of the top box hastily, and the smoky smell of Harris tweeds rose to his nostrils. He cut the string of another and dragged out an armful of made-to-measure shirts. Rapidly, in a perfect snowstorm of tissue paper, he flung on his new garments, and with hardly a glance at the glass in his haste he dragged on his old trench-coat over them, clapped his ancient slouch hat on his head, and with his glories discreetly eclipsed from the watchful eyes of Monks, slipped quietly out of the house and went round to the garage, where his employer had already got the car out and started her up. Murchison looked at the long, lean bonnet of the two-seater, and saw that she was a thoroughbred. At one time in his chequered career he had driven a van, and he reckoned that there was nothing much he couldn't do in London traffic, but this craft was an altogether different story, and he was thankful that his employer had got her out of the garage.

He took her out into the traffic of the Gray's Inn Road, moving gingerly in second, feeling her jump at the slightest touch on the accelerator; feeling also how lightly she answered her helm and the vice-like grip of the brakes. He thought of the old death-cart he used to trundle around, and wondered what would happen when he put this thoroughbred into top gear, and how long she would run in second without boiling.

Murchison had never driven a decent car before, and once he had got used to the way the thoroughbred jumped under him, he began to feel the fascination of it, and when they reached the North Circular Road he let her out, amazed how easy she was to handle and how she held the road as compared with the slithering, labouring van he was used to. So this was the kind of toy rich men played with, he thought to himself, not without a touch of bitterness, and seeing a luxurious limousine in front of him he first hooted for the road and then took it, cutting in shamelessly out of pure cussedness, to the great amusement of Brangwyn, who caught a glimpse of the chauffeur's face as he wrenched at his wheel.

Presently they turned into the long road that goes on and on and on till it stops at the sea-wall of Holyhead, and Murchison, now quite at home with the car, began to fling the miles over his shoulder. Brangwyn, watching the needle of the speedometer creeping round the dial, chuckled to himself, thinking of that ancient scene outside the walls of Troy, and wondering whether, metaphorically speaking, the body of Hector was not tied on behind. Achilles had come out of his tent in style.

Murchison was too busy getting the hang of the unfamiliar car to do much thinking for the first part of the journey, but as they skirted the edge of the Black Country and ran along a ridge of high ground and he saw the Welsh mountains lift over the horizon, it suddenly occurred to him to wonder whether they would reach their objective in time, or whether Ursula Brangwyn, tempted out for a lonely walk by the fine day, had fallen into the hands of Fouldes and unspeakable abominations. The road stretched straight and empty before them; he trod on the accelerator, and the speedometer gave up the unequal struggle. It was only Brangwyn's admonitions which persuaded him that the relative crawl of forty miles an hour was not a suitable speed at which to take a large car through the narrow streets of the ancient city of Shrewsbury.

CHAPTER 18

Murchison's guess had been correct, Ursula Brangwyn had been tempted out by the fine spring day, and the opportunity Astley had foreseen came to pass. Unaware of the treacherous spy-hole created by Monks, she believed the very existence of the cottage high up on the flanks of Snowdon, invisible from any road, to be unknown to friend or enemy, and, unsuspecting, had set out in the glorious air and sunshine over a high path used only by shepherds when moving their flocks from one mountain pasture to another. It was the only way out from the little valley in which the farm lay, unless one were to go down a steep and rock-bound track that led in half a mile or so to the main motor road over the passes, upon which no pedestrian would set foot if he had the choice. The task before anyone spying upon the movements of Ursula Brangwyn was simplicity itself, provided he knew the rudiments of rock-climbing; he had only to make his way up an easy chimney within stone-throw of the hotel on the neck of the pass, and nothing but a grass slope lay between him and the sheep-path leading to the high pastures.

The path made its way up a steep couloir and came out on to the top of a ridge, one flank of which fell away in precipices to the pass, and the other sloped steeply to the south, with a far-off glimpse of the sea. The air was like champagne and the sky like a sapphire. The faint barking of a dog came from high up the slopes to the great peak, and moving dots of white showed that sheep that had strayed too high during the night were being rounded up and brought down to safer pastures. It was a task the dogs attended to unsupervised each morning.

The girl paused, leaning on her stick, to watch the wonderful working of Welsh sheepdogs. Two dogs were at work, a biggish grey beast, who at close quarters was wall-eyed, and a little black bitch with a white waistcoat, who was famous all over Wales and had a row of cups engraved with her name on the mantelpiece in the farmhouse. There was no question as to which was the master-mind of the two; the wall-eyed gentleman did as he was bid.

The sheep, unflurried and obedient to the familiar dogs, were being worked steadily down the slopes towards the path, and Ursula could see Gwennie's white waistcoat flashing as she galloped in and out among the boulders, turning like a polo pony on the proverbial sixpence. So absorbed was she in watching the organized strategy of the two canine experts that she did not hear a footstep approaching over the short mountain turf, and it was not until a voice almost in her ear said, 'Good morning, Ursula,' that she swung round with a violent start to find Fouldes at her elbow, his climbing boots and the coil of light rope on his arm indicating the way he had got to her.

'Are you pleased to see me?' he enquired.

Ursula took a firm grip on herself. She must not panic, and at all costs she must avoid sliding off into that queer, passive, dream-like state that Fouldes knew so well how to produce in her.

'I cannot honestly say that I am very pleased to see you,' she said, as steadily as she could, for his presence, as always, shook her self-control. 'I think it would be very much better that we should see no more of each other, and let there be the clean cut that has a chance to heal.'

'I think otherwise, Ursula. I think it very much better that we should see something of each other, and then the breach that is between us will have a chance to heal.'

'It cannot heal, Frank, now that you have thrown in your lot with Astley.'

'You shouldn't believe all you hear, Ursula. I assure you that it gets twisted out of all recognition by the time the Sunday papers have done with it.'

'Alick confirms most of it, Frank.'

'Two of a trade never agree. You can hardly expect Alick to love Hugo after he has bagged his best pupils.'

'It's no use arguing, Frank. You know my decision. It would be much better for both of us if you would accept it as final and leave me alone.'

'I am not going to leave you alone, Ursula. You belong to me, and I am going to have you. What is all this tomfoolery about that hulking secretary of Alick's? Where in the world did he pick the chap up? He looks like an out-of-work bruiser who has been sleeping under hedges. What is he supposed to be? Chucker-out to Alick, or lounge-lizard to you? I don't admire your taste if it's the latter, Ursula.'

'What he is supposed to be is no business of yours; nor of mine, either.'

'Then, dear lady, why get so pink about it?'

Ursula turned on him furiously. 'I don't know what you are trying to insinuate, but it is abominably insulting.'

'Then if you don't know what it is, what makes you think it is insulting? I seem to be touching a tender spot, my dear. Are you and Alick trying to replace me with the bruiser?'

'I refuse to discuss the matter.'

'Then Hugo is right, and that is the game. My God, Ursula, what a game! And with that tramp? I can hardly believe it of you. How can you do it? Where's your sense of decency? If you won't have me, at least have something that's clean and tidy.'

'I don't want anything further to do with you!' Ursula was choking with wrath, for Fouldes had come pretty near to expressing her own opinions where the unfortunate Murchison was concerned.

'Ursula, you can't do this thing. It is too revolting. The fellow is only fit to carry a sandwich-board. What can Alick be thinking of? Has he taken leave of his senses? How can you pair off with a man like that? And you of all people, Ursula. The thing's impossible on every plane. Don't be foolish, child; if Alick is prepared to let you in for a thing like that, surely even you must see that you can't trust him blindly.'

'I - I won't discuss the matter with you.'

'Yes, you will. Come here, Ursula. Look me in the eyes. No, don't turn away, look at me. Yes, you've got to.'

'I - I won't!' cried Ursula, fuming her head aside, but feeling as if her feet were rooted to the ground.

'Yes, you will. You've got to look at me. You can't help yourself, and you know it. Ursula, look at me. Ursula, look at me. Ursula look at me -'

'I won't! I won't!' Ursula's voice rose in a high scream.

Sounds carry far in the thin mountain air, and canine ears are sharp. She saw the dogs on the high slopes stop and turn their heads. The spell was broken. With a supreme effort Ursula pulled her feet out of the vice that seemed to hold them, and turned and ran for her life down the steep mountain path, Fouldes after her. In a dozen strides he had overtaken her, and throwing his arms round her, held her helpless. She screamed shrilly, struggling desperately against the grey shadows that were closing in upon her from behind, bringing with them an overwhelming desire to sleep. It was this sinking into oblivion she was struggling and screaming against much more than the force the man was using on her, and which she hardly felt. She had no hope that anyone would hear or any help would come. There was no one nearer than the summit of Snowdon. She screamed and screamed, and struggled like a mad thing because it was the best way of defeating the terrible, creeping inertia that was stealing over her, rising from her feet, so that they were rooted to the ground; rising to her waist; rising to her breast. When it reached her eyes she knew she would be unconscious, and would obey Fouldes like an automaton, and he could have his will of her.

Her screams redoubled as she felt the creeping paralysis rising and rising like a tide. She was rigid now to her shoulders, like an Egyptian mummy in its bandages. Only her head and her screaming mouth were free, and the tide was still rising. On the high slopes the dogs too appeared paralysed, not knowing what to make of the scene being enacted below them. Then some waft of the hill-wind blew up the slopes, and Gwennie caught a familiar taint, and like an arrow from the bow she was off at full gallop, stretched out literally *ventre á terre*, her beautiful white waistcoat in the dust that flew up behind her on the wind-dried slopes, ears blown back by the wind of her speed and plumed tail streaming behind like a banner. One of these struggling humans belonged to her! She ran up Fouldes' back as if it had been a bank, and caught him by the back of his neck in her powerful jaws. It was only the woollen muffler he wore that saved him from having his spine broken, and her long white fangs were unpleasantly near his jugular.

He dropped Ursula perforce, and, reaching over his shoulders, caught the dog by her forepaws and dragged her from her hold, her snapping jaws catching his wrist as she slipped, and inflicting a nasty wound. He kicked her in the belly with his heavy nailed boots, and she rolled over, howling. But in a moment she was up again and flew at him like a hairy fury, her eyes glaring with savagery.

He had dropped his stick to have his hands free to catch hold of Ursula, and he dared not stoop to recover it lest the infuriated dog should get him by the throat, so he confined himself to trying to kick her in the face with his nailed boots as she circled round him, snarling like a fiend. If the other dog had deserted the sheep and joined in the fight Fouldes would have been in a bad way, for sheepdog are not only powerful for their size, but amazingly quick. But Wall-eye was too well trained to do that. It was an understood thing that only one dog left the herd at a time, the other remaining to hold them together and keep them from scattering and wasting all the work that had gone before; so he stuck to his job, only relieving his feelings by strangulated yelps of excitement as he watched the glorious scrap going on below him. He had been thrashed too often in the days of his youth for leaving the sheep to join in a fight to dare to budge.

Gwennie was circling round Fouldes, trying to get behind him again, but as he had merely to turn on his heels in order to face her she could not manage it. If he had been content to do this he could have worn her out, but the cruel streak in his nature got the upper hand, and as she ventured in too close he drove at her face with the sole of his nailed boot. Ursula shrieked as she saw the nails go straight at Gwennie's beautiful brown eyes. But the dog was too quick for him - she ran in under the boot and toppled him over like a ninepin, and then settled down to worry him. Luckily for him, what she got hold of was a large mouthful of the seat of his baggy plus fours, which so delighted her that she gnawed it, and worried it, entirely ignoring his vulnerable face and throat, until it came away in her paws, and she stood back panting, with half a yard of Harris tweed hanging from her mouth. She cast one look of utter scorn at the prostrate man, and then, with a jerk of her head at Ursula to indicate that she should follow, trotted quietly down the path towards the farm, looking round every few yards to see that her charge was doing as she was bidden. Ursula, more dead than alive, tottered after her, and fell into the protecting arms of Mrs Davies in the farmyard, while Gwennie stood by, gently waving her plumy tail and bearing her trophy with pride.

'Surely to goodness, now, it iss the seat of a gentleman's trousers!' exclaimed the scandalized Mrs Davies. 'Thanks be to God it iss not hiss throat! Ach now, Miss Ursula bach, come you within, and I will make you some good tea, with a drop of Mr. Davies' whisky in it, indeed. Then you shall tell me what it iss all about, whateffer.'

The good Welsh-woman bustled the girl into the kitchen of the farmhouse, took the great black kettle from its hook over the primitive stove, and poured fresh water and a scatter of tea-leaves into the brown earthenware teapot perpetually stewing on the hob, and drew off the ferocious tea-soup that rejoices the heart of the Welsh. Into this she poured a liberal lacing of Mr. Davies' private supply of whisky, which he, being a deacon, kept for the sick sheep. This potent concoction, which has saved the life of many a shepherd on a wild winter night, she gave to the shuddering girl, and stood back with satisfaction to watch the colour come back to her blanched cheeks and her trembling cease. Gwennie, too, administered such consolation as was in her power by laying the seat of Foulde's trousers gently at her feet; a most touching tribute, for Gwennie valued that trophy highly.

Mrs Davies knew that Ursula had been the victim of a disastrous love affair, and had come away to the secluded cottage to avoid the attentions of an undesirable lover, and it did not need any explanation to tell her quick Welsh wits what had happened. She urged upon the girl the desirability of coming down to the farm instead of remaining alone at the cottage, since the cause of all the trouble was evidently in the neighbourhood and bent upon more trouble, and that of a highly unpleasant nature, for Gwennie was not a dog that would have attacked unprovoked. She could see from the girl's reddened and abraded wrists that considerable violence had been used with her, and that but for Gwennie there might have been more serious damage.

But nothing would persuade Ursula to remain at the farm. She dreaded Mrs Davies' perpetually clacking tongue, and longed for nothing so much as silence and solitude. The dogs, she knew, would give ample warning and protection in the unlikely event of the approach of Fouldes. So the two women walked up the gully to the cottage, and Mrs Davies, after piling up the fire with logs, wisely left the shaken girl alone to the company and protection of Gwennie, who refused to leave her.

Ursula felt deadly cold with the after-effect of the shock she had received, and she drew a three-legged stool close up to the bonfire Mrs Davies had set going, and stared with unseeing eyes at the flames climbing from log to log. Gwennie lay at her feet, watching her with anxious eyes, fully aware of her distress. Sheepdogs are not bred for their looks, but for their brains, and generation after generation only the cleverest workers have been allowed to reproduce their kind; the result is that they represent the professional classes of the canine world, and can do everything, including talk quite fluently to those who understand their language. That they understand the spoken word, and not the mere tone of the voice, is proven by the fact that a dog accustomed to be worked in Welsh cannot be worked in English. Mrs Davies could leave a dazed and hysterical girl in the care of Gwennie with perfect confidence that she would be fetched if anything went amiss.

It had never occurred to Ursula that anything more than her dignity had been in danger from Fouldes' violence; the thing she most dreaded was his sinister influence over her. To call it hypnotic merely classified, but did not explain it. It was the enemy within the gates that she dreaded, the unregenerate side to her own nature, that Fouldes had learnt to play upon so cleverly, her developed mediumship making her highly suggestible and an easy victim to his machinations. And, although she knew all this, and knew exactly how she was being worked upon, it did not make her any the less susceptible. No one could appreciate better than she could how cleverly Fouldes had found the weak spots in her armour in appealing to her fastidiousness and snobbery by emphasizing the uncouthness and shabbiness of poor Murchison. Unworthy as she knew it was to point a finger at the shabbiness of an unemployed ex-soldier, she could not help looking where the finger pointed. And yet she knew that all her future welfare depended upon her being able to see in Murchison what her brother saw in him. She had implicit confidence in her brother, and was sure that if he saw big things in Murchison they must be there; but she herself found it impossible to lose sight of the stained and threadbare clothing and the untended hands.

The afternoon's experience had given her a warning that her security was very precarious, and that Astley's grip would close on her if she were not very careful. If she yielded to the attraction that Frank Fouldes still had for the baser side of her nature, she knew only too clearly that she would be following a dangerous witch-light, and that in a few steps she would feel the suck of the slough about her feet, and she would be drawn down and down, and sucked in, till she came within reach of Astley and the slime of ancient and forgotten abominations closed over her head. For Astley was a student of curious literature, and things that never enter the modern imagination were known to him; such things as are hinted at in the Latin notes to Gibbon's 'Decline and Fall of the Roman Empire'; the things, in fact, that brought ancient Rome to her ruin. Astley did editorial work for a publishing house whose printing-press was in Constantinople and its distributors in Brussels and Buenos Aires. Ursula had seen some of its productions, and they were illustrated, and she was under no illusions as to the part for which she was cast. And yet Fouldes had a fascination for her, and Astley's terrible house had a fascination for her. It was as if these were two sides to her - the extreme fastidiousness that gave her her appreciation of the fine nuances of the most sophisticated culture and that made her make of life an art; and another side, a side that made her kin to the Maenads that followed Dionysus and tore fawns to pieces in their mystical frenzy; and, even baser, the woman who crept out of the mediaeval walled towns by night to go to the witches' sabbath and 'kiss the buttocks of the goat.'

This side of her horrified her; and yet, denied it, life seemed savourless. Love and marriage, if it meant no more than housekeeping and child-bearing, had no attraction for her after she had realized the possibilities revealed to her by Fouldes. She was puffed in every direction as if caught in a cyclone. Fouldes was her true mate, and yet she knew that mating with him meant unspeakable degradation and an early death. Murchison, pressed on her by her brother as her only hope of salvation, was distasteful to her by his roughness and boring to her by his savourless normality. But behind Fouldes loomed Astley, slug-like in his fleshy foulness; and to go to Frank meant to come into the hands of this high-priest of evil.

The moment she was in the presence of Fouldes she was conscious of the broad streak of cruelty that lay in his nature, side by side with his almost feminine charm. She knew that nothing would satisfy his love for her but complete domination; his love, under the tuition of Astley, had become like the coils of an anaconda, that would first crush her into helplessness and then cover her with slime and swallow her.

But, although she realized all this, the moment she looked into his face after she had been away from him for a while she thought only of his fascination, and that his love could call forth aspects of her nature and give her a completeness of fulfilment that she would not find in the love of a better man. There were times when she thought that to burn with fulness of life in a fierce flame was a greater good than long life and peace; when she was sorely tempted to throw off all restraints and give herself to Fouldes utterly. But then the shapeless, vulture shadow of Astley would loom over him, and she would remember that there were horrors not to be faced.

Her brother had assured her, pledging his unrivalled knowledge of strange sciences to back his word, that if she would consent to mate with Murchison she would not be disappointed. She thought of Murchison as he had lain asleep in a heap in the corner of the seat in the roof-garden, and wondered by what alchemical process her brother proposed to transmute that leaden metal into fine gold. He was dull and he was rough, and both her dual selves revolted against him. Fouldes loved subtleties and sophistication, and he burnt like a flame. How could she take the one, having known the other?

Murchison was not like Fouldes; there was no ease of relationship with him. To contact him was like walking into a cliff in the dark. Frank had been possessed of a rare gift of imagination, and had excelled in those finer arts of life that make the companionship of a cultured man so agreeable to an intellectual woman. He had a marked feminine side to his nature, just as there was a streak of the masculine in herself, or so she liked to think. But Murchison was all male, and the pure maleness of him jarred on the streak of the male in her; whereas Frank, with his two-sided temperament, had been able to give place to the positive side of her nature. Frank drew her by his sympathy, whereas Murchison made her want to fight him.

But that afternoon had been a shock to her. She had realized with horror how strong was the baser side of her nature; how eagerly she

161

desired to steal forth to the witches' coven and embrace the goat-god. But she had also realized as never before the extent of the demoralization that had taken place in Fouldes. There was a blanched pallor about him which she suspected to be due to drugs, and a curious goat-like, inhuman expression in his eyes: and when Gwennie attacked him he had been like a wild animal. Face to face with him, her disillusionment was complete; how it was that his power over her kept renewing itself was a mystery to her.

She made up her mind that at the next opportunity she would go into matters fully with Murchison; give him her views, and ask for his, and if they could come to a satisfactory understanding she would make up her mind to go ahead with the experiment her brother pressed on her so urgently. It simplified things considerably that there were no personal reactions between herself and Murchison, and so she could speak to him man to man, as it were. It was somewhat galling to her feminine pride to realize this; nothing could be more certain than that she had not made a conquest in that quarter; Murchison would do what he could to help her in order to please her brother, to whom she knew he was devoted; but here was no knight-errant rescuing damsels in distress. He would hunt dragons as part of his day's work, but the damsel, once rescued, would be shoved in the nearest nunnery.

She ought to take what Murchison was willing to give in the spirit in which it was offered, and be grateful to him for his kindness. People did blood transfusions for perfect strangers in hospitals. Why should she not let Murchison do what was needful for her, provided he were willing? And she gathered that he was. She would be a fool to die for want of a blood transfusion because she did not feel able to make a personal friend of the donor. She knew that, according to her brother's theory, the establishment of a magnetic flow between them would create a very strong bond; that, in the words of Scripture, her desire would be towards him and he would rule over her, a state of affairs she could not possibly envisage.

But she questioned the truth of this, despite her respect for her brother's knowledge of the strange arts they were working in. If Murchison had really desired her, he might have been able to hold her, once the magnetic circuit were formed. But as he so obviously did not want her, and was only willing to do her a kindness, she doubted if anything except a bond that was little more than electric would be formed between them, which a few days' absence would serve to break.

CHAPTER 19

There are only three gates to Wales: Gloucester, Chester and Shrewsbury, and it was at Shrewsbury that the two men crossed the Severn on their hasty journey north, and entered a new spiritual atmosphere. From time to time they passed the ruined walls of castles designed to keep the Kelt to his mountains, and presently the road began to wind up the narrow, wooded valleys that lead into the heart of the Snowdon range.

Twilight fell swiftly among the woods, and Murchison switched on the powerful headlights. There was a sense of primitive wildness in the air, and he had a curious feeling that they had left civilisation behind.

They stopped to ask the way at a fork in the roads, and a black-eyed, sharp-featured man answered in a sing-song, lilting voice, obviously struggling with an unfamiliar language. Murchison had never realized before that one could leave England behind inside the British Isles.

They were following the windings of a river mile after mile, and presently Brangwyn said, 'You had better get into second, Murchison, it is steeper than you think.'

Presently the trees gave out, and heathery hillsides lay dappled in the fight of the newly risen moon. On and on they went, and the wind grew very cold. The engine was labouring in good earnest now, and Murchison changed down without waiting to be told. Then the valley narrowed and granite walls closed in on them, with snow lying in the gullies, and a plume of steam began to rise from the radiator.

And still they climbed. Then suddenly Murchison found his headlights ranging into empty space.

'This is the top,' said Brangwyn. 'Ease her over gently. It's like the side of a house, going down the other slope.'

Murchison eased her over as bidden, and saw what looked like the starry heavens upside down under his front wheels, as the opening pass yielded a glimpse of the plain below, with all the scattered lights a-twinkle.

'Steady on the bend,' said Brangwyn, 'we turn off just here.'

'Right or left?' said Murchison.

'Left man, left. Good God, don't turn right! It's a one hundred foot drop!'

The headlights revealed a gap in the dry stone walling that flanked the road, and Murchison swung the car into it.

'Get into bottom gear,' said Brangwyn. 'This is where she sits on her tail.'

They were bumping over a rough cart-track that wound up a narrow gulch into the very heart of the range. The rock walls closed in behind them, and they might have been among the mountains of the moon. The headlights made the road as bright as day in that confined space, and some very worried mountain sheep ran panic-stricken ahead of them, baaing piteously. A sheepdog came cantering out of the shadows, told the car what he thought of it in a few eloquent barks and then turned his charges neatly on to the grass at the roadside, showing more sense than most drovers. Another sheepdog answered him from near at hand, and then they heard the cry of new-born lambs and smelt the acrid odour of penned sheep. Then lights appeared round a corner of rock and a hurricane of barks saluted them. Murchison saw why it was that no one but a rock-climber could come upon Ursula Brangwyn unawares. The wavering light of a lantern came bobbing towards them, and he stopped the car.

'Why, surely to goodness now, it iss Mr. Brangwyn!' exclaimed a high-pitched, staccato voice.

'Good evening, Mrs Davies, and who did you think it was? Good Lord, woman, what are you doing with that gun?'

Murchison saw a tall, gaunt woman step into the glare of the headlights, with an old-fashioned, single-barrelled shot-gun in the crook of her arm and a perfect pack of hounds at her heels.

'Well, now, I did not know who it wass. Mr. Davies, he hass gone to send you a telegraph. We haf had trouble here.'

Murchison felt a horrible coldness close about his heart, and sat as if turned to stone in his seat.

'What's the matter, Mrs Davies?' he heard Brangwyn say in a very quiet voice.

'Oh, it iss not too bad, Mr. Brangwyn, it iss not too bad. Miss Ursula she hass been frightened, but she iss not hurt. Gwennie took care of her. She wass fetching the sheep from the high hill, and she saw Miss Ursula wass being frightened, and she came down, and she tore the trousers off him, Mr. Brangwyn. Yess, Gwennie bach, you did well.'

Murchison looked round to see who the termagant was who had

performed this feat, and a little black collie with a pretty white waistcoat ran up and stood with her tongue out, looking self-conscious.

'She iss a little lion, iss Gwennie, and so wise. You haf no dogs in England like her, Mr. Brangwyn.'

Murchison looked at the high, domed forehead and wide-set eyes, so different to the torpedo-heads of the prize collies on the show bench.

'I am very grateful to Gwennie,' said Brangwyn. 'She is a fine little lass.'

'Ah, Mr. Brangwyn, she does not speak English.' Some rapid gutterals translated the compliment into Welsh, and Gwennie acknowledged it with a wave of her tail and disappeared into the darkness.

'Is my sister up at the cottage, Mrs Davies?'

'Yess, she iss at the cottage. She would not come down to the farm, and I could not make her. But do you not go up there, but wait here. I will go up and tell her who it iss. She may be frightened, as I wass. She may think it iss that man come back if you drive up in the dark.'

Mrs Davies disappeared into the darkness, followed by the dogs.

'Well, Murchison, you're less confiding than I am. What do you make of her? Would you trust her?'

'I'd trust her all right, sir. She's a first-class old dragon. I don't suppose Fouldes would have come on here after Gwennie'd eaten his pants, but if he had, she'd have blown his shirt-tails off as soon as look at him.'

A shrill cry and wavering of the lantern called them on, and Murchison drove the car across the little Alpine meadow in which the farmhouse stood, rounded a projecting rocky corner, and saw a low, whitewashed cottage with a grey slate roof in front of them. Flickering firelight shone from its windows, and the tall form of Mrs Davies stood in the open doorway, but there was no sign of Ursula Brangwyn.

Mrs Davies hastened to meet them as they climbed stiffly out of the car.

'It iss well you haf come,' she said. 'I do not like the way she looks. No, not at all.'

They went up a narrow flagged pathway across the small forecourt surrounded by low whitewashed stone walls. The open door led straight into the single room that occupied the whole of the ground floor, save for a little lean-to at the back. The air struck warm and sweet as they entered, for a large fire of pine-wood burnt in the primitive grate at one end. A magnificent Welsh dresser, jet-black with generations of elbow-

165

grease, occupied the best part of one wall, but its shelves held books instead of crockery. A couple of high-backed settles made an ingle-nook of the fireplace, and on them were piled bright-coloured cushions to relieve their hardness. Rugs covered the uneven flags of the floor.

The lamp was unlit, and it took a moment or two for Murchison's eyes to become accustomed to the flickering light. Then he saw that Ursula Brangwyn was sitting on a three-legged stool in front of the fire with her back to the room. She was dressed as for walking, save that her hat had been flung aside and her dark hair was dishevelled. There was mud on her shoes, and she looked as if she had returned to the house after her adventure, sat down by the fire, and had not moved since.

'Hello, Ursula?' said her brother.

'Hello, Alick?' said the girl, without turning her head.

Brangwyn crossed the room and sat down on the settle and studied her face. Murchison, embarrassed, hung back in the shadows by the door. No one spoke.

At length the girl broke the silence. 'Did Mrs Davies tell you what happened?'

'Yes,' said Brangwyn.

There was silence again for a while. Then the girl spoke once more.

'Alick,' she said, 'I'd have gone with him if the dog hadn't driven him off.'

'I told you you would,' said Brangwyn. Once again silence fell, and there was no sound in the room save the hissing of the sap in the pine-logs and the slow tick-tock of an old clock. Again the girl broke the silence.

'I'll have to take Murchison, Alick, he's my only chance. What shall we do about it?'

'Murchison is here, Ursula,' said Brangwyn.

'Oh!' cried Ursula, and turned round so suddenly that she nearly over-balanced her three-legged stool.

Murchison came forward out of the shadows.

'Good evening, Miss Brangwyn,' he said.

He took off his old trench coat and sat down on the settle beside Brangwyn, and stared into the fire. These few revealing words of Ursula Brangwyn's had caught him like a blow in the face. Ever since that night when they had danced the dance of the earth in spring together he had felt an ever-strengthening bond with her; Astley's coarsely spoken words had confirmed his intuition, for Astley, foul brute though he was, was very far from a fool. Brangwyn's generous cheque had gone in new clothes as surely as 'a livelier iris changes on the burnished dove,' and it had seemed to him that he had shed his old, thwarted personality when he put off his garments of humiliation. But at Ursula Brangwyn's words something that had hitherto held firm in Murchison through all his difficulties gave way at last, and he was the same man who had once spent an evening discussing pros and cons with a friend of his who had turned motor-bandit. Brangwyn rose from the settle. 'I'll go and put the car away,' he said.

'Let me do it for you, sir,' cried Murchison, leaping to his feet, only too thankful for an excuse to make his escape.

'No, my lad, sit down. You don't know where it goes. Besides, I want to have a word with old Davies he ought to be back by now.' He wished to leave the two together to come to an understanding as best they might, on the same principle that small boys at public schools used to be taught to swim by throwing them into the water. He could not conceive of any other way in which Ursula could pick up the brick she had dropped. He went out; and Murchison had perforce to re-seat himself beside the silent girl, who stared at the fire without speaking.

Murchison could not make out how far Ursula Brangwyn was lost in her own thoughts, and how far she chose to ignore his presence. He slid himself into the corner of the settle that Brangwyn had vacated, so as to get some rest for his back, weary from the long drive, and before he knew where he was he had dropped off to sleep.

But Ursula Brangwyn was quite alive to his presence. Her silence and averted face were due to sheer embarrassment. It was beyond her power to break the silence. She had had three shocks that day; firstly, her stormy encounter with Fouldes; secondly, the realization of her appalling faux pas with Murchison; and, thirdly, the discovery that an entirely new individual had appeared when he peeled off his terrible trench coat and came forward into the firelight. Was it possible that tailoring could make such a difference to a man? Was this the same individual who had looked so ungainly in his soiled and shabby reach-me-downs? Ursula hated herself for being so sensitive to appearances. If Murchison had been dressed like this when she had first seen him, she would not have regarded him as a nauseating pill that she had to hold her nose and swallow. If one did not mind a certain ruggedness of feature, he might be considered a fine-looking man. Why, oh why, had she not been able to see beneath the rough exterior as her brother had done? She remembered Murchison's kindness, almost tenderness, when she had had her upheavals at the flat, and the infinite comfort of it. If only he would be like that again she would open her heart to him and tell him of the horrible panic-fear and helplessness that descended on her, and of her desperate need to hold on to him lest she be swept away and lost for ever.

She would tell him of the morbid fascination Fouldes had for her, and his horrible power over her, and how her bondage could only be broken in one way - by someone coming forward vicariously and stepping into Fouldes' place; replacing his unclean, epicene magnetism with wholesome, normal, male magnetism, such as should flow naturally between a man and a woman, thus drawing her back to normal life in spite of herself.

If she told him all this, surely he would understand that her unlucky remark was not quite as bad as it sounded?

She would tell him that she felt quite differently about him now that she had seen him again. That the love-philtre so cunningly compounded by her brother was beginning to work in her veins, and her craving for Fouldes was fading. She would tell him that it was her wish now that the barriers between them should be thrown down, and that they should become one on the plane of earth, as they already were in the invisible kingdoms by virtue of what had been done in the rite of the earth in spring.

This rite, she knew, had really been a marriage rite - a marriage that depended entirely upon function for its validity. If no magnetic circuit sprang up between them when the power was invoked, no marriage took place; if magnetism began to flow from the one to the other, the marriage had actually come into being, and only needed to be ratified on the physical plane.

Her brother had assured her that if love were not possible between them, there would be no power in the rite, and nothing would happen; but that if power came down, she would know that a very wonderful mating was in store for her. She had trusted him, and had given herself up to the rite, body and soul, and let the tremendous forces it invoked and focused sweep through her. The rite had succeeded far beyond even her brother's expectations; she knew that, though he would not say very much; else why had he been so urgent that she must not come near Murchison again until he had had some training lest the forces that formed a circuit between them should become too strong for his control, and should 'short' in one of those psychic upheavals so dreaded by those who pursue strange arts?

But, although she now ardently wished that the barriers between them should be cast down, she could see that it was going to be easier said than done, especially since her luckless remark had twined them with barbed wire. But a start must be made, and she had nothing to thank but her own snobbishness that it was so difficult.

She raised her eyes from the fire and turned towards the silent man to speak to him, and discovered that he was sound asleep. A sudden wave of anger shot over her. So this was all the regard he had for her? Having come to her side in her time of greatest need, he had so little real concern for her that he had not even been able to keep awake! She had no realization of the effect of that hot, dimly-lit room on the exhausted man. Murchison had driven an unfamiliar car over two hundred miles at high speed, with no pause save for petrol, and if he had known that he would be shot at dawn for sleeping at his post it is doubtful if the result would have been any different. But Ursula Brangwyn had no realization of the stresses of life, and no mercy for those who succumbed to them. Her new-born feeling for Murchison died a sudden death and he became once again a nauseous pill, with the added bitterness of this injury to her scorned beauty.

The door opened, and Brangwyn entered the room. Hearing no sound of voices, he imagined his sister to be alone.

'Hullo?' he said. 'What have you done with Murchison?' wondering arduously what sort of a row the pair of them had had.

Ursula pointed silently to the heap on the settle.

'Good Lord!' exclaimed Brangwyn. 'What's the matter with the fellow?'

'Nothing, so far as I am aware,' said Ursula. 'He just went peacefully off to sleep.' Brangwyn looked at him.

'Dead beat,' he said with a smile, greatly relieved.

'Then in that case,' said Ursula icily, 'it would have been best if he had gone to bed.'

Brangwyn came and sat down beside her, and laid a hand over hers.

'My child,' he said, 'we have done over two hundred miles in five hours, and Murchison has never driven my car before, which means that we have both risked our necks; you must not be too exacting.'

Ursula hung her head. Once again she was being made to feel ashamed where Murchison was concerned. It was as if yet another layer of his uncouth exterior had peeled off and she had had a glimpse of something fine that lay underneath. The furious drive from London was of the authentic tradition of knight-errantry. To average forty miles an hour, as he had done, over that long distance, including the passes, meant some very high speeds on the open road, and all this in an unfamiliar car. Murchison's falling asleep began to appear in a new light. It was, in fact, more of a tribute than an insult. He had run himself out for her, and here was the visible evidence of it. Her heart softened towards him once again. Brangwyn picked Murchison's feet up by the ankles and put him full length on the settle, from which he had looked in danger of sliding off. Murchison merely grunted. It was Ursula herself who went up to her room and brought down a rug and put it over him.

Then Mrs Davies came in with a large pot of savoury stew, and Ursula and her brother had their meal, leaving Murchison to have his sleep out on the settle.

CHAPTER 20

Murchison could not imagine where he was when he was aroused by Mrs Davies' entry with a broom next morning.

'Ach, Mr. Murchison!' she exclaimed. 'I would haf gifen you a bed at the farm if I had known! Haf you been there all night?'

'I think I must have been, Mrs Davies. I've no recollection of going to sleep. I must have just dropped off, and they left me here.'

'Dear to goodness now, you could not haf been very comfortable.'

'I slept too soundly to know whether I was comfortable or not. All I want is a jug of hot water and somewhere to have a wash and a shave.'

Mrs Davies led him into the lean-to, which was fitted up as a little kitchen, boiled him some water on an oil stove and left him to get on with his ablutions at the sink.

'I say, Mrs Davies?' he said, coming out with a shining morning face. 'Do you think you could give me something to eat? I am ravenous, and I don't suppose the Brangwyns will be down yet awhile. I missed my supper last night, you know.'

'Yess, indeed!' exclaimed the hospitable Mrs Davies, bustling about with a frying-pan while he helped her by blowing the embers of the wood fire into flame with the bellows. 'Miss Ursula, she will not be down yet awhile; she iss a naughty young lady, she will not get up in the morning. But then she iss not like us working folk.'

('No, damn her!' thought Murchison. 'She certainly isn't.')

All his resentment against the unfortunate Ursula returned with a rush. Why should she skim the cream off life without effort? Take all and give nothing? He did not choose to remember that life was not being particularly creamy for Ursula at the moment; that it was, in fact, a pretty bitter draught.

He disposed of three eggs, half a dozen rashers of bacon, the best part of a home-baked loaf, and a large pot of black tea in a manner that completely won Mrs Davies' heart. Then he went out into the spring sunshine to escape from her broomings and brushings, and there Brangwyn presently joined him, and they strolled together up the steep

171

couloir, in the mouth of which the cottage stood.

It had evidently been the bed of an ancient glacier, for the marks of the grinding ice could be clearly seen on the cliffs that bounded it. A breadth of turf, smooth as a lawn, and dotted here and there with boulders left behind by the ice, clothed what had once been the bed of a prehistoric river. The high rock walls sheltered them from the wind, the sun blazed down out of a cloudless sky, and the mountain air was magnificent.

'Tradition has it,' said Brangwyn, 'that it was up here that Keridwen minded her cauldron.'

'Who might Keridwen be?' enquired Murchison.

'She is the Keltic Ceres, and her cauldron is the prototype of the Graal. Ursula, in her better moments, likes to identify herself with Keridwen; but I tell her she is not an Earth-mother.'

'No, more like a moon-goddess,' said Murchison, forgetting his resentment against her for a moment. 'I didn't think the part of the earth in spring quite suited her.'

Brangwyn glanced at him covertly, and wondered how much he had guessed of the significance of that rite. They walked on up the path in silence for a time until it came out on to the steep slope of the mountainside.

'Hullo? Look at that!' exclaimed Murchison, pointing to a trampled patch of ground, with some shreds of woollen material lying about on it. 'This must have been where they had the row yesterday. What a swine the chap is! Could you possibly imagine a more isolated place to attack a girl?'

'A swine the lad is now, right enough, but he was by no means a swine when I first knew him, Murchison. This piece of work lies at the door of Astley rather than Fouldes.'

' "A rose by any other name would smell as sweet," ' said Murchison sulkily, staring across to the far horizon, where a line of silver marked the sea. It annoyed him that his feeling for Ursula Brangwyn would not change over into hatred and contempt as it rightly should, but kept on surging up in great waves of sweetness and bitterness.

'It is curious that you should have likened Ursula to a moon goddess,' said Brangwyn conversationally. 'For that is the symbolism we have been working with in the winged bull formula.'

'You told me she was,' said Murchison irritably, still staring out at the horizon. 'You said she was Isis, and Isis is the same as Luna, isn't she?'

'Yes,' said Brangwyn. 'And that's curious, for Luna is also the same as

Diana, and you remember how the dogs made it hot for Acteon when he annoyed Diana? These symbolisms work out in a very odd way, though nobody has ever been able to explain how it comes about. You meditate on the set of symbols which make up a formula and soon they begin to express themselves in your life. I have seen it happen over and over again. Have you ever noticed how meditation on the black Calvary cross of sacrifice always brings suffering and renunciation?'

'Can't say I have. Never having done any,' said Murchison, with his back still to his companion. Brangwyn stared at the broad back, wondering what on earth had upset Murchison, for upset he obviously was.

Suddenly he turned round with a short laugh, and the expression of his face was not pleasant. 'If I remember aright, from the scanty remains of my classical education, Diana was given to blood sacrifices.'

'So she was,' said Brangwyn, wondering what all this was leading up to. 'But we are not in Aulis these days. Diana, I trust, is a reformed character.'

'The symbols never change, Brangwyn. If you start on them at all you have got to see them through.'

Brangwyn looked at him, wondering where this knowledge came from.

Murchison laughed again his harsh, barking laugh, that Brangwyn had never heard before, and that he did not particularly care about.

'Is it part of my job to murder my predecessor?' he asked.

'What in the world do you mean, Murchison?'

'Well, you remember the priest of Diana in the Arician Grove? He always held his job by virtue of having murdered his predecessor, didn't he? And that was the only qualification required of him.'

'It will not be necessary for you to murder Fouldes,' said Brangwyn quietly. 'It will be quite enough if you put his nose out of joint. Shall we go back to breakfast?'

'I believe the priest of Diana in the Arician Grove was always a runaway slave, or some other scallywag,' said Murchison pleasantly. 'So the symbolism fits me just nicely.'

('Ursula must have trodden on his corns particularly badly,' thought Brangwyn to himself. 'It is going to be a pretty kettle of fish if these two start quarrelling.')

They strolled back down the couloir to find that Ursula had at last put in an appearance. Her brother thought that she looked remarkably fresh and radiant, considering the experience she had been through the previous day, but Murchison paid no attention to her. His dark mood did not seem to affect his appetite, however, for he did ample justice to a second breakfast.

'I wonder if you would take the car and run over to Llandudno, Murchison, and see what you can do in the way of shirts,' said Brangwyn. 'I feel as grimy as a collier after our run yesterday. What would you like to do, Ursula? Would you like to go with him for the run?'

Murchison expected her to decline, but to his surprise she accepted, alleging that she would be glad of the opportunity for a little shopping herself. They started off in the brilliant mountain sunshine, dropping down the steep pass to the plain, and making their way through wide valleys to the coast.

It was not until they went to have a cup of coffee in a cafe, at the girl's suggestion, that there was any conversation between them.

'I want to talk to you,' said the girl abruptly.

'Yes?' said Murchison, raising his eyebrows enquiringly.

She lifted her eyes from her cup, where she had been prodding the sugar with an absorbed preoccupation, and for a moment she hated him. He was so terribly heavy and unresponsive and slow in the uptake; and she disliked blue eyes, anyway, they were so insipid. But there was no backing out now; he was sitting looking at her with a questioning air, and looked as if he would continue to sit till the day of judgment. She felt that no help would be forthcoming from him, and that she must take the initiative and make use of him if he were to be any help to her at all.

She returned to the consideration of her coffee to get away from his unblinking gaze. At length she managed to speak, though she could not look up.

'I had a pretty bad fright yesterday.'

'So I gathered. It was a good job for you the dog was handy.'

'It wasn't so much that. I don't suppose he would have done me any real injury. It was myself I was scared at - the extent I am under his influence.'

'I think he would have done you a pretty real injury if you had held out,' said Murchison.

'What makes you say that?' Ursula looked up, surprised.

'Astley said he would use violence if necessary.' He thought it well for her to know that, so that she should not take risks, strong in her own conceit. It would do her all the good in the world to have a bit of her self-sufficiency taken out of her. She needed to know what it would be like to be up against even a man as slightly built as Fouldes if the gloves were off.

174

'Who did Astley say that to?'

'To me.'

'When?'

'Yesterday.'

'Where?'

'In a pub.?'

'What were you doing with him in a pub?'

'Making him tight.'

'Why?'

'So's he'd talk.'

Ursula returned gaze for gaze with Murchison.

'Will you tell me frankly why you are doing all this?'

'Because your brother pays me to, Miss Brangwyn.'

Ursula blushed crimson and dropped her eyes to her cup again.

'Did you think I was doing it for you?'

The girl looked up, speechless and white with anger.

'No, I'm not doing it for you. I'm not such a fool as all that,' said Murchison.

'It seems to me,' said Ursula, speaking with difficulty, 'that you and I might as well give up the idea of trying to work together.'

'Well, what is it you want from me?'

Ursula was speechless. She knew what her brother's ideas were, and she gathered that Murchison also knew now.

'Do you know what you'd say of me if I were a woman? You'd say I was a prostitute.'

Ursula half rose from her chair, but the man's eyes held her. She did not think that blue eyes were insipid now. They were terrible. She thought they were the cruellest eyes she had ever seen.

'I know your brother picked me out of the gutter. I know I'm well paid. But there are some things I draw the line at, and you're one of them. I don't like you any better than you like me, Miss Brangwyn, but I'll do my job of work with you because your brother wants me to, and because you need it, but there it begins and ends. As long as you understand that, it's all right, and if you'll tell me what you want, I'll do my best to carry it out.'

'I don't want anything!' cried Ursula furiously. 'It's an utterly impossible situation. I have told my brother so all along.'

'I think so, too,' said Murchison sulkily. 'I'll cash in my checks when we get back.'

'I shan't go back with you. I absolutely refuse to drive back with you.

I shall stop at an hotel for the night, and my brother can fetch me in the morning.'

'All right. Which hotel would you like to stop at?'

'That is my business.'

'No it isn't, it's mine also. It is up to me to see that you don't fall into Fouldes' hands. That's what I'm paid for.'

A shadow fell across the table.

'If you don't like your escort, Ursula, perhaps you would care to accept mine?' They looked up, startled, to see Fouldes standing over them smiling. He drew up a chair and sat down at their table, still smiling.

'I gather, Mr. Murchison, that your attitude is not altogether acceptable to Miss Brangwyn, which is hardly to be wondered at, and I am going to give myself the pleasure of asking you to mind your manners.'

Everything disappeared before Murchison in a blaze of wrath. He knew that he was at a disadvantage with the subtler man, for he could not very well use force in the restaurant. He also knew that he had quarrelled with Ursula without provocation, and been insultingly rude to her, and that she was very angry, and justifiably so. And in addition to all this he had let his employer down very badly. Why had he suddenly rounded on the unfortunate Ursula for a question that intended no offence? He didn't know himself. She had only asked him why he was putting his heart and soul into the job of rescuing her from Fouldes, and had got insulted for her pains. It was the very thing to fling her into Fouldes' arms. Fouldes knew it, too. He had evidently heard their angry tones, if not what was actually said, and was quite alive to his advantage. Ursula Brangwyn, as proud as Lucifer, would go over to his side simply to spite Murchison. He saw that she was gathering her furs about her. Fouldes, smiling maliciously, drew back her chair as she rose. She turned her back on Murchison, and Fouldes put her furs around her shoulders.

Murchison got to his feet. The other's smile began to fade. All the cards were in his hands, but he did not like the look on the Yorkshireman's face.

Murchison was a slow mover till he got going, and none of the other occupants of the cafe guessed that there was a row in progress. He lurched clumsily forward, and Fouldes, light as a stag, gave back.

'Don't let us have a scene in public,' he said.

'You'll have what you make,' said Murchison.

Fouldes gave back again. 'Go out and get into my car, Kitten,' he said. 'There is no need for you to be involved in this. I will get the management to deal with him.'

Murchison felt himself to be battling at a disadvantage with quicker wits than his. Moreover, he had lost his self-control and could not trust himself. The old berserker rage that had so often betrayed him was rising within him, and he knew that once that broke bounds every man's hand would be against him. If he took the law into his own hands the management would send for the police; if he did not, Ursula Brangwyn would walk out with Fouldes, betrayed by his own savage temper.

He felt like a baited bull fuming frantically on his elusive tormentors. The image of the bull brought back to him all the scheme of things that Brangwyn had half hinted and half explained, and it seemed to him as if everything worth having in life were collapsing about his ears. It was not his job he thought of; to do him justice, that never entered his head. It was the down-rushing power of that marvellous ritual of the earth in spring. He would lose all that; he would lose all the possibilities it opened up, dimly though he guessed them. Ursula and he were bound together by that ritual. However much he hated her, or she hated him, that experience shared had established a bond between them. And Fouldes was taking her from him. Taking her to unspeakable degradation. The blind fury of the wild beast in defence of its mate surged up within him, and the berserker rage burst bounds.

He caught Ursula round the waist.

'You're coming with me,' he said, and before anyone could interfere he swept her out of the shop, pushed her into the car, sprang in himself, and was flying down the wide street at sixty miles an hour.

CHAPTER 21

It did not take them many minutes at this gait to get clear of the town. A road between half-built houses led down to the shore, and he turned the car down it; in a few moments they had bumped over the loose sand of the dunes and come to a standstill beside the line of seaweed that showed highwater mark, the wide and treacherous flats of the bay stretching before them almost to the horizon.

He stopped the engine, and there was dead silence except for the crying of gulls. He stared out over the flats at the distant sea with unseeing eyes. Ursula Brangwyn, the breath knocked out of her, stared at him. What had provoked this storm that had suddenly come out of the blue? What hidden forces had been unleashed by her unthinking words - Why are you doing all this? Why was he doing it? Her question had certainly touched him on the raw, and his answer had been the answer of outraged pride.

He turned slowly round. 'I wish to apologize,' he said. 'I am afraid I let you in for a good deal of unpleasantness. I am exceedingly sorry. I hope you'll forget it if you can. I don't know what possessed me to speak as I did. I didn't mean to.'

'There is nothing in that,' said Ursula quietly. 'I have thought no more about it. We both spoke hastily and said a iot more than we meant. But I wish I knew what it was all about. It blew up so suddenly, all out of nothing.'

'I don't know what it was about any more than you do,' said Murchison moodily, resting his elbows on the steering-wheel and his chin in his hand, and staring out over the desolate flats to the far-off sea. 'I suddenly got mad with you. I don't know why. I felt I was in a very false position with you, and I resented it, as I suppose any man would who isn't a pot-hunter.'

'It is a very queer position for both of us,' said Ursula.

'Very,' said Murchison, continuing to stare at the distant fine of breakers.

'Can you see the end of it?' asked the girl tentatively.

'No, frankly, I can't. But I can see a most awful bust-up on the way. I think we're playing with fire, if you ask me.'

'In what way?'

'Need we be crude? You weren't born yesterday. You know the way of the world, I take it. You are a very attractive woman, and I am a very lonely man. You aren't my style, and I'm not yours, and no good could come of it. And, anyway, I have no money.'

'Need that worry us?' said Ursula in a low voice.

'It has begun to worry me,' said Murchison. 'I thought I could do what you needed in cold blood, but I find I can't. I'd be only too glad to lend you a hand, both for your own sake and your brother's, but I can't rely on myself, and you can't rely on me. I gave you a sample of my temper just now, so you see what it's like; and there's more of that where it came from, good and plenty, believe me.'

'I-I think it will be all right,' said the girl in a low voice.

'I don't, and perhaps I know more about it than you do.'

'Mr. Murchison, don't worry about it. It will be all right. I know what I am saying.'

He turned and looked at her sulkily.

'I think you are talking through your hat,' he said.

'No, I am not. I know what I am talking about. It is the result of that ritual we worked together, the dance of the earth in spring.'

'I have been let in for this thing in the dark,' said Murchison angrily.

'So have I!' So have I!' cried the girl. 'My brother has forced both our hands. But, all the same, I think it will be all right. I can see that now.'

'Well, I can't,' said Murchison, 'and I think I had better drive you back.' He pressed the self-starter. Ursula bent forward and switched off the ignition.

'No, we have got to finish this now we have started.' She laid her hand on his arm, and he frowned and drew away angrily at the touch.

'Do you know that we have gone too far in this thing to back out?'

'I don't know anything about it. I have been let in for this without my knowledge or consent.'

'Yes, I know you have, and so have I. My brother has been quite unscrupulous. But, all the same, it will be all right. I can feel that now.'

'It depends on what you call all right. Your standards mayn't be the same as mine.'

Ursula took a firm hold on herself. 'I should call this all right - if we were able to work the rite of the winged bull together, with all that it means.'

'And what does it mean?'

'It means a very curious spiritual bond between a man and a woman. It means much more than ordinary marriage ever could.'

'It means a very invidious position for the man, Miss Brangwyn, if he is placed as I am.'

'In what way?'

'Well, surely you know how I am placed? You don't need telling that twice, do you?'

'I know nothing of your affairs, Mr. Murchison, except that your father was in the army, and you would have been, too, if the war had not put an end to his career.'

'Then I had better tell you something about my affairs, Miss Brangwyn, and then perhaps you will understand the situation a little better than you do now.

'I went into the army straight from school; my father was killed within a week of my joining up. I came out of the army at nineteen with a subloot's gratuity, which my brother took for board and lodging, instead of starting me off in a career with it, and I have never had a career of any sort, shape or description. I've never even driven a car before. I drove a van. That was how I learnt to drive. So far as I can see, I never shall have a career now. I shall be lucky if I end up with a sandwich-board. I have been out of work a great deal oftener than in it, and that demoralizes a man. The only way I could make anything is in crime, and that is what I shall probably take to. I have a friend who is a motor-bandit. When I leave your brother I shall look him up.

'That's my past, Miss Brangwyn, and my prospects, so perhaps you can see now why I hesitate to commit myself in any way.'

'My brother thinks that you have very exceptional capacities, Mr. Murchison, and I know you could have a very good career with him if you were willing.'

'Yes, but am I willing?'

'Well, aren't you?'

'God knows. I'd be a fool not to, placed as I am. Yes, I suppose I am. I don't know what possesses me to play up like this. I suppose it's the dying kick of my self-respect.'

'What do you mean? Surely we are not asking anything of you that can hurt your self-respect?'

'Depends on your standards, dear lady. I don't suppose there ought to be anything on God's earth that could hurt my self-respect.'

'It seems to me that you have got a very bad inferiority complex and

180

are being very silly,' said Miss Brangwyn.

'Yes, I expect you're right. Shall we go home?'

'I think we had better. I wouldn't ask you to drive me if there were any other mode of conveyance.'

'There is.'

'What is that?'

'You can hire a car at Llandudno junction, and we are quite near there. Or, if you can drive yourself, I will drop off there, and you can take the car back to the farm and I will take the train to London.'

'Very good, drive me to Llandudno junction.'

He started up the car without a word, and they bumped laboriously back on to the main road, or so he thought.

But they had not been driving very long when the road came to a dead end at an abandoned coastguard station, and they found themselves with an arm of the sea barring further progress.

'Damn it all!' said Murchison savagely, 'where are we?'

'I'm afraid I don't know,' said Ursula miserably. 'I believe the main road turns inland somewhere about where we left it. We must be on the wrong road. We shall have to go back the way we came.'

He swung the car round impatiently; but he was used to a short-chassised van, and miscalculated the steerage-way required by a thoroughbred, and before he knew what was happening the front wheels were in the ditch and he had as much hope of shifting the car as he had of moving mountains.

'My God!' was all he could find to say. Ursula burst out laughing and slipped her hand through his arm.

'It's no use,' she said. 'The stars in their courses won't let us part. We have got to be friends.'

'Oh, my God!' said Murchison, looking at her as she sat half turned towards him with her lips parted in laughter.

'Shake hands?' said Ursula. 'You've been a beast to me, and I've been a cat to you. Shall we call it square?'

'Right you are,' said he, struggling to get himself in hand, and giving her a brief handshake. 'Now what are we going to do? Is it far from here to the nearest village where we can 'phone?'

'A good way, I should think, when you come to walk it. We have been travelling down this road for quite ten minutes, and one covers a good deal of ground in that time in a car.'

'Do you think you can manage to walk back, or will you wait here while I go and phone a garage?'

'I couldn't possibly walk it. I've only got patent leather pumps on my feet.'
'Well, then, you'll have to wait here, and I'll be as quick as I can.'
'Very good.'
'If you'll get out, I'll lift the seat out and put it inside this barn, you will be much more comfortable in there than in the car at this angle.'

They got out of the heeled-over car, and he did as he had suggested, making Ursula as comfortable as possible with rugs and her mink coat, and a packet of papers. Then he set off on his walk.

He was thankful to be alone. As always, Ursula Brangwyn went to his head at close quarters. He had used the right word when he had told her brother that he found her glamorous. She was like Lilith beguiling Adam. He remembered that Astley, who, God knows, wasn't particular, had called her Morgan le Fay, the witch-sister of Arthur, to whom Merlin had taught all enchantments. He had been reading about her in the books Brangwyn had put in his room, and had been struck at the time by her likeness to the pictures of the Keltic enchantress.

He had never believed it possible to dislike any woman quite so much. He hated her because he had been rude to her; because she was rich and sophisticated, and he was rough, uncouth and driftwood in life's stream, unless he were prepared to be a pensioner of her brother's, who was quite willing to stall-feed him handsomely provided he would marry her. But, above all, he hated her because she attracted him so tremendously, and the only terms on which he could have her were terms which his pride would not allow. Murchison, striding down the sandy road in the worst of tempers and the oldest of mackintoshes, felt he had every justification for hating the unhappy Ursula Brangwyn in her mink coat.

He had hardly gone a mile, however, when he saw on the other side of the creek that flanked the road at that point a youth fishing for eels. He hailed him, explained the situation, and bid the youth take himself off at top speed to the main road, which was at no great distance as the crow flies, hail a passing car, and send a message to the nearest garage. Then he set out to return to the derelict coastguard station, hoping against hope that none of his messages would miscarry. It had been impossible to give the youth a note to deliver because of the width of the creek.

His walk had cooled him considerably, but it had not been long enough to lessen his smouldering sense of resentment against life in general, and Ursula Brangwyn in particular. In fact, it seemed as if every wrong life had ever done him - the career that had never got started, the home that could never be his, all the thwartings of his natural instincts, all the hammering of the square peg into the round hole to which he had been subjected for the best years of his life - everything seemed to gather up and focus on to Ursula Brangwyn, who fascinated him, but whom he did not like, and whom he could never hope to meet on an equality.

He asked himself, as he walked back at a more leisurely pace over the sandy road, whether he would have asked her to marry him if he had been in a position to do so, and decided that he probably would, so great was the fascination she had for him, but it would certainly have turned out very badly. What could you expect if a girl married one man in order to get away from another, for whom she really cared? And, anyway, apart from her mink coat, she was pretty worthless. No girl who was any good would ever have got mixed up with a chap like Fouldes. This seemed incontestable to him, and deprived Ursula Brangwyn of any vestige of claim to his consideration that she might ever have possessed.

Then there came to him, in his evil mood, a bright idea. She had robbed him of every vestige of self-respect, and he did not suppose she herself could be blessed with an overplus of that commodity, judging by the way she had behaved with Fouldes. Why not make the best of both worlds and exploit her as she deserved to be exploited? It was true that his father's son would not have tolerated that idea, but the unemployed man who had drifted rudderless all these years took it in and welcomed it. He knew that Ursula Brangwyn had got to have him, and had now definitely made up her mind to take him. He could see that she was getting quite keen on the scheme her brother had propounded, for some reason best known to herself. The fact that the scheme was no longer distasteful to her gave him a sense of power over her; it made her a suppliant for his favours, instead of a reluctant yielder to her brother's pressure. And with the discovery of Ursula's changed attitude there came to Murchison a desire to repay on her all the humiliation he had received from life; he wished that Ursula Brangwyn in her mink coat should know humiliation as he had known it, because she had been willing to marry him without wanting him in order to get herself out of a scrape; because, although she was fascinating to him, he was a nauseous drought to her, only to be got down under the compulsion of dire necessity.

He would damn well rub her nose in it. It should be fifty-fifty as far as humiliation went, and life should pay up something on account towards the arrears it owed him.

Ursula Brangwyn, left alone in the open-fronted shed looking out to sea, came to the end of her own delicate Turkish cigarettes and started on one of Murchison's papers, made a wry face, and extinguished it. Then, being very bored and rather worried, lit it up again. It was better than nothing, and after she had smoked a few whiffs she found it better than she had expected. It was largely the contrast with the previous Turkish that had made it taste so foul.

And, as she did so, she thought of the man in whose pocket these cigarettes had been. She was doing exactly the same thing with him as she had done with his cigarette - first rejecting him as distasteful; then accepting him under the compulsion of necessity; and then finding him not so bad after all. As she inhaled deep lungfuls of the strong Virginia, she came to the conclusion that Murchison's type of cigarettes were considerably more satisfying than her scented Turkish when one was really in need of consolation. And the same applied to Murchison.

He was the most extraordinarily satisfying person when he took you in hand. Life had been lived at a high level during those few seconds when he caught hold of her and literally flung her out of the cafe and into the car. And the one thing above all others that she felt was that she could trust him; that he was absolutely reliable. And she knew that her brother felt the same about him, and she had great confidence in her brother. She felt rather ashamed of herself that she had not been able to see the possibilities in Murchison when she first met him, but had had to wait for a well-cut suit to reveal them to her. She was not taking his present *difficile* attitude too seriously. She was twenty-seven, and had seen something of life under her brother's roof, and she guessed that hurt pride was at the bottom of Murchison's trouble. His words, 'You are a very attractive woman,' had been balm of Gilead to her sore soul. She had been under the impression that he was lending himself to her brother's schemes for no other reason than a financial one; or, at best, out of pity. There had been times when he had been extraordinarily kind. She suspected that he was more attracted by her than he was willing to admit, even to himself; and because he felt himself to be in an invidious position with regard to her, he was ruffling up his feathers in this alarming manner. But for all his mutterings and threatenings her feminine ear caught another note now and again in his voice.

She was turning all this over in her mind, when suddenly, dark against the light, a man stood in front of her, having approached noiselessly over the loose sand. She could not see his face, and because he was tall she jumped to the conclusion that he must be Fouldes, and, screaming aloud, scrambled to her feet, standing at bay in the corner of the barn, her face livid with terror.

184

'Good Lord, what's the matter?' exclaimed the man, coming into the barn, and she saw that it was Murchison.

'I thought it was Frank,' she said, feeling weak and shaken and very foolish, for she saw at once that Murchison was not moved to sympathy on this occasion by her display of weakness.

She dropped down on the cushioned car-seat again, and drew the rug over her lap.

'No,' said the man, 'I'm afraid I'm not Frank. Sorry, but it can't be helped.'

She was not sure whether he was making one of his rough jokes, or whether he was being nasty.

He, too, dropped down on the sand.

'May I have one of my fags.' he said. She passed him the crumpled packet, and then gave him a light from her little gold lighter. His eye caught the hall-mark as she held it towards him, and he did not love her any better.

'I have been thinking things out,' he said, between puffs at the newly lit cigarette. 'And I have got a proposition to put before you.'

'Yes?' said Ursula tentatively, wondering what in the world was coming.

'If I have got the hang of the job right, your brother wants me to marry you in order to cut out Fouldes, on the principle that one nail drives out another. Is that so?'

'Yes,' said Ursula faintly. 'But there is more to it than that.'

He ignored the latter part of her remark and went on.

'I told him that I would do anything I could for you, but I definitely would not marry you. Did he tell you that?'

'No,' said Ursula, still more faintly.

'He seems to think, however, that the proposition is not a practicable one without marriage. Is that so?'

'I don't know,' said Ursula miserably.

'Well, he seemed to think so. Now the proposition I have to put up is this. I am not willing to marry you for keeps, because I honestly don't think it would work. But I will marry you and live with you for a year if you like, provided the arrangement is subject to three months' notice on either side. I mean by that, that if I provide the evidence any time after the year is up you will undertake to divorce me within three months, and I, on my side, will undertake to provide you with evidence any time you want it. I will do this on condition that you or your brother, it doesn't matter to me which, will put me through a university course in civil

185

engineering, and give me a start overseas.'

He looked at Ursula, and saw that she had gone as white as a sheet, and a pang of compunction shot through him. But her next words removed it.

'I suppose that is a reasonable proposition,' she said, 'I know my brother intended to make some sort of financial arrangement with you.' Her head was held very high, but he saw that her mouth was quivering.

'We'll take that as settled, shall we?' he said, and rose to his feet. He wanted to get away from her; having shot his bolt, the sight of her was unbearable to him.

She rose, too, and they stood facing each other. He would not have believed that it was possible for him to desire to hurt and humiliate any living being as he desired to hurt and humiliate her as she stood there, looking white and frightened, in her mink coat, with her gold net purse lying at her feet, where she had dropped it in her agitation, spilling out its valuable contents on to the sand.

'Well,' he said, 'as we are now formally engaged, I think that "a kiss or two is justly due, as, from, and between us both," ' and he took her in his arms.

The moment he felt the touch of her soft lips on his, his evil enchantment left him. He held her from him at arm's length, and stared in horror at her white face.

'My God!' he said, 'what have I been doing?' and he turned on his heel and walked hastily out of the barn, to come face to face with the breakdown gang that had arrived unheard over the sandy road.

It did not take the powerful derrick long to get Brangwyn's car out of the ditch; but when they did so, they found that the steering-gear had been wrenched and the car was practically uncontrollable.

'We'll pull her on the tow-rope to steady her,' said the foreman of the gang, 'and you must keep on straightening her out as she bears to one side. I think the lady had better come on the van with us in case you run into the ditch again.'

So on the journey back to civilisation Murchison had the company of a chatty youth in greasy overalls, and there was no opportunity to say any word of explanation or apology to Ursula.

At Llandudno junction, to which the breakdown van towed them, they went into a little hotel to have tea while the car retired in disgrace to the garage.

'Is there any way of letting your brother know what has happened to us?' said Murchison. 'We shall be pretty late getting in.'

'You can get at the farm quite easily,' said Ursula. 'Phone the hotel at the top of the pass, and they will send a boy up to the farm with a message.'

Murchison turned into the office to do his phoning, and when he came out the Boots informed him that the lady had taken a bedroom and gone to lie down, as she did not feel well.

Murchison ordered tea for one sulkily. He could hardly blame Ursula for not desiring his company after the way he had behaved towards her.

CHAPTER 22

Ursula, for her part, lay on an ice-cold bed under a clammy eiderdown, trying to console herself with hot tea, and thinking that she had never felt so miserable in her life. Her only consolation was that she had got Murchison's cigarettes.

The cold-blooded cynicism of his proposition had been a terrible shock to her. And yet, could she justly deny that the proposition which had been put before him was just as cold-blooded? She was surprised to find how greatly Murchison's defection had shaken her; for she had come to rely on him far more than she had realized. The reliability of Murchison had become a kind of article of faith with her; for all her reluctance towards him, she had come to look upon him as a form of fire insurance which would prevent the worst from ever befalling her. It seemed as if her world had collapsed about her ears. Murchison's integrity, her brother's insight and knowledge - both had been weighed in the balance and found wanting, and if these two men failed her, where had she to look for security? Was there any good faith in the world? She did not question her brother's good faith, but the fact that he could have been so deceived in his judgment of a man as he had been in Murchison made her feel that she could never rely on him again.

But the thing that amazed her most was her reaction in the face of Murchison's treatment of her. She ought to have snubbed him soundly and told her brother that he must choose between them. If Murchison stayed, she went. And yet here she was, meekly accepting his insults and wondering what she could do to propitiate him and put things right, and telling herself that if anything could justify such behaviour towards a woman, it was the treatment Murchison had received at her hands.

Outwardly, of course, she had been civil enough, except for that terrible *faux pas,* which had been quite unintentional, and which was not really nearly as bad as it must have sounded in Murchison's ears. But on the inner planes she knew that she had committed magical sin in taking all that Murchison had to give and giving back to him nothing. That was just plain vampirism, and nothing else.

She felt sure that the upheaval in Murchison was due to some check in the workings of the mysterious power that they had set in motion when she had played the part of the earth in spring and he had played the part of the life-giving sun. The old rites were potent, whether the forces they stirred were cosmic or subconscious. She had given herself up to draw out the magnetism latent in him, and had drawn the whole man to her. She herself had felt new life and hope flow into her, but there had been no return flow on the circuit; there had been no new hope for Murchison in his thwarted life. In spite of all that her brother kept on telling her, she had felt in her heart that there would be no building of the uncouth Murchison into the fabric of her sophisticated existence; there was no place in it for him. She had agreed in her heart when he had said that he would be used as scaffolding, and pulled down and carted away when he had served his purpose. She admitted frankly to herself that if she had really believed what her brother had told her concerning the relationship that would build up between them if the magic worked, she would never have permitted the attempt to be made.

It had never occurred to her before to consider what would be the effect of all these experiments on Murchison, till his words gave her the key. 'You are a very attractive woman, and I am a very lonely man.' What must it have meant to that man to have heard her words, 'I shall have to take Murchison, Alick?'

How far were his reactions to be attributed to hurt vanity, and how far to a much deeper wound? It was difficult to think of pique and petty spite in connection with Murchison. She did not think she had been far out when she had flung at him the taunt of an inferiority complex. How could a man of his calibre, placed in his circumstances, have escaped it? She thought of the Oxen of the Sun bowing their mighty necks to the peasant's yoke. Murchison was a tremendous force. She realized that more clearly at each contact she had with him.

And she had also begun to realize and appreciate another characteristic that distinguished Murchison - he was extra-ordinarily unselfish. He had been quite willing to let her use him as scaffolding, giving her the most sacred thing a man had to give a woman, and then, when she had had all she needed from him, quietly to withdraw. 'Greater love hath no man than this.'

Ursula felt bitterly grieved with herself that she had not realized the nobility of Murchison. She had trodden under foot something very sacred and very rare. There were few men who could or would have done what Murchison had done. And because she had not met him half-way and taken up her share of the task to which they had set their hands, it proved too much for him, and he had gone down under it. She had not given herself to Murchison, and he felt it, even if he did not understand it, and it was this that was upsetting him. If there had been a return flow of magnetism from her to him, how wonderful would have been their relationship by now. She sat up miserably, hugging her knees and thinking of it. Her brother was right, this could be a very big thing; but was it spoilt beyond repair by her snobbery and folly? She made up her mind that next time Murchison approached her he should have no cause to complain of her lack of response. The kiss in the barn had taken her by surprise and she had been too startled and upset for any response to be possible; but next time he kissed her she determined there should be a flow and return that should seal their union, and the Mass of the Winged Bull would begin.

She wondered whether the hotel people would tolerate it if she sent for him to come up to her room and talk to her, and concluded that as they were highly respectable, chapel-going Welsh they probably wouldn't. She snuggled down under the eiderdown that the warmth of her body was gradually airing, and had almost dropped off to sleep after all the alarums and excursions, when a knock at the door announced the chambermaid with a note. She tore it open, wondering who in the world was writing to her. It was on the hotel stationery, and addressed her as dear Miss Brangwyn, and was written in a sprawling schoolboy hand that exactly matched Murchison's whole personality.

'Your brother has just been through on the phone to me in answer to my message. I told him of the trouble we had with Fouldes following us around' - ('But you didn't tell him about the trouble you have had with me,' thought Ursula, 'or you wouldn't be at such pains to make it clear that it was only the trouble with Frank you have told him about, so I think you are ashamed of yourself.') -'And he says that we are not to return to the farm, but to wait here for him, and he will bring your things down by car from the hotel, and we are to return to London by the night mail.' And he was hers faithfully, Edward Murchison.

Ursula was very much relieved. She had dreaded the return to the farm under Mrs Davies' sharp eyes. The farm, too, was full of painful memories now. She would far sooner be back with Murchison in the flat. She decided that the best way to handle Murchison in his upheaved condition was to leave him until he cooled down, and then ask her brother to stage another rite of the earth in spring, and she would send across to Murchison such a return flow of magnetism that all barriers would go down between them. Meanwhile, her attitude should just be quietly friendly, refusing to take offence.

She decided that it might be as well to give Murchison an opportunity to apologize if he wanted to, for she had judged from his expression of horror after he had kissed her that he had wakened up to the enormity of his behaviour, so she arose and put on her frock and went down to the lounge of the little hotel. Murchison was not there, but through a half-open door she caught a glimpse of him playing a game of billiards with a stranger, so her scheme went astray, and she had no word with Murchison till her brother appeared in a hired car loaded up with luggage which Mrs Davies must have done wonders to get packed in so short a time. Murchison, summoned from his game by the sound of his employer's voice in the hall, presented a wooden countenance and refused to meet Ursula's eyes.

They got a first-class carriage to themselves on the Holyhead express. Ursula, who had a very genuine headache by now, refused dinner, and they left her lying at full length on a seat, with a pillow under her head and a rug over her and her face to the wall, like Ahab.

'I say, sir,' said Murchison as soon as he was seated in the dining-car with his employer. 'We've had the hell of a row, Miss Brangwyn and I.'

Brangwyn raised his eyebrows. 'What's it all about, Murchison?'

'Dashed if I know, sir. I suddenly exploded, without any provocation whatever. In fact, she had the patience of Job with me. I think I've put my foot in it properly.'

Brangwyn smiled. 'It won't do my lady sister any harm to have a good rowing occasionally. In fact, it is what she needs.'

'I don't know about that, sir. What I did was pretty unpardonable.'

Then a commercial traveller joined them, and insisted on entering into the conversation, so further confidences were impossible, and Murchison ate his dinner in a miserable silence while Brangwyn coped with a loquacious son of Erin travelling in bacon.

191

CHAPTER 23

Ursula had had some sleep on the train, thanks to the liberal use of aspirin, but she had no more sleep after they got back to the flat towards midnight. And as she sat up in her rose-pink bed to look at the clock, she wondered whether Murchison, up in his flat, were sleeping any better than she was. As a matter of fact, he was of the type that sleeps like the proverbial second mate, and his troubles were over for the time being.

As soon as it began to get light Ursula got up, had a bath, put on a walking costume, and went out. To her surprise, she found Monks taking down the shutters of the second-hand book-shop. She knew him well, and greeted him cordially, glad of the sight of a familiar face.

'Good gracious, Mr. Monks!' she said. 'Whatever time do you open shop?'

'Taint so early as all that, miss,' he replied. 'It's gettin' on towards seven. I've got to get the place swep' up before I open.'

He did not tell her that news of her precipitate return had been telephoned from Wales the night before.

'You're up early, miss. Never known you do this before.'

'I slept on the train, and then couldn't sleep again when I got to bed.'

'Would you like a cup o'tea, miss? I got the kettle on the gas-ring, just goin'to make one for meself'

She followed him into the shop, where the sound of a kettle singing vouched for the truth of his words.

'Taint quite bilin' yet,' he said. 'I'll put through a phone call while we're waitin', 'cos I'm afraid I may miss the feller if I leave it too late.'

He was truly thankful that the automatic telephone had come in, and that he had not got to cry a number aloud in her presence. All unsuspicious, Ursula Brangwyn sat down and heard him, after a considerable wait, address an unknown interlocutor.

'This is Monks this end. Will you tell the boss right now that the goods 'as arrived, and I 'ave 'em in the shop.'

A simple message, but efficacious, for Ursula had hardly finished drinking her cup of tea when a taxi drew up outside the shop, and in walked Astley.

She rose to her feet, startled, wondering what extraordinary coincidence it was that brought him there; guessing that spies were at work, but quite unsuspicious of Monks, who had been with her brother some years and was deeply in debt to him for many kindnesses. In fact, Monks would probably have been paying the penalty for embezzlement at that moment but for the charity of Brangwyn.

'Yessir?' said Monks briskly, as if Astley were a complete stranger.

'All right, my man, all right,' said Astley, brushing him aside as if he had never set eyes on him before. 'I wish to speak to the lady.'

'Yessir,' said Monks, and vanished into the little cubbyhole where he had made the tea, leaving Ursula alone with Astley, who was between her and the door.

'Well, Ursula, what about it?' said Astley.

'There is nothing about anything, Mr. Astley. Good morning,' said Ursula, and rose to depart. Astley shut the door, turned the key, and dropped it into his pocket. The heavy shutters were still up, the streets deserted at that hour, and Ursula Brangwyn was most effectually a prisoner.

'Mr. Monks!' she called out, but there was no reply, and the significance of the telephone call she had heard suddenly dawned on her.

She turned on Astley. 'Will you kindly unlock the door?' she said.

'No, my girl, not till I've had a talk with you. Won't you sit down?'

'I prefer to stand. This interview cannot be very prolonged, for I shall start screaming as soon as I hear a passer-by.'

'I think you would be wise to hear what I have to say before you make any decision. You might regret it afterwards if you didn't. Am I right in thinking that you and Murchison are proposing to work the Mass of the Bull?'

'No, we are proposing to work the Mass of the Winged Bull, which is a very different matter.'

'A distinction without a difference, as far as I can see,' said Astley. 'Well, my dear child, whatever you are proposing to work, it won't come off. Murchison is a cock that won't fight.'

'My affairs are none of your business,' said Ursula.

'But your affairs are my business, my dear child, because you and Frank are already pretty deeply committed to me in the matter of the Mass of the Bull. Now listen, Ursula, and be sensible. You are in a very bad nervous condition, and you cannot get right, as you very well know, until what you have begun is finished off. You think you can do it with

Murchison, but I know that you cannot, because Murchison has other fish to fry, and he won't polarize with you. In other words, my dear child, you have a rival.'

The explanation fitted the circumstances so exactly that Ursula felt her heart turn to stone within her. Astley saw his advantage, and followed it up. 'Read this,' he said, and handed her Murchison's letter.

She read it in silence, and stood with it in her hand for several minutes without speaking, staring into space. Astley did not break in upon her thoughts, but stood concentrating upon her with the intent gaze of the hypnotist.

At length she raised her eyes and said, 'Yes, I see your point. What do you suggest?'

'I suggest that you and Frank take your lives into your own hands and do the thing that it is in your hearts to do. He is your real mate, Ursula, and you know it. This oaf of Brangwyn's is no possible mate for you, even if he were willing, and he quite obviously is not. You would have been happily married by now if your brother had not started poking sticks into the wheels.

'You come back to me, Ursula, and you will feel the power beginning to flow again. It will bring life to you, Ursula. See, it is beginning to flow now. You feel the power flowing into you, Ursula. You cannot resist it. There is no resistance in you.'

He made the hypnotist's passes over her, unlocked the door, beckoned her to follow him, and winked over her shoulder at Monks. He put her into the taxi and they drove away. Monks hastily relocked the door, and decided that he would not open the shop early that morning, and then he could not be questioned as to whether he had seen Miss Brangwyn go out.

An hour later Brangwyn said to Murchison, 'I don't think it is any use waiting for Ursula, so we will start our breakfast.'

But Murchison was not disposed to start his breakfast. He pecked at his food in a discontented fashion, fidgeted, and stared at the door.

'I suppose she's all right?' he said at length.

'Why shouldn't she be all right?'

'I don't know. I just wondered if she was.'

Brangwyn went on with his breakfast, but Murchison continued to drink tea and fidget, and would not eat anything.

At length he said, 'Why don't you send the char up to see if she is all right?'

'Because Ursula would not be at all pleased at having her beauty sleep disturbed. She is not an early riser at the best of times.'

After breakfast Brangwyn moved over to the fire with the Times, and Murchison went up to his flat. As he passed the door of Ursula's apartments he saw that it was slightly ajar. Obeying a sudden impulse he pushed it wider and looked in, and saw that both sitting-room and bathroom were empty, and the door into the bedroom stood ajar. He looked over the rail of the gallery and saw that Brangwyn was intent on his paper, so he tiptoed silently over the thick carpet and peered into the bedroom, taking a chance that he might come upon Miss Brangwyn with nothing on.

The bedroom was empty, her nightgown lying across the tumbled bed. She had obviously got up and dressed. But where was she? Hoping against hope he raced up the stairs to the roof-garden, but it stood empty in the spring sunshine. He leapt down the stairs three steps at a time, and Brangwyn looked up from his paper to find his secretary standing over him, his usually ruddy face as white as a sheet.

'She's gone out,' he said.

'Has she?' said Brangwyn. 'Well, there's no need to be unduly alarmed about that. Why shouldn't she go out if she wanted to?'

'My God, I am alarmed, though!' said Murchison. 'I think she's gone to Fouldes.'

'What makes you think that?'

'I gave her a terrific wipe in the eye yesterday. I bet she's done it out of sheer pique. I told her I'd marry her if you made it worth my while, but I wouldn't live with her longer than a year.'

'What on earth possessed you to tell her that?'

'God knows. I think I was mad. I suppose what she said about having to put up with me upset me.'

'Have you got fond of Ursula, Murchison?'

'Yes, I've got very fond of her.'

'Well, my dear boy, don't let that affect your judgment. There is no need to jump to the conclusion that because she isn't in the flat something has happened to her. Wait and see whether she comes back for lunch or not. If she doesn't come back for lunch, and doesn't phone, then we'll start getting worried, not before.'

'I *know* something has happened to her, Brangwyn.'

Brangwyn looked at him, and his own uneasiness increased. The magical bond he had wrought between Murchison and Ursula was such that he thought the man's feelings were a pretty good indication of what was happening to the girl. He had never seen the stolid and controlled

Murchison like this before.

'What do you suggest doing, Murchison?' he asked.

'I suggest that I look Astley up and tell him that I've had a row with you and would like that job he promised me. Then I shall get my nose in there, and may be able to sniff something out. Astley will know where she is, even if she isn't actually there, and it may leak out if I ply him with whisky and pump him.'

'That's an excellent idea, Murchison. But don't tell him you've had a row with me. Tell him you haven't got much to do for me and have plenty of time on your hands, and you've dropped in to see him, and find out if there is anything doing in your line. I'll give you a few papers you can take him to act as a ground-bait.'

Murchison made his way cross-country on foot to the down-at-heel district in North London, at no great distance from Brangwyn's flat, where Astley's superlative visiting card said he lived.

The house itself was a large corner house painted a symbolic black, relieved only by leprous white patches where the neglected paint had scaled off, oddly reminiscent of the dark-skinned, pock-marked Astley. The whole effect of the place, with its uncleaned windows and unwhitened steps, was that of the shabby sophistication of a *passee prostitute*.

Murchison rang the bell, and waited some time for an answer; and then the door was opened to him by an enormous grinning negro, a great deal blacker than the dusty butler's blacks that he wore. Murchison was shown into an inner hall even dustier than the butler. The furniture was the kind of furniture that appears in American films of ancestral British homes.

Almost before he had sat down, Astley appeared and greeted him as if he were a long-lost brother.

'Hullo, my dear chap? What brings you round to see me?'

Murchison saw him run his eye over the new blue suit of first-class tailoring, and guessed it was his prosperous appearance that was obtaining him this cordiality.

'I managed to lay my hands on a few papers that looked to me like what you wanted,' he said. 'At any rate, they came out of the safe. I hope they're the right ones. I took a long chance to get them.'

'Splendid, my dear chap, splendid! Let's have a look at them. Oh, damn it all, these aren't the ones. I've got these already, through Fouldes. Sorry, Murchison, these are no use to me,' and he handed them back.

Murchison declined to take them, and looked as sulky as was

compatible with a hard struggle to keep a straight face.

'Well, what about a bit on account?'

'My dear chap, these are no use to me. These are not the ones I asked you for. You deliver the goods, and you'll have no cause to complain of your treatment. Come and have a drink.'

'Well, I don't mind if I do. Brangwyn keeps the decanter locked up.'

They went down a passage to what had evidently been a billiard-room when the house had belonged to decent city fathers, and which was now Astley's study. It was a chaotic apartment, strewn with papers and books, and surrounded by dusty book-lined walls. In one corner was an antique statue of the kind that the British Museum keeps locked up. Over the littered mantelpiece was a study of Pan and the nymphs which left nothing to the imagination. It was the room of a scholar, a sloven and a sensualist. Like the rest of the house, it bore the mark of lavish expenditure and negligent upkeep.

Murchison lowered himself into a massive leather-covered armchair, such as must once have graced a West-end club, and felt the broken springs digging into him. Beside it was a spittoon so full of cigar-ends that there was hardly room for the ash of his cigarette. There were several bottles and glasses standing on a side table, but none of the bottles were full, and none of the glasses were clean.

Astley rang the bell, and a girl appeared. Murchison stared hard at the girl and wondered whether Ursula Brangwyn would ever come to look as she did. The girl was thin to emaciation; her eyes sunken in her head and surrounded by black circles; her lips carmined with so vicious a lipstick that she looked as if she had been kissing the wet paint on a pillar-box. Her clothing consisted of an exceedingly figure-revealing *djibbah* of dingy green. She looked like a sickly and unclean nymph who had had altogether too much attention from Pan.

Astley demanded a bottle of whisky. The nymph shook her head with a faint smile.

'Dash it all!' exclaimed Astley, feeling in his pockets, 'I've got no change. I say, Murchison, lend me a quid, will you?'

Murchison handed him ten shillings. Astley gave it to the girl, who disappeared, to return in a few minutes with a bottle.

'Steady on for me,' said Murchison. 'I don't generally take spirits at this hour of the day.'

'Lucky feller,' said Astley. 'They're the only things I can take. Everything else plays up my digestion.'

While Astley was busy with the syphon, Murchison slipped half his drink into an aspidistra which stood conveniently to hand; he wanted all his wits about him for the forthcoming interview.

'Well?' said Astley, when they were comfortably settled with their drinks and cigarettes. 'How are you getting on with old Brangwyn?'

'So-so. I've had the hell of a row with the girl, though.'

'Have you really? What about?'

'I got sick of playing lounge-lizard, and let her have it in the neck. I fancy my job's a bit precarious. She'll get me chucked out if she can. Luckily for me, old Brangwyn loves me. By the way, I suppose you heard there was a fine old shindy with Fouldes up at Brangwyn's place in the mountains? An old sheepdog ate the seat out of his pants. No end of a lark. We've been watching her like a cat at a mousehole ever since. Brangwyn thinks she means to go off with him.'

Astley smiled.

'Oh, he thinks, does he? And where does he think she is at the present moment?'

'Tucked up in her little bed, I suppose. At any rate, she wasn't down when I came out.'

'Would it surprise you to learn that she is in this house at the present moment?'

'Gee whizz, is she really? Won't old Brangwyn be wild! But I suppose that means my job's at an end. He won't want a watchdog any longer if she's definitely bolted. What's his chance of getting her back, do you think?'

'None. I'll see to that.'

'I say, for God's sake don't let her catch sight of me. I don't want any tales of my visits to go back to Brangwyn.'

'You needn't worry. Nothing will go back to Brangwyn.'

Astley's certainty, and the curious sense of power behind the man struck cold at Murchison's heart.

Abruptly Astley changed subject.

'Are you a handy man with tools?'

'Pretty fair. The saw is mightier than the pen in my case.'

'Got any time on your hands?'

'Yes, lots. Brangwyn said he'd be out to lunch, and I could have a day off. I'm not to know there's a family catastrophe, am I? I shall stroll home when the pubs shut and hear the news for the first time.'

'Care to lend me a hand downstairs? I'll show you something interesting.'

'Yes, rather. I'm only killing time. Don't exactly want to spend the day calling on my sister-in-law.'

This was a chance beyond all expectation.

Astley rose laboriously from his chair, and Murchison realized what a wreck the man was. He could only just get up without assistance. According to the Sunday papers, Astley dealt in the elixir of life that bestowed immortal youth. Murchison thought that he was no testimonial to his own preparations.

'This is an odd house, this is!' said Astley. 'It was built before the railway came this way, and the bridge that takes the road over the railway is raised on a good-sized embankment that completely swamps our two lower floors. This floor we are on now is, strictly speaking, the drawing-room floor. The original ground-floor is the basement, and we've got a kind of sub-basement that nobody knows anything about.'

They returned down the passage to the hall, and descended a staircase to murky kitchen quarters, where Murchison caught a glimpse of the dingy nymph engaged in washing up what looked like a belated breakfast. Astley inserted a key in a cupboard door, swung it open, and revealed another stairway apparently descending into the bowels of the earth. An extraordinary aroma arose to meet them, compounded of stale incense and something else, which was vaguely familiar, but Murchison could not identify it at first. Then the bleat of a billy-goat greeted them, and he guessed who the second thurifer was.

'Old boy hums a bit, doesn't he?' said Astley. 'I must get someone to clean him out. Voluntary workers are extraordinarily slack.'

They entered a large room which seemed to extend under the whole house, with the superstructure supported on pillars which had obviously not been put up by a professional. Murchison eyed those pillars, and thought that one fine night the house would probably sit down on top of Astley and his crew when they were at their rites.

The room reminded him of the room in Brangwyn's basement devoted to the same purpose, save that it was much larger and decorated in Egyptian red and black. The effect of those two colours in juxtaposition was peculiarly sinister. In the centre of the room was what looked like an old-fashioned table-tomb such as crusaders repose on in country churches. It was covered with a black velvet pall, and a cushion at the head showed that it was intended for someone to lie on. Murchison remembered what Brangwyn had told him about the Black Mass, and wondered what scenes had been enacted with that tomb for a centre-piece.

At the far end of the room was a low platform reached by three shallow steps. Astley led the way on to this, put aside the heavy black draperies that formed its background, and revealed a door, which, on being opened, gave access to a lumber-room, half carpenter's shop and half general storage. There was a bench strewn with tools, and a quantity of timber pushed under it.

'Can't very well send for a firm to do jobs like ours,' said Astley, 'so we have to get busy and do 'em ourselves. I'd be glad if you'd lend me a hand. I'm no use with tools nowadays. I get goes of neuritis.'

Murchison believed him. He was lucky not to get goes of blindness, considering the way he was lowering the whisky.

'What I want you to make is a cross.'

'Right you are,' said Murchison. 'What sort of a cross?'

'One big enough to crucify a six-foot man on.'

'My God!' said Murchison. 'Who's going to be the corpse?'

'No one's going to be the corpse. It's only symbolic. Your arms rest in webbing slings. It's perfectly comfortable.'

'No accounting for tastes. Let folk have what they like, that's my motto. Shall I use some of this timber?'

They got to work. Astley measuring and marking competently enough, and Murchison in his shirt-sleeves doing the sawing, till they were interrupted by the dingy nymph, who came to tell Astley that he was wanted on the telephone.

'Damn!' said Astley, who was evidently enjoying himself at the carpentering. 'Carry on, will you, Murchison, I won't be longer than I can help.'

Murchison downed tools as promptly as any trade unionist the moment the door closed behind Astley. He had observed another door at the opposite end of the room, and he wanted to see where it led to. He shifted aside the lumber till it could be got open wide enough for him to slide through edgeways, disposing the lumber so as to look as if it had not been disturbed, drew the enormous bolts that secured it top and bottom, coaxed it open on its rusted hinges, and slipped hastily through. He knew that Astley had a considerable distance to go to the phone, and prayed that his interlocutor would be loquacious.

He found himself in what was evidently the area of the original basement, to judge by the gullies of the drain pipes. It had been roofed over, and Murchison saw that the whole house had moved up a storey when the railway came, as Astley had described. He struck a match and discerned a mouldering flight of steps in one corner. He groped his way up these till his head met an obstruction, struck another match, and saw what looked like a trap-door above him; pushed it, found to his joy that it yielded, put his head and shoulders cautiously through, and found himself in the coal-cellar, empty save for a heap of swept-up coal-dust in a corner. This was a bit of all right. The coal-cellar would certainly have access to the present area, and it ought to be a comparatively simple matter to use this route as an emergency exit from Astley's temple of the black arts. It would also be an equally simple matter to get in the same way should need arise, provided one did not mind risking being charged with burglary.

Well pleased with his discoveries, Murchison slipped quickly back to the lumber-room, dusted the coal-dust off his hands, gave the hinges of the door a drop of oil, re-arranged the lumber so that it did not appear to have been disturbed, and yet allowed of the door being opened, and got to work on the cross again, looking as if butter would not melt in his mouth, and was so engaged when Astley returned from his telephoning.

The massive cross, made of old floor-boards, was soon knocked together, and with the help of the butler, who looked like a second edition of Jack Johnson, Murchison got it through into the temple and up-ended it on the platform and jammed its foot in a slot, securing it in position with struts from behind. It was a pretty stout piece of work by the time it was finished, and Murchison reckoned that anyone who was fastened to that cross would have to stay there.

'There; we'll leave the girls to paint that black,' said Astley, viewing the job with satisfaction. 'Come upstairs and have a drink.'

Murchison wondered whether he were going to be offered lunch in return for his exertions, which had not been inconsiderable, the cross being a heavy piece of work, but there were no signs of it in that hugger-mugger household. He was particularly anxious to avoid any quantity of Astley's whisky on a stomach that was pretty empty by now, having had practically no breakfast, so the aspidistra again received a libation. He had always heard that aspidistras were very hardy plants, and he hoped this one would live up to its reputation, for this was its third glass of whisky that morning.

'Did Brangwyn ever do any rituals with you?' enquired Astley when they had settled down to their drinks.

Murchison thought frankness best, as he did not know how well-informed Monks might be concerning the doings in Brangwyn's basement, and any attempt at dissimulation would have put Astley on his guard; indeed, this might be a test to see whether he were whole-souled or not.

'We did one,' he said. 'Pretty mild, but quite interesting.'

'What did you do?'

'Old Brangwyn recited poetry, and the girl and I pranced about. Nothing happened.'

'Nothing could happen under those circumstances. Would you like to see a ritual where something really happens?'

'Yes, rather; you bet I would.'

'Let me see, tonight's the 18th, and it's full moon on the 21st, that's Thursday; the paint on the cross ought to be dry by then if the girls get the first coat on today. We'll have the show on Friday night; you come round then, about eight, no, make it nine, in case Fouldes' train is late. And, look here, how'd you like to go on the cross?'

'What do you mean? Run crooked?'

'No, nothing of the sort. Someone has to stand in front of that cross looking as if he were crucified. You'd have nothing to say, just stand there and look pleasant.'

'Arm-aching job, isn't it, spread-eagled like that?'

'Not at all, your arms are suspended by webbing slings; it's perfectly comfortable. I've been on crosses for hours at a time, meditating.'

Murchison stared at him, thinking what a diabolical crucifix it must have been that was thus contrived, and amazed that any human imagination could have conceived such a bizarre blasphemy as the pot-bellied, bulldog-jowled, bottle-nosed mulatto on a cross.

'I don't mind as long as it's not too much like hard work. What am I supposed to be, stuck up there like a stoat on a barn-door?'

'You are supposed to be the Saviour of the World.'

'God help the world!'

Astley chuckled. 'You'll have a lovely time. We have the dance of the virgins round you.'

Murchison had no idea what kind of blasphemy was intended by the dance of the virgins, but he was pretty sure it was a misnomer.

'Does the Brangwyn girl take part in this show?' he enquired.

'You bet she does. In fact, she is the show. That's why we have to wait for Fouldes.'

'Is she willing?' Astley's face suddenly changed from its leering good humour:

'She will be by then!'

CHAPTER 24

As no food appeared to be forthcoming, Astley, like many heavy drinkers, being a very scanty feeder, Murchison, who was feeling pretty hungry by now, took his leave.

'Find your way out?' said Astley, who seemed to find it an effort to stir when once he got into his deep armchair.

Murchison nodded and took his departure.

No one was about in the dusty hall, and he marvelled at the thoughtlessness of Astley, who could give a perfect stranger the run of the house in this casual fashion.

He opened the hall door and stepped outside, nearly kicking over a bucket of dirty water as he did so, and there, at his feet, was Ursula Brangwyn on her knees, cleaning the steps.

'My God!' he said, incapable of any other form of greeting. If he had found her lying dead he could hardly have been more taken aback. The fastidious Miss Brangwyn cleaning Astley's filthy steps!

She scrambled to her feet when she saw him, and they stood facing each other.

'What are you doing here?' she asked in level tones, looking him straight in the face with angry eyes.

Murchison was nonplussed. He did not know what to say. If he confessed he was spying on Astley she might betray him and so put a stop to his activities. But if he did not, what conclusion would she draw, and what would her attitude be towards him?

She settled the matter for him.

'I have seen your letter to Astley,' she said.

'Have you?' said Murchison, whose wits worked slowly when it came to words.

'And I think you are a thorough cad to treat my brother like that when he trusts you.'

Murchison flushed scarlet at her accusation, but did not know what to reply. Was she speaking in good faith, or was she trying to draw him?

'May I ask you a question?' he said, turning the tables on her as the

203

best way of escape from his dilemma. 'What are you doing here yourself.'

'I will tell you what I am doing here, and then you can tell my brother. I have made up my mind. If you had been different it might have been different, but as it is, I am better off with Frank, and any way,' she said with a bitter laugh, 'I do not think there is very much to choose between you.'

'I would do anything in the world to get you out of here, Miss Brangwyn. Won't you come back to your brother with me? Come just as you are, and we'll get a taxi.'

Ursula laughed again. 'Are you going to fling me into a taxi as you did into the car at Llandudno?'

'No,' said Murchison quietly, 'I shall never make that mistake again.'

Ursula looked at him with a puzzled expression. 'What do you mean?'

'It would be no use. You would only run back again. If you will take one step, I will take you the rest of the way, but you have got to do that, this time.'

'Do you imagine I would take one single step towards you after the way you have behaved towards me?'

'God knows. Is it any use saying how frightfully sorry I am?'

'No, none. There are some things that cannot be apologized for.'

'Well, I suppose we'll have to leave it at that. But, if there is anything I can do to help you, I will, gladly.'

'The best thing you can do is to go away and leave me alone.'

'I shan't do that. While there's life there's hope. I shall hope to get you out of this place as long as you're above ground.'

'It's not the slightest use. I shan't come. I've made up my mind.'

'You may change it before Astley's finished with you. I shouldn't care to be in your shoes after the way he looked as he spoke of you.'

'What do you mean? Has he been discussing me with you?'

'Yes.'

'What did he say?'

'He told me what he intended to do with you. I asked him if you were willing. He said you would be by the time he wanted you.'

'What did he say he intended to do with me?'

'I gathered it was the Black Mass.'

'No, it isn't.'

'Well, it's as near as makes no matter.'

'Whatever it is, it is not your business.'

'It's any decent man's business when a thing like this is afoot!'

'What do you propose to do about it then?'

'Wait and see.'

'Mr. Murchison, you had better be careful what you do. I know of three men who died in this house.'

'Is that a threat?'

'No, it isn't. Honestly it isn't. It's a warning.'

'What do you want to warn me for? I thought you wanted to be rid of me?'

'So I do, but I don't want to see you murdered. Do go away and leave things alone. You can do no good. My mind is made up.'

'So is mine.'

'I don't think it is any use discussing it any longer. Good-bye.'

Ursula Brangwyn turned in at the door and slammed it behind her.

Murchison stood looking at the door for quite a long time. Then he looked down at the bucket at his feet.

'Good Lord, what a girl!' he said, shaking his head sadly. 'She's left her bucket outside!'

He picked up the bucket and the swab, and Astley's steps had such a sluicing as they had never had in their lives.

Ursula Brangwyn went into the inner hall, feeling as if her knees would give way under her. She was trembling all over with excitement after her passage of arms with Murchison. Why was it that he was always able to affect her so powerfully? She sat down in one of the broken-down chairs to recover. What an utter rotter the man was. How completely Alick had been taken in over him. It was too bad. First Monks, and now Murchison, and he had been so good to both of them. Alick would be heartbroken when he found out about Murchison, for he had thought such worlds of him. For some unaccountable reason Ursula Brangwyn found herself very near tears.

To pull herself together she went out to finish her task on the steps. Astley had set it her as a test, saying it would be very good for her, and she knew he was right, for anything more alien to her nature and experience than to clean steps could hardly be imagined.

She opened the door and stepped out, and was amazed to find that the bucket was empty, the steps all neatly cleaned, and the filthy swab wrung out and hung on the bucket. Who had done the job? It could only have been one person. Ursula looked down the street to see if he were still in sight, but he was not. Was the man who had cleaned those steps for her the same one who proposed to rob her brother who trusted him? Yet she could not get away from that letter. There, in Murchison's own handwriting, was the statement. She knew his handwriting, for she had seen his other letter.

She went slowly up to her room, locked the door to safeguard herself from intrusion, and sat down on the narrow camp-bed with its army blankets. Astley believed in training souls by driving them hard along the line of greatest resistance. If they yielded, the job was done. So Ursula Brangwyn had the worst room in the house, a mean slip of a room, cut off from a larger one by a very inadequate partition, and looking into the well of the house, so that it got neither light nor air.

But the upheaval of her disillusionment over Murchison had been so great that she neither knew nor cared what her surroundings were like.

She got her handbag out of a drawer and drew from it Murchison's letter, written on the notepaper of the little Welsh hotel, and read it through again. For the first time it struck her that Murchison's two letters, the one to Astley and the one to her, were quite different. She took out the one he had written to Astley, and that Astley, with his usual carelessness, had not troubled to recover from her after giving it to her to read, and re-read that also, her blood boiling at the references to herself.

What an extraordinary man Murchison was, an absolute Jekyll and Hyde. Which was the real man? The Murchison who had cleaned the steps for her, or the one who had written this revolting letter to Astley? It was curious, comparing the two letters, to see how the essential Murchison came out in the second and longer one. It was exactly the way he spoke; she could see the man rise before her as she read it, and her eyes filled with tears for some unknown reason. The first letter was not a bit like him. Or, rather, it was like him at his worst. Like he was the day they had had lunch together in her brother's absence, and she had thought him such an appalling lout. The letters were puzzling. The handwriting was obviously identical, and he spelt faithfully with one 'l' in both letters, and yet the letters did not seem as if they were from the same man. What was the answer to the riddle? Who had written the second letter if Murchison had not? For her whole case turned on that letter and his perfidy. And yet Murchison, when taxed with it, had not denied that it was his letter. She read it through again. The turn of a phrase struck her as familiar. Then the answer to the riddle leapt to her mind. The letter had been written by Murchison at Alick's dictation. This was Alick trying to express Murchison, and doing it successfully. The other letter was Murchison trying to express himself, and entirely failing to do so.

Then, if that were the case, her violent reaction had been entirely groundless. The man who had shown her such kindness and understanding when she had had her nerve-storms at the flat, and the man who had cleaned the steps for her, were one and the same person. And possibly the alleged rival, in whom Astley had rubbed her nose with great gusto, might be as fictitious as the rest of Murchison's pseudo-perfidy. Though Murchison had never betrayed his feelings by word or deed, there had been times when there had been a look in his eyes - but then one could never be quite sure. But if he had been fond of her, and had overheard her unlucky words in the cottage on the night of his arrival, they must have wounded him very deeply, and the quarrel at Llandudno had been the result.

But, in any case, her feelings had undergone a revulsion. That one kindly act in doing the steps for her, an act that one could not conceive any member of Astley's entourage as even imagining, had swung her completely round. The man who had done that was someone quite out of the ordinary. She decided that even if she and Murchison could not polarize, she would not remain any longer in Astley's sordid and dangerous house. She had been an utter fool ever to enter it again after her previous experiences there, which would not bear thinking of. She took off her borrowed overall, put on her hat, powdered her nose in front of the fly-blown glass, and went downstairs.

In the hall she met the butler, who, grinning widely, leant his back against the door. 'Will you kindly open the door?' she said. 'I am going out.'

Grinning still wider, he put out a hand like a Brandenburg ham and pushed her gently into the inner hall and shut the door behind her.

CHAPTER 25

Brangwyn had been afraid to leave the flat lest he should miss a phone call from Murchison, and time went slowly as he waited, feeling sure that Murchison must be hot on the trail or he would have turned up before that. He found it impossible to settle down to anything. It was long after lunch-time, and still no word from Ursula. Obviously Murchison's intuitions had been right, and she had either been decoyed away or had gone of her own accord.

One bright spot, however, stood out in the unsavoury and dangerous business - Murchison's confession of his feelings for Ursula. Brangwyn was satisfied that this was something much more than a mere stirring of the senses. Murchison, in his thwarted and solitary life, was quite accustomed to having his senses stirred, and took it for what it was worth - the voice of neither God nor the Devil, but a matter of endocrinology. The great bull was unfolding his wings at length, and Murchison knew the difference.

He wondered how the two of them would get on if they settled down together. Murchison was not an easy-tempered man, circumstances having taken their toll of him, and Ursula was fastidious and exacting. Murchison, he knew, would not be willing to live in his wife's pocket, nor to take money he had not earned. He himself would dearly have loved to keep them with him, to work and experiment together, but he doubted whether Murchison would consider this sufficiently like work to accept a salary for it.

His meditations were interrupted by the sound of a key in the door, and in walked the subject of them, and said without preamble,

'She's with Astley.' Brangwyn whistled. 'Have you seen her to speak to?'

'Yes. What do you think she was doing? Try and guess?'

'Something improbable, I take it. Saying her prayers?'

'No, washing the steps.'

'You don't say! That's one up for Astley! I really admire that man. There is nothing that could possibly do Ursula more good. I hope he makes her peel potatoes as well. But how did you find her, and what had she got to say for herself?'

'She seemed all right. But then, of course, she has only been there a few hours, and Fouldes isn't back from Wales yet. Astley is going to do the Black Mass or something of that sort with her as soon as Fouldes gets back, and what do you think? He has offered me a walk-on part!'

'What do you mean? Asked you to take part in the ceremonial? But you aren't initiated. There's a catch somewhere, Murchison.'

'That's what I thought. But it's too good an offer to refuse, don't you think? It's a chance in a million to get one's nose in there at the critical moment. I bet I wreck that Mass!'

'I bet you do, too. But you will have to watch your step. Astley's up to something.'

'I have got an idea what his opening gambit will be, but haven't a notion about his follow-up. I thought perhaps you might know, as it's your line of country.'

'What is his opening gambit?'

'All in due order. What do you suppose I have spent the morning doing?'

'I've no idea.'

'Carpentering with Astley in the basement. And what do you suppose we have been making?'

'Heaven alone knows. What could Astley want? A coffin?'

'No, a cross big enough to crucify a six-foot man on.'

'Good God, Murchison, what are they playing at?'

'I've no idea. Astley swore it was symbolical. You just stand in front of it with your arms suspended by slings from the cross-bar and pretend to be the Saviour of the World. My guess is that when you are safely spread-eagled on that cross, someone comes along quietly and tightens those slings so's you can't budge and then gives you beans. I made that cross of old floor-boards and strutted it up with iron stays. You could slaughter an ox on it.'

'I don't envy the person who is cast for the part of Saviour of the World.'

'Neither do I. And it's me.'

'You? Is Astley going to truss you up on that cross? He's up to something all right. But, Murchison, you're never going to walk into that trap, are you? I don't suppose he would go as far as murder, but there is not much else he would stick at. You are in for a pretty ghastly experience, once he gets you fastened to that cross.'

'I've been thinking things out, and I'll tell you what my idea is. I think your sister is safe enough till the day after tomorrow, when the ceremony comes off, because Astley will want her in good form for the ceremony. What's left of her after that ceremony won't bear thinking about, to judge from Astley's expression when he talked of her. My suggestion is that I turn up at the ceremony with a revolver in my pocket and you hang about outside, and if I don't come out at the appointed time you fetch the police.'

'You won't have any pockets to put revolvers in at that ceremony, my dear boy. You will be lucky if you have a loin-cloth.'

'Gosh, it's going to be a chilly job on that cross.'

'No, it won't. That will be the least of your worries. The temple will get as hot as a Turkish bath when the ceremony gets going.'

'Well, it's an odd do, anyway. I say, what else do you think Astley has got down in that basement? A stinking old billy-goat. Would you believe it? And didn't he hum! They couldn't have cleaned him out for donkey's years.'

'What a menage!' said Brangwyn. 'And there's my ultra-faddy sister in the midst of it! But, look here, my dear fellow, why should we wait till the day after tomorrow to do anything. If you can get access to Ursula quite freely, it is obvious no coercion is being used, and we might be able to persuade her to come away, or even take her by the arms and march her out.'

'Don't you believe it, Brangwyn. She was planted on those steps for me to fall over. Astley knows what he's about. And in any case, you couldn't budge her. I did my darnedest, and she rated me like a pickpocket for my pains. Astley had shown her the blessed letter we compounded, and she'd swallowed it, hook, line and sinker, and blackguarded me for having betrayed your trust. She'd have smacked my faced for two twos.'

'I'll bet she would! Do you remember what was in that letter, Murchison?'

'Yes, by gosh, there was a reference to her, wasn't there? I'd forgotten all about that. And I didn't attempt to explain that letter. I daren't, in case she'd rat on me. Oh, my Lord, what a mix-up! No wonder she wouldn't accept it when I tried to apologize. I say, sir, this has put the lid on. I'll get her out of Astley's dive if I die in the attempt, but I'll have to clear out afterwards.'

'Don't let us cross our bridges before we come to them. I am inclined to agree with you; she is safe enough till they start the Mass, and then,

God help her. But we can't do anything until the little fool learns her lesson, and sometimes, Murchison, I can't help feeling she would deserve all she got if we let her go through with it.'

'I dunno about that, sir. She's probably been told a pack of lies. She can't be expected to realize what she's up against.'

'When I think of you going on that cross, Murchison, to save that little idiot from the results of her folly -'

'I don't mind, sir. It will be rather a lark.'

'I am not so sure of that, my boy. Astley is a dangerous brute, and as cruel as a fiend. He knows we won't want the publicity of a prosecution because of Ursula's reputation. I am certain you are in for a pretty painful experience, and I only hope you will take no permanent harm.'

Time passed slowly for the two men at the flat until the day of Ursula's ordeal came round. Brangwyn took Murchison down to Scotland Yard, and they had a long talk with a man high up, to whom Brangwyn's connections gave him access. Murchison saw the outside of a stout folder, held together by a strap to keep it from bursting, which contained Astley's record in the files of the CID, and in response to a telephone call they sent over another, nearly as stout, from Scotland house, which contained an account of his doings in subversive politics.

'Have you never had the chap under lock and key?' he asked.

'Never,' was the answer. 'The worse the criminal, the harder he is to catch. You may rest assured we shall leave no stone unturned if you call us in; but I quite understand that you do not want any publicity for Miss Brangwyn's sake, and, of course, we have to work in the full glare of publicity.'

The time passed at length, however, to Brangwyn's great relief, for he was exceedingly anxious about his sister, in spite of Murchison's belief that she would be immune till the ceremony started; for he knew a great deal about the possibilities of subtle evil in that terrible house of which Murchison had no suspicion.

The two men walked across the murky district behind Euston together. Brangwyn wished to see Murchison enter the house so that he could, if necessary, swear to his presence there. It was a silent walk. Murchison was trying to visualize all possible contingencies and provide against them, and Brangwyn was much more anxious than he cared to admit, and was debating whether he ought not, after all, to withdraw his consent to his companion's scheme for permitting himself to be fastened helpless to the cross of sacrifice, and insist on the police being invoked forthwith, although he knew only too well that Ursula would refuse to be rescued or interfered with until she had learnt for herself what the actualities of the Black Mass were, and then, alas, it might be too late to help her. Brangwyn was not so old fashioned as to think that a single experience of the seamy side of life could ruin a woman; but the kind of evil that is wrought with ritual disintegrates character in a peculiar way, and in Ursula's already highly nervous state the result was not unlikely to be definite mental unbalance.

At the corner of Astley's road they parted, for they did not wish any of Astley's hangers-on to see them approaching the house together. It was arranged that if Murchison did not return to the flat by three o'clock in the morning, it was to be concluded that there had been foul play, and Brangwyn had a letter in his pocket to that effect. It was their intention, however, to get Ursula out without invoking the police if possible, in order to avoid the disgrace of the publicity, for there could be no question but that Astley, cornered, would be an exceedingly ugly customer. Brangwyn confirmed Ursula's statement concerning three men who were believed to have met their deaths at Astley's hands; but in each case their bodies had been found in smashed up motor-cars in one or another of the home counties, and it was impossible to say whether the head injuries that had caused their deaths had been inflicted at the time of the smash, or whether a dead body had been in the car when it was despatched to destruction from the top of a steep hill. All that was known was that three associates of Astley's, after a quarrel, had died in the same manner, and, although there was no evidence to go to a jury, the finger of suspicion pointed at him uncompromisingly.

Murchison, with no other weapon in his pocket than a small electric torch, was admitted into the dingy black house by the grinning black butler, who conducted him downstairs to the depths with such expedition that he suspected it was desired that his presence in the house should not be known to certain of its inmates. The butler took him straight into the underground temple. It was brightly lit with electric light, and pictures and statues were displayed about it of a nature that brought Murchison up all standing with a gasp, which caused the butler to go off in a fit of giggles. From the chairs ranged round the walls Murchison gathered that an audience of no inconsiderable dimensions was expected, but at present the room, though all lit up and heated almost to suffocation by a powerful anthracite stove, was empty, save for the billy-goat, tied up in a corner, looking like a dilapidated hearthrug with the evil eye, and smelling to high heaven.

Murchison and his escort crossed the big room and entered the lumber-room behind the platform, where the carpentering had been done.

'You will be kind enough, suh, to get ondressed and put this on,' said the butler holding out a brief length of roller-towelling. Murchison began to strip without protest, and the butler, seeing that he had a willing victim, left him to his own devices while he went to tend the stove. Murchison availed himself of the opportunity to slip his electric torch into the towel twisted about his middle, and added to it, as an afterthought, a stout chisel, a formidable weapon in a ruthless hand. He wished he had had his trench-coat, which he had left in the hall, to use as a dressing-gown while waiting. He strolled back into the temple to stand by the stove and keep warm, using his eyes diligently. He observed that a single big master-switch controlled all the small switches on the switchboard near the door, so it was evidently the practice to switch all the lights off suddenly at certain points in the ceremonies. If this happened, all sorts of chances would occur, and he hoped and prayed that this was one of the ceremonies in which it was done.

At that moment Astley entered, and the billy-goat suddenly became stricken with panic fear, backing away to the length of its rope and bleating piteously. Astley paid not the faintest attention to it, but came hastily over to Murchison.

'I say, old chap, do you mind waiting in the workshop?'

'Not if you'll lend me a dressing-gown, but it's a bit chilly in there with nothing on.'

'Here, take this.' Astley hastily flung over his bare shoulders a voluminous black velvet cape that lay over the arm of a kind of throne on the platform at the opposite end to the great cross, which was almost invisible against its black velvet background now that it was painted.

Astley pushed Murchison into the lumber-room in a great hurry and shut the door behind him. Obviously his presence was to be kept a secret for some reason or other.

He took advantage of being unobserved to take a thorough inventory of his surroundings. He opened the door into the area, to make sure that its hinges worked easily and silently; and, discovering among the tools on the bench a stout iron bar that might have been a very large case-opener, but looked suspiciously like a burglar's jemmy, he put it outside the door. Then he sat down on an empty box and lit a cigarette, a grotesque figure in his black velvet cloak, naked except for a loin-cloth, with his shock of fair hair, as always, standing up in all directions, and, as always, in want of cutting.

213

He guessed by the sound of voices and the scrape of chairs that the audience was beginning to arrive. Then the negro butler put his bullet head round the corner and beckoned, and shedding his cloak, Murchison stepped out into the brilliantly lighted room where the ceremony was to take place, and heard a gasp of astonishment go up from the assembled audience.

He was certainly a startling figure with his milk-white skin, inherited from his Norse ancestors, his ruddy face, heavily muscled limbs and shock of fair hair like a sun-god's halo.

'You stand here, suh,' said the butler, backing him up to the cross, beside which stood Monks of the book-shop, got up in a kind of verger's soutane, who exchanged grins with him. In fact, both Monks and the butler were grinning altogether too much for his liking.

'Put your 'ands through the loops, sir,' said Monks.

Murchison did as he was bid, slipping his wrists into stout webbing loops that hung from the ends of the cross-bar, and in an instant there was a jerk, and the butler and Monks had pulled those loops tight and buckled them, and added a strap round his ankles as well.

'Here, steady on,' he said, 'that's too tight to be comfortable.'

But Monks and the butler had already quitted the platform, and left him alone to face the staring room.

There were, perhaps, forty persons present, all clad in flowing robes of various primary colours, making a very gay assembly, and all masked, so it was only by the feet of the front row that he could tell who were the men and who were the women, and he judged that they were fairly evenly divided. Then an organ, and quite a good one, began to play, and in came a procession, consisting of Astley, Ursula, Fouldes, a couple of strapping young fellows armed with swords, and the butler and the unhappy goat bringing up the rear.

Astley was a sight for the gods, all in cloth of gold and crimson, with a towering head-dress of scarlet feathers, not unlike a Red Indian Chief. Ursula wore a white velvet cloak with a cowl, that enveloped her from head to heel; the cowl was drawn over her head, hiding her face, all except her small pointed chin, and from underneath the robe gleamed the shimmer of a silver tunic as she moved. Fouldes also wore a silver tunic, but a black cloak. The two young men were respectively in black and white, and the billy-goat wore his own dingy fur.

Astley took his seat on the throne on the far platform, the two young men behind him. Fouldes faced the billy-goat across the open space in the centre of the room, and Ursula came forward to the table-tomb that stood almost at the foot of the cross. She put her foot on a stool at the side of it, the butler gave her a hand, and she sprang up on to the altar and lay down, her feet within a yard of Murchison's own feet. The white velvet cowl encircled her head, and she lay with her eyes closed, like one dead. Murchison stared at her, thinking he had never seen any living being quite so white.

Astley called his temple to order with a resounding rap of a gavel, and everyone sat up straight and stopped whispering. But across the sacred silence cut a very secular voice.

'Excuse me, sir, before you start, could I have the straps slacked off. They are uncomfortably tight.'

A murmur of shocked surprise ran through the audience. Astley paused, evidently taken aback, and wondering how he could best restore the atmosphere of religious awe that had been shattered by the matter-of-fact Murchison.

'That' - he replied in portentous tones - 'is one of the tests of the Degree. You are bound upon the Cross of Suffering as the Saviour of the World, and it is by your sweat of agony that power is exuded for the work of the rite we are about to perform.'

He rose to his feet, and with slow pacing steps came sweeping across the hall in his flowing robes. Ursula lifted her head from her cowl and stared at Murchison with startled eyes, an expression of horror gradually growing in them as the significance of the scene dawned on her.

Astley mounted the platform at the foot of the cross, went round behind Murchison and encircled his throat with his hands. Murchison thought he was going to be strangled, and his startled eyes met Ursula's. She read in them his fear, and half rose on her elbow as if to protest.

But Astley did nothing so crude as to exert pressure on Murchison's windpipe. His thumbs felt for the two spots in the neck where the carotids cross a muscle, and he pressed there with a ju-jitsu grip. Murchison saw the room swirl and go dark as the blood supply to the brain was cut off, and his head fell forward on to his chest and his whole figure sagged down, hanging by the arms in a dead faint, the true image of the Crucified One. Astley stepped back and surveyed his handiwork with the satisfaction of an artist, and then swept back with stately pace to his throne. The organ struck up at a sign of his hand, and the ritual began.

One by one he picked up his officers with question and answer, even the miserable billy-goat replying to his cue with a despairing bleat as the butler stuck a pin into him. Ursula lay motionless, staring at Murchison as he hung limply from the cross, his face ashen-grey, his hands nearly black.

Fortunately his faint did not last long, the blood supply speedily re-establishing itself as soon as the pressure of Astley's thumbs was removed. He lifted his head, and stared dazedly about him, unable to realize where he was or what had been done to him. The intolerable strain on his arms made itself felt, and he struggled to get upright and relieve it. But his feet had slipped through their strap during his faint, and he could not get his balance. It was an ugly sight as he struggled on the cross, and the audience held its breath, spell-bound, watching it, stirred to God knows what intensity of decadent emotion by the spectacle.

At length he got on to his feet and heaved a sigh of relief, met Ursula's horrified eyes and half smiled at her. Then he turned his attention to the ritual, watching for anything that should give him a cue. Astley was chanting translations from some of the more recondite Greek poets - the passages that are not included in the versions prepared for the use of schools. Murchison glanced down, and saw that Ursula was still gazing at him with a fixed intensity.

The ritual went on, chant and response and intoning making an impressive ceremony. Monks marched round with a censer that smoked like a factory chimney and smelt worse than the billy-goat. Astley waved his arms and boomed at intervals. Murchison leant back against the cross and watched it all.

And as he stood extended on the black Cross of Sacrifice watching it all, a strange feeling began to steal over him. Everything became unreal on the physical plane and real in some other dimension, and he himself, stretched on that cross, willingly suffering for the sake of another who despised and rejected him, felt himself actually becoming a saviour by the power of sacrifice and vicarious suffering, and for the first time he had a glimpse of the significance of the Christian doctrine. What his brother had been unable to accomplish in his comfortable and aesthetic church, Astley accomplished without meaning to in a rite intended to invoke all evil and stimulate every depraved emotion.

Then the alleged virgins began to dance in diaphanous draperies, and Murchison was devoutly thankful that Ursula had her back to the performance.

Finally, Astley struck his pedestal a resounding crash, the organ went off full blast, all the lights went out, and Murchison knew they had got to business at last, and tensed himself for whatever might be forthcoming.

The thing that was immediately forthcoming startled him so that he nearly cried out, for it was a small cold hand on his bare chest, and a voice that whispered, 'It's me, it's Ursula!'

The hand ran down his arm to the strap that held it, and after a moment's struggle the buckle was cast loose and the arm dropped down, drawing a gasp of agony from him in the pain of the bending. In another second the other arm was also set free, and, bending down, she unstrapped his feet. He put a numbed arm round her shoulder, and half dragging her, half supported by her, got behind the draperies at the back of the platform and out into the workshop. She switched on the light, as could safely be done behind these draperies, and they stared at each other silently. Ursula had left her cloak behind her, and was clad only in a straight silver tunic held round the breast by a band, her feet bare.

'Come on, quick!' he said, seizing her by the wrist with one hand and picking up the cloak Astley had wrapped about him with the other. He threw the cloak over her shoulders, opened the door leading into the area, thrust her through it, switched off the light, and followed her, after pulling the lumber back into position so as to block the door and make it look as if nothing had been disturbed. Then, electric torch in hand, he guided her up the steps that led to the trapdoor.

'Hold this, will you?' he said, thrusting the torch into her hand; she took it, and he put his hands against the trapdoor and pushed. But nothing happened save a trickle of coal-dust through the cracks and a sound of crunching. The trapdoor would not budge. It was held down by a weight too great for his strength to move, strain as he would, and it dawned on him that a load of coal must have come into the empty cellar since his last visit, and that a ton weight probably rested upon the trapdoor.

He turned a horrified face towards Ursula.

'Stymied!' he said.

At that moment they heard noises from the carpenter's shop which sounded as if someone were pulling down piles of lumber in the search for them. They listened, holding their breath, till the sounds died away and the light disappeared from the cracks of the door.

'What are we going to do?' whispered Ursula.

'Sit here and wait, and stick it as best we can till your brother comes.'

'Does my brother know you are here?'

'Yes, that's all right, don't you worry about that. He goes for the police if I'm not back by three.'

'What time is it now?'

'Goodness knows. Getting on for eleven, I should think. We'd better sit down and make the best of it.'

They sat down in the angle of the area steps so as to have the wall to lean their backs against. Ursula, drawing the thick black velvet cloak around her for what warmth she could get, accidentally brushed Murchison's bare back with her wrist.

'Good gracious!' she said, 'you've got nothing on!'

'Yes I have. I've got half a yard of roller-towelling.'

'Oh, but you can't sit like that for three or four hours. Here, have half my cape.'

He felt a fold of velvet come over his shoulder and Ursula snuggle up against him, but he made no attempt to draw the cloak round him, but left it hanging loose, very draughty for both of them.

'I want to say something,' came the girl's voice in the dark.

'Yes?'

'I'm awfully sorry I was so rotten to you the other morning.'

'Perhaps you realize now that I did not betray your brother?'

'Yes, of course I do. But why didn't you explain?'

'I was afraid you might give me away.'

'I shouldn't have.'

'How was I to know that?'

'Will you forgive me?'

'What for?'

'Everything. I have been rotten to you, and you've been simply wonderful to me.'

'That's all right. I'm glad if I've been able to help you.'

'But do you really forgive me for - for everything?'

'There's nothing to forgive that I know of. I don't bear any ill-will, and never did. I'm sorry I lost my temper that day in the car, and if you'll accept my apologies for that, we'll call it square.'

'I believe I owe you a great deal more than my life tonight.'

'You had better wait a bit before you return thanks for that. I haven't got you out of this yet. We are still sitting on Astley's area steps, quite as likely to die of pneumonia as of murder.'

At that moment rays of light burst through the cracks of the door leading into the lumber-room, and they knew that the search was not yet over. They heard a sound of lumber being shifted away from the door.

'We have got to face this,' said Murchison. 'It is no good taking it lying down. I guess I can bluff him. He won't dare murder two of us together.'

He rose, an electric torch in one hand and the iron bar in the other, went forward to the door, banged on it with the bar, and called in a loud voice:

'Hullo, Astley, looking for us?'

'Hullo, yourself!' returned Astley, with a most deceptive affability. 'Having a Mass of the Bull on your own out there?'

'What's the next item on the programme?'

'I thought of inviting you to come in and finish the Mass.'

'Supposing we won't?'

'You soon will when you get a sulphur candle lit under you.'

'Suppose I show fight?'

'You'll get the worst of it.'

'How about the summons for assault next morning?'

'There won't be any summons for assault.'

'Why not?'

'Because there will be no one to bring it.'

'Looks to me as if someone were going to get murdered.'

'I have envisaged that possibility.'

'Are you quite sure we are both thinking of the same person?'

'Who may you be thinking of?'

'I am thinking of the first person who comes through this door.'

'What is going to happen to him?'

'He will get a tap on the head with an iron bar. And I shall hit to kill, Astley. I know three men have died in this house, and if you corner me I shall fight to a finish.'

'We shan't trouble to corner you, we shall leave you there. You won't last long in this weather.'

'I shall last till the police arrive.'

'And when do you expect that to be?'

'Three a.m.'

'And how can you be so precise about time?'

'Because that is the arrangement with Scotland Yard.'

There was a dead silence in the lumber-room, and a muttered consultation could be heard.

'I am not sure that I believe that yarn, Murchison.'

'Please yourself about that.'

'We shall simply deny that you have ever been here, and I don't suppose you have advertised your comings and goings.'

'Brangwyn walked with me to the end of the road and saw me enter the door.'

'Do you expect us to believe that?'

'Please yourself once again.'

'What do you suppose Brangwyn would say if he saw a certain letter I had from you?'

'He wrote it.'

'What?'

'Well, I wrote it at his dictation.'

There was another dead silence from the other side of the door, not even enlivened by a whispered consultation.

'Look here, Murchison, if we let you and the girl go, will you keep your mouth shut?'

'Sure.'

'Well, if you open yours, I shall open mine, and to some purpose too; she won't dare show her nose in decent society again.'

'If you open your mouth, Astley, I'll lay for you till I catch you, and I'll disable you for life.'

'Well, what about it? Like a free pass to go quietly?'

'Right you are. But I say, Astley?'

'Yes?'

'If you murder one, you'll have to murder both, you know, and I've already been down to Scotland Yard with Brangwyn to discuss this stunt, and they have a letter from me to say I'm here.'

'All right, don't worry. I don't want the trouble of disposing of your corpses. It isn't worth it. *I'm* not in love with Ursula.'

The door swung wide open and a flood of light poured into the draughty darkness of the area.

'Come on, Miss Brangwyn,' said Murchison, not daring to turn round.

He felt Ursula's hand clutch his, and advanced through the low doorway, iron bar at the ready, drawing her after him.

Before him were Astley, the butler, Monks and the two young men in black and white, complete with swords, and in the hands of the butler was an iron bar, the fellow to Murchison's.

'You had better get some clothes on,' said Astley amiably. 'We don't want the house disgraced.'

'No damn fear. Think I want to be scragged while I'm half in and half out of my trousers?'

'Please yourself. Only don't say you come from here.'

'All I want is a taxi, and you can chuck my duds into it. If anyone comes near me, I'll brain him.'

He pointed towards the door.

'You go first, all of you,' he said.

'Anything to oblige. Come along, boys,' said Astley, who knew how to lose gracefully. And in any case he did not greatly care, not being, as he said, enamoured of Miss Brangwyn. Fouldes could kick up a row if he liked. He led the way towards the door, the others trooping after him.

'I'll lead, I think, in case of trouble,' said Murchison, motioning to Ursula to follow him.

They came out into the now empty temple, and the first person they came face to face with was Fouldes, now back in the dinner jacket of civilization. Involuntarily Ursula drew close to Murchison's side. Fouldes saw the movement, and for a long moment he stared at the pair of them without speaking, and then, God knows what demons of drink or drugs possessing him, struck Murchison full in the face. Murchison sprang back, iron bar upraised. Luckily some streak of sanity prevailed, and he dropped the bar and came for Fouldes with his bare hands. They were much of a height, but Murchison was the heavier and the hardier man. The result was a foregone conclusion. Fouldes was exceedingly quick and active, Murchison slower because of his weight and type, but he had the advantage of being stripped, against the man in a dress-shirt. It was not so much a fight as a chase. Fouldes made a dash for the door, but Murchison headed him off. They dodged round the altar on which Ursula had lain, and Murchison nearly had him. Murchison was fighting mad in one of his berserk rages; his eyes had that strange, shining, blue, insane look of the Norseman in a tantrum, and Fouldes sincerely believed that he would die if Murchison laid hands on him, and the fear lent wings to his feet. Ursula, watching the man she had once loved and feared being chased like a frightened hen, felt his influence over her break once and for all.

It was obvious that Fouldes was faster than Murchison, and could turn in a shorter space, and the clutter of furniture in the room was to his advantage; but it was equally evident that Fouldes was panting and straining, whereas the deep-chested, heavily-muscled Murchison was going like a steam-engine; it was only a matter of time till he ran the other man down; it was impossible for Fouldes to get out through the door, as Astley and his party blocked it, thoroughly enjoying the fun and showing no signs of assisting him.

Finally, the end came when Fouldes made a bolt across an open space, tried to turn, and ran smack into Murchison. In a second his head was in chancery under Murchison's arm, and Murchison was pounding his face to pulp. He twisted round, got hold of the fold of skin under

221

Murchison's ribs, and made his teeth meet in it. Murchison gave a snarl of rage, picked him up, raised him at arm's length above his head, and flung him from him with all his strength. He hit one of Astley's homemade pillars, and knocked it flying.

'My God!' said Astley, as Fouldes lay in a crumpled heap almost at his feet, blood pouring from a nasty scalp wound. 'We don't want any more corpses here. We've had too many already.'

Murchison blinked, and stared round him with the look of one suddenly wakened from sleep. Astley bent down and examined the unconscious man, who stirred and groaned.

'Ribs gone, and badly concussed. I thought you'd broken his spine! Look at my pillar! The bally house will come down. Here, you, get out of this. We've had enough of you.'

'All right. Lend me that cloak.'

'Take it. Take anything. Only go.'

Murchison wrapped about him the white velvet cloak Ursula had worn. He did not bother with his iron bar, nor to guard against possible attack from the rear. All the fight had gone out of everybody. The butler phoned for a taxi from one of the big stations; Murchison and Ursula, looking like the fag-end of a very rowdy fancy-dress ball, got into it; Astley flung Murchison's clothes in after them, and somebody rushed up with Ursula's frock and handbag, and flung those in too.

The drive home was silent. Ursula glanced up shyly at her companion once or twice, but he only presented to her a grim profile, and stared steadily out of the window.

CHAPTER 26

Brangwyn, watching the clock anxiously as the hands crept towards two, heaved a sigh of relief as he heard a key inserted in the lock; the door opened, and in came Ursula and Murchison. Ursula went up to her brother without a word and put her arms round his neck and hid her face on his shoulder. He put his arm round her and patted her back, and then held out his hand to Murchison. They exchanged a grip in a silence that was more eloquent than many words. Then Murchison turned and went off to his own quarters, leaving Brangwyn alone with his sister.

Murchison arrived down at breakfast next morning looking rather subdued and white.

'How's Miss Brangwyn?' he enquired, seeing that the table was only laid for two.

'Pretty bad. I was up with her all night. At seven this morning I sent for a doctor, and he gave her an injection of morphia and took her off to a nursing-home.'

Murchison made no comment, but sat staring at the table in silence. Finally he said:

'Perhaps it's just as well.'

'What do you mean?'

'I'd like to get off without seeing her again, if you don't mind, sir'

'What do you mean, Murchison? You are not going to leave us, are you?'

'I think I'd better. I've had as much as I can stick!'

'But, my dear fellow, I don't want to lose you. Even if you and Ursula can't hit it off, I should like you to remain on as my secretary.'

'That's asking a bit too much, sir. This business has gone pretty deep with me, and I couldn't stand it.'

'Are you sure you know where you stand with Ursula?'

'I know where I get off, sir, and that is much more to the point.'

'I'm frightfully sorry about it, my dear boy. This is a bitter disappointment to me, but I won't press you to stay if you don't feel you can. What do you want to do?'

'I'll go round to an employment agency and put my name down, and see what turns up. I suppose Miss Brangwyn will be at the nursing-home for a few days?'

'Certainly that. Don't rush your choice. You are due for a month's wages from me in any case.'

'Thanks very much, sir. I don't want to land myself out of a job. I've had too much of that sort of thing.'

It was with a heavy heart he climbed the stairs of a very superior employment agency in Piccadilly to which Brangwyn had sent him with a letter of introduction. But he found it was a very different matter applying for a post in his good clothes and with his first-class reference to what it had been as a down-and-out. The clerk was almost cordial.

'I think we can fit you up with what you want, if you are willing to go abroad?'

'Delighted! Nothing I should like better. Where to, and when?'

'Egypt, in about a month's time!'

'Well, I should have like to have gone sooner, but I can hang on till then if it's worth it.'

'Very good. You go round to the Savoy and see Mr. Agassiz. He's a Heinz; do you mind that?'

'What in the world's a Heinz?'

'A mongrel Levantine from Alexandria, the world's very worst. We call 'em Heinzes because fifty-seven varieties have gone to the making of 'em, see? This fellow is as rich as Croesus, and he's apparently been having trouble with his poor relations and he wants someone as a kind of boydguard-cum-secretary.'

'Sounds all right. I ought to be able to put the fear of God into a Heinz's poor relations.'

'Very good. Take this card and go and see him, and let us know if you get the job.'

Murchison took a bus to the Savoy and interviewed a small, skinny, sallow-cheeked little man, with eyes like black currants and greasy ringlets all over his head, who scuttled about the expensive suite like a hen in traffic all the time he was talking, too nervous to sit down.

He jibbed at the five pounds a week Murchison boldly asked for, but finally closed at four when he heard that Murchison was a good revolver shot. He would not require his new servitor till he sailed for Alexandria in a month's time, and he absolutely declined to contribute a halfpenny towards his support during the interregnum. He could take it or leave it.

Murchison took it. He still had the balance of Brangwyn's cheque in hand. The Heinz spun like a Japanese waltzing mouse as he shooed Murchison out of the suite, and he heard the door being locked behind him.

'You've got a beauty, sir!' whispered a waiter in passing.

Murchison returned to the flat, and told Brangwyn of his doings.

'I am glad you are fixed up, my lad, though I shall be very sorry to lose you. But if you don't like your Heinz, and he does not sound attractive, you can always come back to me.'

They ate their lunch in silence. Murchison seemed depressed and dispirited in a way that Brangwyn had never seen him before. He had often seen Murchison sullen and brooding, or resentful and up against life, but he had never seen him with all the kick gone out of him like this.

He had thought, from Murchison's attitude, that he must have definitely received his *congé* from Ursula; but when he had visited her during the morning, and his arrival had roused her momentarily from her drugged daze, the words that came from her were to ask for Murchison, and to mutter that he had nearly died on the cross.

After the breakfast conversation with Murchison he had resigned himself to the disappointment of his hopes and accepted his magical experiment as a failure. But now he was not so sure. Murchison had frankly admitted he had come to care for Ursula, and at the present moment, brooding over his coffee, looked about as thoroughly broken-hearted as a man could look; and the one thing Ursula had wanted to know in her semi delirium was whether Murchison was all right, and, reassured, had become quiet and dropped off to sleep. Actions speak louder than words, thought Brangwyn, trained to watch the language of unconscious gesture.

And as he watched Murchison staring into space with miserable eyes, oblivious of his companion, a deep-laid plot began to hatch in his mind.

'Murchison,' he said, 'if you haven't got to go to your Heinz for a month, I wonder whether you would do a job for me?'

'Yes, rather, sir. What is it?'

'I shall have to give up the cottage in Wales. It is far better that Ursula should not go back there after all that has happened. It will be full of painful memories for her. I want to find another place as a retreat. Do you think you could hunt about and find one for me? I am a wretched hand at house-hunting.'

'Rather, sir. I'd love to do it. What part of the country are you thinking of'

'I had thought of the East Coast, up Yorkshire way.'

'That's my native heath. I'll soon hunt you up something.'

'Splendid. Go ahead. I want to have somewhere to take Ursula when she comes out of the nursing-home. Can you catch the afternoon mail-train for Llandudno junction and pick up the car? You will want it for this job.'

'Yes, easy. I'll slam a few things into a suitcase and get off. Give me some particulars of the sort of thing you want, and the price you are prepared to go to.'

It was a tremendous relief to have something to do, and especially something to do that should take him about the country in the open air. Brangwyn could not possibly have found a better medicine for his sore soul.

Murchison enjoyed the amenities of a first-class smoker to Llandudno junction (Brangwyn wouldn't let him go third), and then revelled in the driving of a six-cylindered thoroughbred cross-country to the East Coast, even though much of the route lay through the Black Country.

Finally he crossed the Humber and came into his own land. It was late afternoon as he approached the sea. He was making for a little village that had been the scene of summer holidays during his childhood. There were people about there who might remember him as a small boy in a sailor-suit, getting into every imaginable kind of mischief. Moreover, his name was one to conjure with in that district, for his forbears had owned it for many square miles. His objective was a farmhouse, about a mile from the village, right down on the beach among sandy dunes, where a stream that came from the moors ran out to the sea. It was here that they had always stayed, his father and mother and himself and an old Nanny; for his brother was a young man at the University by then, and despised holidays at a fishing village.

He planned to go and see the old couple who owned the farm. They would know every house in the neighbourhood that was to let. They must be getting on by now, for they had seemed old when he was a small boy; but then everybody who has a beard seems old to a child, and the old man was bearded like a pard, and the old lady, too, for that matter.

He passed through the village, and turned the car off the main road on to a rutted track, much overgrown. It was little more than a path, and he had to push the car through with some anxiety as to Brangwyn's varnish. Curious how things shrink from what you remember them to be as a kid. He had thought it a decent road down to the farm.

Finally he pushed through a small wood of wind-blown firs and came out into the farmyard itself. Curious, he thought, that no dog gave warning of his approach, for the door stood hospitably open. But as he drew up to it he saw the reason. The curtainless windows stared blank as the eyes of a dead man. The house was empty and deserted, and the broken door swung idly in the wind.

Murchison felt as if the bottom had dropped out of the universe. This was the last straw, everything had gone from him.

The comfortable farm and the kindly old couple were the one link he had with happier days, and now that was broken. The empty house affected him out of all proportion to its practical significance. The words ran in his head of a text from which his brother had preached a sermon of entirely different import - 'He came to His own, and His own received Him not.'

Secure in the solitude of the deserted homestead, Murchison folded his arms on the steering-wheel and laid his head on them.

When at length he raised his head, a red-gold beam of the setting sun had penetrated a rift in the cloud-bank to the west and lit up the stained whitewash of the old walls and set the windows ablaze. The place seemed alive again for the moment, as if firelight were shining out of the windows, as he had seen it shine out of the windows of Ursula's mountain cottage as he had approached it, dead-beat, but full of strange hopes, only to hear the casual words that had revealed to him his real position.

And with the memory there flashed into his mind a sudden idea that perhaps the farm itself might suit Brangwyn for his place of secret retreat, and his depression lifted as suddenly as the beam of the setting sun had struck through the rift in the clouds. With a new eagerness he got out of the car and entered the open door. The setting sun shone straight in at the windows, filling the place with temporary cheer. The floor was deep in drilling leaves and the droppings of roosting birds, but it was dry and weather tight. The big kitchen would do for Brangwyn's living-room; the sacred parlour for his dining-room; and the big scullery out at the rear for his kitchen. An active wench on a cycle would make nothing of the mile from the village.

Murchison made his way back to the village, and received a warm welcome at the local pub when he made himself known. The landlady being a daughter of the old couple, whose pigtail he had often pulled in the days of his youth; the farm was her brother's property, brother produced forthwith, and a more than modest price demanded for the farm and the few acres immediately surrounding it that gave it complete seclusion with their wind-swept woods and barren dunes. The land was useless for farming, and no one wanted it.

Murchison went over to the post office, put through a trunk call to the flat, and announced his find to Brangwyn, to be received with acclamation.

'It sounds absolutely right to me, provided you can vouch for the water supply. Close with it at once, and put the decorators in. I want it ready at the earliest possible moment to take Ursula to. She is jabbing at the nursing-home.'

'How is she?'

'Better than she was, but far from right. She can get no natural sleep, and with her nervous temperament the doctors are very shy of drugs, so we are between the devil and the deep sea.'

Murchison slept at the pub, and next morning accompanied the landlady's brother to the local solicitor, and the conveyancing of the farm to Brangwyn was put in hand. The brother himself proved to be the local handyman, decorator, maker of hen-coops, and undertaker, so down they went to the house and looked over it with a view to repairs. Practically none were needed, save to the door, that had apparently been forced by tramps or trippers.

Paint, whitewash and distemper were the chief requirements, so the job did not promise to be a big one, or a prolonged one.

Murchison was good at staff-work, and the farmhouse was taking shape rapidly. At the end of the week he was able to move in and camp out in it. The days slid by unnoticed, and almost every day there was a letter from Miss Brangwyn containing instructions and little personal friendly touches, and she always signed them 'Ursula', so that he came to the conclusion that Christian names were cheap in the set in which she moved. He watched the post for those letters, and yet they only kept open the wound that he wished would start to heal.

While waiting for the varnish on the floors to dry, pending the arrival of the furniture, Murchison got to work on what had been the garden, and unearthed the precious remains of certain pink and white moss-rose bushes beside the gate. And there was a sweet-briar under the window of the old kitchen, that was now the living-room; and lad's-love beside the door. Then he raided a neighbouring wood for primrose roots, already in flower, and lined the path to the gate with them. An enormous van with a trailer arrived, barging its way as best it might down the overgrown lane, and Murchison spent a strenuous day helping to lift furniture into its appointed place, as sketched on a plan by Miss Brangwyn.

Altogether, he was thoroughly enjoying himself, and what with the strong sea air and active work had been able to push his worries to the back of his mind. The Heinz seemed no more than a bad dream, fading from memory, and he had half forgotten that the sands were running low of the month's notice he was working out with Brangwyn. He seemed to have struck his roots into the old place with every spadeful of earth he turned, and ever slap of whitewash he laid on the walls.

Then there came disillusionment. The lorry from the railway station came lumbering down the lane and deposited a large packing-case in front of the door. Murchison, left alone by the departure of undertaker-decorator at the end of his job, lugged it into the living-room, which now had its curtains up, and prised it open, pulled off the covering newspapers, and discovered that it contained all Ursula Brangwyn's things from the cottage upon the flank of Snowdon. Here were books, pictures, ornaments, rugs, cushions - all the things he had seen about her in that room that had seemed so full of her personality, and in which he had heard the fatal words spoken that had shattered his dream. Here was the very rug that he had slept under that night on the settle. Out of a book fell snapshots of herself and Brangwyn, taken in front of the cottage. He picked them up and studied them. Here was a laughing Ursula, a very different person to the one he had known. Evidently the snapshot had been taken before her trouble came upon her. He held the little photo in his big hands and studied it closely. He wondered what Ursula Brangwyn could be like to those she cared for. She looked a really jolly girl here, not in the least die-away and supercilious. The eyes of the photo looked straight out at him, and he stared back at them.

'My God!' he said, 'this won't do!' and hastily thrust the photos back into the book they had come from, and proceeded to get on with the unpacking.

Presently he came to a layer of china, and found that Ursula's garments had been used as packing for it. Here was her rose-pink dressing-gown; here was the frock in which he had first seen her, faintly smelling of the scent she always used. Here were her slippers, her gloves, her silver-backed brushes. Murchison sat down on the edge of the packing-case and stared at the litter around him. It was like clearing up after a death, than which there is no more ghastly experience if one had loved the one who died. Murchison did not know that it was possible to feel such intensity of emotion.

He went out and stood at the back door for a time, looking out to

229

sea. Then he strolled slowly round the house to the front, where the little bit of garden he had unearthed was beginning to make a brave show. Slowly it dawned upon him that in ten days' time he was due to join his Heinz and sail for Alexandria, and that would be the end of his association with the Brangwyns. He asked himself desperately if it were possible to rescind his decision and stop on with Brangwyn as secretary, as he had been pressed to do, and decided for the twentieth time that bad as the pain of the wrench might be, it would be infinitely less than the long-drawn-out agony of being in close touch with Ursula Brangwyn. Moreover, he did not feel he could trust his self-control. He had already broken out once with her, in the barn on the Conway shore, near Llandudno. It would not be fair to let Brangwyn in for unpleasantness. No, it was best to stick to his decision and go while the going was good. If he delayed, he might lose his reference.

He returned to the house, and grimly, as a kind of martyrdom, he carried Ursula Brangwyn's things up to the room she had chosen, and put them away in the drawers and cupboards for her, hung her pictures, and spread her pink eiderdown on the bed.

CHAPTER 27

In the very hour that Murchison was undergoing the martyrdom of handling Ursula's intimate personal belongings, their owner was sitting up in bed in a luxurious nursing-home, and saying to her brother, 'Alick, do you think Murchison would come and see me?'

Brangwyn hesitated for a moment, and then crossed the Rubicon.

'No, Ursula,' he said. 'I don't think he would.'

'Why ever not?' Ursula's voice was sharp and startled.

'Well, my dear, he has made up his mind that you have no use for him, and he prefers to cut his loss.'

'Oh, but Alick, that isn't the case at all. I like him tremendously.'

'You do not seem to have given him that impression, Ursula. At any rate, he's through with you.'

'Oh, but Alick, that's impossible. There is such a tremendously strong bond between us. What has happened? What has put him off me?'

'Your own words, my dear, "I shall have to take Murchison." He wasn't having you on those terms, and I don't blame him.'

'But I don't feel like that now, Alick. I feel quite differently.'

'Then you had better tell him so, and tell him plainly and quickly, for he is due to sail for Egypt in ten days' time.'

'Is he leaving us? But why? Oh, Alick, he can't do that. Why is he leaving us?'

'Because, my dear, I think you have upset him pretty thoroughly.'

'Oh Lord, I didn't mean to. What have I done? Can't we get things straightened out?'

'I don't know, Ursula, whether you can or not. Murchison told me he did not want to see you again.'

'But he must! I must talk to him. I must explain things. Oh, Alick, I don't want him to go! Can't you do anything?'

'I have done what I can, my dear, and it was no use. The only person who can do anything is yourself.'

'But what can I do if he won't meet me? Is it any use writing to him?

231

Or will that do more harm than good?'

'I think that things like this, Ursula, are very difficult to put right by letter. You had better see him.'

'But Alick, you say he won't see me?'

'Neither he will, my dear, if he knows it. So your only chance is to walk in on him when he isn't expecting you.'

'Oh dear, I can't make the running like that. Alick, can't you do anything?'

'No, Ursula, you are the only person who can do anything.'

'But what can I do?' Ursula was beginning to cry.

'Go straight to him and tell him how you feel and ask him to stop.'

'But will he stop? He is so dreadfully formidable when he is angry. Oh, Alick, I daren't!'

'You will have to do it, or lose him altogether.'

'Oh, Alick, I can't lose him! He mustn't go. I'll do anything.'

'Then I think the best thing to do would be for us to go down to the farm as soon as you are fit to travel, and for you to confront him face to face and say your say.'

'But will he listen to me? Have I damaged things beyond repair?'

'Ursula, I think that if you handle him the right way, he will fall into your hands like a ripe plum. He is very much in love with you, you know, and that is what all the upheaval has been about.'

'Is he really? Do you really think he cares for me? Then why does he want to leave me?'

'Because if you are very fond of someone, and that one is not fond of you, it hurts very much to be around with them. At least it hurts a man. I can't answer for a woman.'

'I think I would sooner have half a loaf than no bread. If I were Murchison I should have stuck on as your secretary.'

'A man is not built that way, my child. You have a few things to learn yet that you do not know. But there is no time to lose if you want to catch Murchison before he leaves. When do you think you will be fit to travel?'

'I'll be fit tomorrow, if I can get nurse to wash my hair tonight,' said the bed-ridden Miss Brangwyn.

The next morning Murchison received a wire, 'Arriving 3.15 for a few days. Please meet.' Brangwyn had decided that a wire would be better than a letter, as so much less could be explained in it.

Murchison told Mrs Learoyd, who had taken charge of the household, to get a bed made up in the room Brangwyn had chosen for his own, and at the appointed hour pulled on the old trench-coat and the slouch hat of the same vintage, and drove the four miles to the nearest station. It was market day, and there was a considerable crowd on the platform, and it was a few moments before he caught sight of Brangwyn's tall figure among the farmers. He bore down upon him, and was shaking him warmly by the hand, when he suddenly saw a face looking round Brangwyn's shoulder, and there was Miss Brangwyn smiling up at him rather shyly from out of the huge collar of her mink coat. He held on to Brangwyn's hand without realising what he was doing, and stared at her, till Brangwyn, who was getting his fingers damaged, made him let go.

'Well, you two, do I need to introduce you?' said Brangwyn, in an endeavour to relieve an embarrassing situation.

'Oh, er - no. How do you do, Miss Brangwyn? I hope you are better?'

'Yes, thanks, I'm much better.'

'She'll be all right when she gets plenty of sleep. Have you got the car outside, Murchison?'

'Yes, sir. It's outside. Shall I see about the luggage?'

'I'd be glad if you would. Ursula has brought her usual lorry-load.'

Ursula was squeezed in between the two men on the front seat, and her lorry-load of luggage was stuffed into the dickey of the big two-seater. Murchison, with a face like a graven image, drove rather slowly and carefully. Brangwyn made occasional remarks, and got monosyllables in reply. Murchison was exceedingly angry and hurt. This was too bad of Brangwyn. He knew how he felt, and it was cruelty to animals to let him in for this.

Ursula was more than delighted with the farm, and pronounced it her place of dreams.

'But the garden is so sweet!' she cried. 'I thought it was a neglected wilderness.'

'So it was, I expect,' said Brangwyn, 'but someone has been at work on it. Are you the gardener, Murchison?'

'Yes,' said Murchison sulkily.

Mrs Learoyd was in great form, welcoming the owners, but greatly perturbed lest they should not have enough to eat; but Yorkshire standards of high tea would have fed a family of Ursulas. Murchison sat down to the meal with them, but he never looked at Ursula once, and she was reduced to the state when she dared not address a remark to him, but only eyed him furtively, and was near to tears.

They were still at the table when a telegraph boy came banging at the door with a wire for Brangwyn.

'Damn it all!' said Brangwyn. 'Look at that, will you?' He flung a telegram down in front of Murchison, who saw that it was an urgent demand for Brangwyn's immediate return to town from his solicitors. How was he to know that Brangwyn had taken their name in vain and left the wire with Luigi to be sent off at the appointed hour?

'Murchison, I'm afraid I'll have to ask you to run me back to the station again. I'll have to catch the next train back.'

'All right.'

Ursula cast an anguished look at her brother. Was she to return with him, and so lose her chance to talk to Murchison? Or was she, appalling thought, to be left alone with him in this black mood?

'I don't think we've got too much time, Murchison. I think we'd better push off, if you don't mind?'

'Very good, sir. Do you expect to come back?'

'Yes, certainly, as soon as I can.'

'Good job I didn't unload the dickey.'

'That's all Ursula's stuff, my dear chap. I've only got one humble suitcase.'

'Isn't Miss Brangwyn returning with you?'

'No, why should she?' Murchison's eyes met Ursula's for the first time since that first anguished stare, and she saw that he had gone very white.

He was debating in his mind whether he would pack his own suitcase, and insist on returning to London with Brangwyn. But he had the wage-slave's dread of losing a reference, and reckoned that he would have to set his teeth and stick it out while his month's notice ran its course.

It was Brangwyn who broke the silence on the drive to the station.

'I gather you are angry with me, Murchison?'

'It's not for me, in my position, to be angry with you, sir, but I find the situation pretty trying.'

'When I told Ursula that you were leaving for Egypt in ten days' time, she got straight out of bed and insisted on coming down by the next train to see you and try and put things right with you.'

'It's very good of her, but there is no need. I don't bear any ill-will. Why didn't you tell her to leave it alone? You knew how I felt.'

'Because Ursula wished to talk to you herself; and when I realized what she had to say, I knew that she was right, and that she must come. Hear what she has to say, Murchison, before your form your judgment.'

They drove into the station-yard.

'My God, there's the train!' cried Brangwyn.

They raced on to the platform, and Murchison flung the suitcase into a first-class smoker just as the guard blew his whistle. The train took Brangwyn as far as a neighbouring seaside town, and there stopped, and Brangwyn went to a hotel for the night.

Murchison drove sullenly back to the farm. His first thought was to cram his things into a suitcase and retreat to the pub, but he saw that he could hardly leave a girl, just arisen from a bed of sickness, alone in the house, with gypsies and other gentry attracted by a local fair on the prowl. He put the car away and went straight up to his room, and stood there staring out of the window with his hands in his pockets, till Ursula came knocking timidly at the door.

'What time shall we have supper?' she said. 'It's a cold supper. Mrs Learoyd left it on the table; she couldn't stop, as they are going to the fair.'

Murchison came out. 'We'll have it when you like,' he said quietly.

'Shall we have it now?' said Ursula, very meekly.

'Very good.'

It was a dreadful meal. Murchison was perfectly polite, but he never volunteered a remark, and he never looked at her. Ursula, quivering with nervousness, struggled through it as best she might.

This was being even worse than she had expected. There was nothing for it but to take her courage in both hands, and break through the ice with a crash.

'I have come down here to talk to you.'

'So your brother gave me to understand. But there was no need. I quite understood. I bear no ill-will for anything, and I'm only too glad to have been able to do anything for you. I hope you'll get on to your feet now, and be all right.'

'Alick tells me that you are going to Egypt in ten days' time.'

'Yes, that is so.'

'Why are you going?'

'Because I have got a job with a man who lives in Alexandria.'

'But why are you leaving us?'

'Because my job here is finished, Miss Brangwyn.'

'Who says so?'

'I say so.'

Ursula pressed her sweating hands together nervously.

'Will you stop if I ask you to?' she said in a very small voice.

Murchison did not answer, but tense and motionless, stared at the fire. At last he said:

'What good purpose could it serve?'

'I - I would like you to stop.'

There was another long, agonizing silence. Then Murchison spoke again. 'I don't quite know why you make that request.'

'Well, I feel that there is an awfully strong bond between us after all we've been through together, and I think we shall miss each other horribly. I know I shall.'

'So shall I. I don't deny it. But I think it's an unnatural sort of bond, and the sooner we break it the better.'

'But why - but why?'

'Well, Miss Brangwyn, you wouldn't like me for keeps, would you? And this is not the sort of thing to play about with. I think it is better to clear out and be done with it. A clean cut has a chance to heal.'

Ursula could not control her voice sufficiently to speak, and he took her prolonged silence for agreement. He rose:

'If you don't mind, I think I'll get off upstairs. This sort of talk can do no manner of good.'

Ursula sprang to her feet and caught hold of his arm.

'Oh, don't go. You mustn't go. I simply can't let you go. I feel as if the best thing in my life were going out of it. Oh, please don't go.'

He stood looking down at her uncomprehendingly.

'I know I've been an awful beast to you. I'm frightfully sorry. I'll never be like that again. It wasn't the real me. It was the me that was all tangled up with Frank. Oh, please don't go. I'll never be like that again. I won't, really.'

She leant her face against the rough tweed of his sleeve. He stared down at her without moving.

'You mean you really want me to stop?'

'Yes, please. Will you?'

'I don't know. It seems to me to be a pretty difficult situation.'

'But why?'

'Well, you see, I've been unfortunate enough to get to care for you, and I know you don't care for me, and I'd sooner clear out.'

'Are you quite sure I don't care for you?'

'Well - do you?'

'Yes.'

There was a dead silence, till at last Murchison said, 'What are you driving at?'

Ursula let go of his arm and turned away.

236

'I can't say much more than that, can I? I've told you how I feel, and I've asked you to stop. Do you still want to go to Egypt?'

'I never *wanted* to go to Egypt. But the situation looked to me so hopelessly tangled it seemed the best thing to do.'

'Do you still feel like that?'

'I do. I can't see my way through the tangle. I can't ask you to marry me, you know.'

Ursula turned a startled face towards him.

'I haven't a bean. A man in my position can't marry.'

'There's no truth, is there, in what you said in Astley's letter about having other fish to fry?'

'No, not a word; that was only to put him off the scent.'

'Then the only difficulty is a money one?'

'Not the only one. Anything more incompatible than you and me, I can't possibly imagine.'

'And yet you say you care for me?'

'Yes, God help me, I do.'

'And I care for you. Surely the money question isn't going to come between us? We'd be simply miserable without each other. It isn't as if we'd neither of us got anything. I've got twelve hundred a year of my own.'

'I shouldn't care to live in your pocket, you know.'

'Oh dear, what are we to do? Look here, we'll halve it. You have half, and I'll have half.'

'I wouldn't take it.'

'But this is silly. Do you mean to say you will go away, and make us both thoroughly miserable, just because you won't share with me, when I want to share with you?'

She came over to him and put her hands on his shoulders and looked up into his face.

'Look here, you've *got* to stop.'

He put his hands over hers as they rested on his shoulders and looked down at her without speaking.

'All right,' he said at length. 'Do what you like with me.'

'I'd like to make you happy.'

'You'll have your work cut out. I'm pretty sour-tempered.'

'Don't you think you could be happy with me?'

'I could be happy with you if I could be happy with anyone, Ursula. But everything that could go wrong with a fellow has gone wrong with me.'

'I'll take my chance. I know I couldn't be happy with anyone else.

Don't you feel how strong the bond is between us?'

'I feel it all right. But do you mean to say that you feel it too?'

'Yes, I feel it too. Aren't you glad?'

'I don't know what to make of it. I can't believe it.'

'Is there anything in life sweeter than to love and be loved?' said Ursula, and lifted her lips to his. She suddenly felt herself gripped and held very closely. There was not much doubt about Murchison's feelings, even if he were not very good at putting them into words.

He dropped into the big armchair, and Ursula sank down on the hearthrug at his feet and put her head on his knee. After a moment's hesitation he put his arm round her shoulders tentatively, as if expecting to be rebuffed. They sat for a long time like that, gazing at the fire in silence.

It was the girl who broke the silence at length.

'I can hardly believe it is true that the big love has come between us, as Alick said it would. It seems like a dream to me.'

'It seems like a dream to me, too,' said Murchison. 'And I'm expecting to wake up with a head tomorrow. I am wondering whether I am fantasying the whole thing, and you will hit me a tremendous swipe if I act accordingly.'

'Try and see.'

'No fear! I'm taking no chances. You set the pace. You see, I doubt if it's the genuine article on your side. You've been doped with love-philtres, like the Queen in *Midsummer Night's Dream*, and presently you'll sober up and find out that I'm Bottom.'

'I don't think so. I started out by thinking you were the Beast, and then began to realize that you were the Prince.'

'Go on! Put more water with it. Brangwyn's given you an overdose.'

Ursula moved closer to him, and his arm tightened round her.

'Tell me,' he said. 'When did you first begin to like me? What made you change your mind about me?'

'I kept on having glimpses from the very beginning. But the thing that really made an impression on me was when you snaffled me out from under Frank's very nose and simply threw me into the car; and, again, when you kissed me in the barn.'

'Good Lord, I thought I'd have to spend the rest of my life living those things down! I say, Ursula, you realize, don't you, that I didn't really mean it when I said I'd marry you if it were made worth my while? I've perspired every time I've thought of it ever since.'

'Of course I do, silly. I knew that at the time. I knew you only meant to stamp on my toes. But what made you do it?'

'Well, I was having rather a bad time myself, you know, and I passed the kick on to you. But tell me, why did you say you'd have to take me in the same tone as if I were castor oil?'

'Because I'd really begun to want you, and I wasn't going to admit it to Alick.'

'Oh, you little devil! I wish I'd known that. It would have saved me some bad half hours!'

'Did you really mind?'

'I minded frightfully, Ursula.'

'I'm ever so sorry,' she said, slipping her hand into his.

Silence fell between them, and in the silence they seemed to draw very near to each other. They were both weary; the girl because she was only just up after three weeks in bed, and the man worn out with stormy emotions; and they rested in each other. Murchison felt as if something that had been held under pressure till it ached desperately were now flowing freely in relief from the bare contact with the girl. His hand on Ursula's shoulder was enough, with the warmth of her flesh coming to him through the thin silk of her sleeve.

It was the girl who broke the silence again.

'Isn't it wonderful, together like this in the firelight? Alick always said that the great test of a spiritual mating is that there is peace in it. Tell me, are you happy, quietly, like this, at our own fireside?'

'Very happy, Ursula. I did not know it was possible to be so happy.'

They sat together silently in the warm glow of the hearth, watching the little blue flames of the burning driftwood flickering over the embers.

It was once more the girl who broke the silence.

'Did you know that I nearly became a nun?' she said.

'Yes, your brother told me.'

'Do you know why I did it?'

'No, why did you?'

'Because two or three times in the convent chapel I felt the most wonderful sense of peace and fulfilment and protection flow over me. It was the most perfect thing I had ever known, and I thought that if I became a nun and gave myself unreservedly to God that I would have it all the time. But Alick says no; I was too young; and my human life would have been too strong for me. He thinks it is no good to try and give yourself to Heaven until you've learnt the lessons of earth.'

'There is an extraordinary mixture of worldliness and spirituality about your brother that I have never understood.'

'Well, you see, he does not believe that there is any dividing-line between spirit and matter. He says that matter is solidified spirit, as it were. Did you know that the initiates worship God made manifest in nature? It is one of their great secrets. It will work out in our marriage, you will see.'

'In what way?'

'Do you know the words, "Bring the Godhead down into manhood, and take manhood up into Godhead"? Well, like that. That was why Alick would not let me go on at the convent. He said their teaching was all wrong on the subject of sex. And he made me meditate on the symbol of the winged bull to break me of it; but it had been so ground into me that sex was coarse and vulgar and evil that the bull simply scandalized me at first, and I couldn't visualize his wings at all. They seemed utterly inappropriate, as if there were no wings made that could lift that solid lump of beef.

'And I think Frank emphasized that aspect, too, with all his talk of unrepression and being your elemental self. But you can't just - what was it you called it? - up-end the ash-bin. It isn't done. Think what the streets would be like if we all up-ended our ash-bins - too messy for words. The thing to do is not to have an ash-bin, but to burn all your rubbish, as they tell you on the dust-carts. God told St. Peter that nothing He had made was to be considered unclean, and who are we to try and go one better than God? Alick says that sex ought not to be under a taboo because it is unclean, but because it is sacred. Ted, do I shock you, talking like this? You see, I've had it so thoroughly rubbed into me that sex is natural that I forget to blush.'

'Good Lord, no, you don't shock me. I can think of nothing worse than having to cope with a female who had no ideas at all on the subject.'

'Well, those are my ideas - the naturalness of the physical, and the tremendous importance of the subtle, magnetic aspect that lies behind it, which makes marriage something much more than the love affair of two people and their subsequent rows; which makes it God made manifest in nature - life flowing into the world direct from God, and human beings as channels for it. A real marriage, which has a spiritual side as well as a physical, ought to put one in circuit with the whole universe, for one becomes a channel for the life of the race going on; that is why there is no blessing on a marriage when you close the gates of life permanently against incoming souls.'

'I cannot imagine anything more wonderful than opening those gates, Ursula.'

Silence fell between them again, and they watched the fire of driftwood gradually crumble to embers, each deep in the thoughts they shared; and the great bull spread his wings and took off as easily as a bird. Murchison knew instinctively that they had mated, and that nothing now remained to be done but to ratify it outwardly.

END

THE SOCIETY OF THE INNER LIGHT

The Society of the Inner Light is a Society for the study of Occultism, Mysticism, and Esoteric Psychology and the development of their practice.

Its aims are Christian and its methods are Western.

Students who, after due inquiry, desire to pursue their studies further, may take the Correspondence Course. Their training will be in the theory of Esoteric Science, and they will be given the discipline which prepares for its practice.

For further details apply for a copy of the WORK & AIMS of the Society from;

> The Secretariat
> Society of the Inner Light
> 38 Steele's Road
> London NW3 4RG

THE INNER LIGHT JOURNAL, a Quarterly Magazine, founded by Dion Fortune, is devoted to the study of Mysticism, Esoteric Christianity, Occult Science, and the Psychology of Super-consciousness. Annual Subscription £16.00. Please make cheques out to Society of The Inner Light.